STATE GOVERNMENT

CQ's GUIDE TO CURRENT ISSUES AND ACTIVITIES
1991-92

edited by Thad L. Beyle

The University of North Carolina
at Chapel Hill

Congressional Quarterly Inc.

Congressional Quarterly

Congressional Quarterly, an editorial research service and publishing company, serves clients in the fields of news, education, business, and government. It combines Congressional Quarterly's specific coverage of Congress, government, and politics with the more general subject range of an affiliated service, the *CQ Researcher.*

Congressional Quarterly publishes the *Congressional Quarterly Weekly Report* and a variety of books, including college political science textbooks under the CQ Press imprint and public affairs paperbacks on developing issues and events. CQ also publishes information directories and reference books on the federal government, national elections, and politics, including the *Guide to the Presidency,* the *Guide to Congress,* the *Guide to the U.S. Supreme Court,* the *Guide to U.S. Elections, Politics in America,* and *Congress A to Z: CQ's Ready Reference Encyclopedia.* The *CQ Almanac,* a compendium of legislation for one session of Congress, is published each year. *Congress and the Nation,* a record of government for a presidential term, is published every four years.

CQ publishes the *Congressional Monitor,* a daily report on current and future activities of congressional committees, and several newsletters including *Congressional Insight,* a weekly analysis of congressional action, and *Campaign Practices Reports,* a semimonthly update on campaign laws.

An electronic online information system, Washington Alert, provides immediate access to CQ's databases of legislative action, votes, schedules, profiles, and analyses.

The Library of Congress cataloged the first edition of this title as follows:

Beyle, Thad L., 1934-
    State government.

    Bibliography: p.
    Includes index.
    1. State governments—Addresses, essays, lectures. I. Congressional Quarterly, inc. II. Title.

JK2408.B49   1985   320.973   85-9657

ISBN 0-87187-634-5
ISSN 0888-8590

Printed in the United States of America
Copyright 1991 Congressional Quarterly
1414 22nd Street, N.W., Washington, D.C. 20037
(202) 887-8500

STATE GOVERNMENT

Contents

III. POLITICS: PARTIES, INTEREST GROUPS, AND PACS

IV. MEDIA AND THE STATES

V. STATE LEGISLATURES

VI. GOVERNORS AND THE EXECUTIVE BRANCH

VII. STATE BUREAUCRACIES AND ADMINISTRATION

VIII. STATE COURTS

IX. STATE ISSUES

Boxes, Tables, and Figures

TABLES

FIGURES

Foreword

As the fiscal crisis deepens and the budget knives sharpen in Washington, the states are faced with greater financial and programmatic challenges than ever before—and more than ever before, they are on their own. The early years of the Bush presidency have brought little fiscal relief and more transferred costs to the states, continuing and accelerating the trend of the last dozen years. The Reagan era in particular ushered in a massive shift in the balance of federalism. Enormous responsibilities—and the accompanying burdens—were transferred from the nation's capital to the state capitals.

While Washington has drastically cut back many of its basic social programs, struggled with massive deficits, and seemed almost incapable of putting its governmental house in order, the states have considerably expanded their activities, operating with balanced budgets in most cases and taking the necessary steps, however painful—such as cutting spending and raising taxes—to meet their obligations. The energy, enthusiasm, and willingness to experiment observed today at the state level is reminiscent of earlier, happier eras in the national government's existence; the contrast between past and present is stark.

Thad Beyle, one of the country's foremost scholars of state government, has been skillfully charting the trends that are reshaping state government and politics in this series for Congressional Quarterly. The carefully selected articles in this latest compendium recount the results of the 1990 elections for state offices and look forward to the 1991 redistrictings. Updates on current governors, legislatures, bureaucracies, and state courts are included, as are discussions of some overriding issues on the states' agendas, from education and the environment to auto insurance reform and AIDS. News media coverage of state issues and government is also emphasized.

In an age when the federal government is retrenching, both the national government and the localities are looking to the states as never before for leadership. State governments are facing unprecedented challenges, and we need to be more attentive than ever to their agendas. This informative volume, the seventh in the series, helps us to keep up with the states—the new cutting edge of the federal system.

Larry J. Sabato
Charlottesville, Virginia

Preface

State governments are no longer sleepy backwater operations located in far-off capitals where few people know or care what they are doing. They are big-time organizations on a par with many "Fortune 500" companies. Comparing the states and their 1989 general revenues with the nation's largest businesses based on their 1990 sales finds 18 states in the top 50 of these largest organizations. In fact, 30 states had revenues equal to or greater than the top 100 companies in the "Fortune 500" listing.[1]

The "Reagan revolution" contributed to the states' increased visibility and influence. State governments were asked to shoulder more of the domestic policy burden as the federal government coped with the national debt and defense. The states' response to the fiscal challenges of the 1980s became an issue of national as well as local importance. And this heightened role is projected to continue into the 1990s as we see state after state grappling with budgetary problems often caused by having to pick up some of the fiscal slack created by a federal government "preoccupied by the problems of subtraction"[2] and cutting back its support of domestic programs. Certainly the events surrounding the Gulf

crisis and war did little to focus the federal government's attention on the problems of the states and domestic programs.

Richard Nathan of the State University of New York—Albany and Martha Derthick of the University of Virginia recently reviewed what they now see happening in the states: "State governments are on a roll ... they are reforming education and health systems, trying to convert welfare to workfare and building new roads and bridges and other public works." They found that most elected state officials loved this new activism, often seeing governors and legislatures competing "with one another to do more, do it better, and do it faster." Even state attorneys general were coming alive "with populist flair" as they were "fighting mergers that the [U.S.] Justice Department finds acceptable" and "challenging allegedly deceptive advertising by fast-food chains and commercial airlines." Nathan and Derthick argued that one of the most important legacies of the Reagan years would be "this increased activism in state governments" as responsibilities have gravitated from both the national and local levels to the states.[3]

But in the 1990s the states and their elected leaders are finding it difficult to continue on the track of "increased activism" in their states as the economy has led to decreasing revenues for most states. Such activism costs money and that translates into the need for more revenues or higher taxes. When such activism can be conducted "on the cheap"— that is, by not raising taxes—the public is not too concerned. But when it must take additional tax money out of their pockets, they become concerned. Such concern has now forced state leaders into some rather severe policy problems in which they must decide which programs to cut and by how much. Yesterday's heroes are becoming today's political targets for retribution.

The 1991-92 edition of *State Government: CQ's Guide to Current Issues and Activities* includes recent articles from state journals and other publications by those in state government and public interest organizations attempting to define and analyze state issues and agendas. Short background essays introduce the articles and highlight developments in the states.

The organization of this book parallels that of most state government texts. First is politics: the most recent election results, and the roles of direct democracy, interest groups, political parties, and the media. Next are the institutions: legislatures, governors, bureaucracies, and state courts. Finally are some of the issues of primary concern to the states today: raising revenue, disposing of nuclear waste, treating AIDS, reforming insurance, reducing drug abuse, and reforming education. A reference guide for further study also is included.

There are many to thank for their assistance in developing this book. Among them are David R. Tarr, the director of the Book Department at Congressional Quarterly, for his support, and Larry Sabato at the University of Virginia for his recommendations and kind words in the Foreword. This edition reflects the hard work of CQ editor Jerry

Orvedahl and managing editor of the Book Department Nancy Lammers. To them I offer my appreciation.

This is our seventh compilation of the *Guide,* and there is much we have yet to learn. Any errors you find are mine. I hope you will send your comments and suggestions so we might be able to improve the 1992-93 edition.

Thad L. Beyle
Chapel Hill, North Carolina

Notes

1. California ($81.7 billion) fell between third place Ford Motor Company ($98.3 billion) and fourth place IBM ($69.0 billion); New York State ($60.7 billion) was between fourth place IBM and fifth place Mobil Oil ($58.8 billion); Texas ($29.4 billion) fell between eleventh place Chrysler ($30.9 billion) and twelfth place Amoco ($28.3 billion); Ohio ($27.5 billion) and Pennsylvania ($25.7 billion) were between thirteenth place Boeing ($27.6 billion) and fourteenth place Shell Oil ($24.4 billion); Michigan ($22.7 billion), Illinois and Florida ($22.2 billion each) were between fifteenth place Proctor and Gamble ($24.4 billion) and sixteenth place Occidental Petroleum ($21.9 billion), which was where New Jersey ($21.9 billion) was just ahead of seventeenth place United Technologies ($21.8 billion); Massachusetts ($16.0 billion) was between twenty-fourth place McDonnell Douglas ($16.4 billion) and twenty-fifth place ConAgra ($15.5 billion); Washington State and North Carolina ($13.5 billion each) fell between twenty-eighth place RJR Nabisco ($13.9 billion) and twenty-ninth place Hewlett-Packard ($13.2 billion); Wisconsin and Virginia ($13.1 billion each) were at the same level as thirtieth place Digital Equipment ($13.1 billion); Minnesota ($12.4 billion) was at the same level as thirty-sixth place Allied-Signal ($12.4 billion); Georgia was at the same level as thirty-seventh place Sun Oil ($11.9 billion); Maryland was at the same level as fortieth place Goodyear Tire ($11.5 billion); and Indiana was at the same level as forty-fifth place Unocal ($10.7 billion) on the

Fortune "500" listing. From "The Fortune 500," *Fortune* 123:8 (April 22, 1991), 286-305, and the Bureau of the Census, U.S. Department of Commerce, *State Government Finances in 1989* (Washington, D.C.: U.S. Government Printing Office, 1990), 5.

2. Carl E. Van Horn, ed. *The State of the States* (Washington, D.C.: CQ Press, 1989), ix.

3. "Federalism," *State Policy Reports* 5:24 (December 31, 1987), 23.

I. 1990-1991 POLITICS

The Courts Warily Find Their Way
Into the Political Thicket

29

State officials continue to debate the timing of U.S. elections. Some argue that national, state, and local elections should be held at different times to keep separate the issues, candidates, and political concerns of each level. Following this argument, national elections for president, vice president, U.S. senators, and U.S. representatives would be held in even years, as they are now; exactly which year would depend on the length of the term—that is, representatives every two years, presidents every four years, and senators every six years. State-level elections for governor and other executive officials, state legislators, and state constitutional amendments and referendums would be held in "off-years" (nonpresidential election years) or possibly in odd-numbered years. And local elections would be at another time, preferably not in conjunction with either state or national elections.

Others advocate holding all elections at the same time to maximize voter interest and turnout and, not inconsequentially, to increase the importance of the political party as the main determinant of voters' decisions from the top of the ballot to the bottom. But there is not a single Republican party or a single Democratic party to influence voters' choices. At least fifty different Republican and Democratic state parties reflect the unique political culture, heritage, and positions of the fifty states. Add to that the increasing number of independents and other voters who split their tickets, and it is clear that this political party rationale for simultaneous elections will not hold up in the practical world of politics.

Neither side of the timing argument has predominated. During the 1988 presidential election year, forty-four states elected their legislatures, but only twelve elected their governors. Of these twelve states, New Hampshire, Rhode Island, and Vermont elected their governors to two-year terms, which means that their gubernatorial elections alternate between presidential and nonpresidential election years. In 1986, Arkansas switched its gubernatorial elections to the even, nonpresidential years and granted the governor a four- rather than two-year term. Indeed, most states hold their gubernatorial elections in even, nonpresidential years, as in 1990, when thirty-six governors were elected, along with forty-four state legislatures; or in odd years, as in 1989, when New Jersey and Virginia held their state elections, and in 1991, when Kentucky, Louisiana, and Mississippi are holding theirs.[1]

A major reason why some states have shifted their elections to nonpresidential years is because the personalities, issues, and concerns evident in presidential elections often spill over into state-level contests. While presidential elections are stirring events that bring the excitement of politics to the American populace and lead to higher turnout among voters, some state officials fear that the "coattail effect" of the national elections will change the results of their elections and, most important, obscure the state issues that voters should consider on election day.

In 1988, there was an interesting political change as twenty states moved to hold their presidential primary elections on the same date—on the March 8 "Super Tuesday." The twelve states holding state elections in 1988 still ran their primaries and caucuses at the normal time in their political calendars, and thereby kept their national and state political processes separate. It is too soon to determine the effects of this shift on state politics, but one fact is clear: there was an additional primary election in these states. This addition strained fragile political resources, resulting in a diminished pool of those who would work in political campaigns, those who would provide contributions to political campaigns, and, unfortunately, those who would vote in a state primary. Changes are already afoot in some of these states to discontinue their state's participation in this type of a "Southern Primary," while several states in other parts of the country are exploring the possibility of a regional primary.

Over the 1980s and into the 1990s women have been increasingly successful as candidates for top level state offices. In 1986, Republican Kay A. Orr of Nebraska won that state's governorship and Democrat Madeleine M. Kunin of Vermont was reelected to her second term. Women also won forty-two other statewide elected offices, including twelve secretaries of state, ten treasurers, six lieutenant governors, and six state auditors.[2] In 1990, Joan Finney (D) won in Kansas, Barbara Roberts (D) won in Oregon, and Ann Richards (D) won a hard fought campaign in Texas. These women can attribute their success to better fund raising, aid from other office holders who are women, more active financial support and counseling from female corporate executives, and more active support for top female candidates from men.[3]

To some observers, this set of victories by women represents the third wave of recruitment of women into state politics. The first wave, up to the early 1970s, consisted of women winning as widows, wives, or daughters of established male politicians. The second wave through the 1970s consisted of women active in civic affairs shifting their volunteer work and contacts into political affairs. The third wave now evident is of women who have moved up the political ladder by defeating other candidates while keeping their eyes on a higher political goal such as the governorship, much as men have. In other words, the third wave consists of upwardly mobile politicians who happen to be women.[4]

State Campaigns: 1987-90

During the 1987-90 electoral period, there was an uncertainness about our political system. President Ronald Reagan, having been reelected for his second term in 1984, was a political "lame duck": a powerful national politician with no further chances to demonstrate this power at the ballot box. His administration was being shaken by allegations of scandal, and the Iran-contra affair raised questions about his leadership. In response, politicians at all levels of government, especially Republicans, began to put some political distance between themselves and the president. Local and state issues began to dominate the contests for these offices.

To date, the 1988 election of Republican George Bush as president, and the Bush administration, have not seemed to have an impact on elections at lower levels of government. In fact, Bush's victory in 1988 was the first in American history in which the winning presidential candidate's party didn't make any gains down the ballot.[5] However, the recent military success in the Persian Gulf under the leadership of President Bush may change that equation down the ballot in upcoming elections. Of course, that foreign policy success could be considerably tempered by how well the economy is performing at election time.

The three states that held elections in 1987 are traditionally one-party Democratic states: Kentucky, Louisiana, and Mississippi. Democrats again won the major gubernatorial races—though Buddy Roemer of Louisiana subsequently changed his party affiliation to Republican—and continued their control over the state legislatures. Each gubernatorial race was unique. The most lopsided victory was in Kentucky where new Democratic governor Wallace G. Wilkinson, a self-made millionaire businessman with a lack of political experience, conducted the most expensive gubernatorial campaign in the state's history, stressing his "new ideas" approach to governing and winning 65 percent of the vote.[6] Now, in 1991, with the seat up again, there is going to be a spirited contest for the office between several candidates, one of whom was Governor Wilkinson's wife, who wanted to keep the office in the family. She later withdrew.

Louisiana's new governor, Buddy Roemer, a U.S. representative from the Shreveport area, promised a "revolution" in state government, and barely defeated incumbent governor Edwin Edwards (33 percent to 28 percent) in that state's unique open first primary. For Edwards, a controversial and tainted political figure, this loss was the handwriting on the wall. He declined to challenge Roemer to a runoff. This seemed to end Edwards's "Louisiana Hayride" style of governing under the Cajun-French slogan *Laissez les bons temps rouler* (Let the good times roll).[7]

For the state's 1991 political menu, Roemer has now switched to being a Republican; Edwards is back to seek his old seat; and David Duke, the former grand wizard of the Ku Klux Klan, organizer of the National Association for the Advancement of White People, and current state senator, has also entered the contest. Duke, who has a charismatic attraction to some of the state's voters, ran for the U.S. Senate in 1990 and did much better than expected. So this will be the contest to watch for 1991.

In Mississippi, the rise of Republican party strength was apparent as Democratic state auditor Ray Mabus received only 53 percent of the vote in defeating a moderate Republican challenger. The state has not had a Republican governor since the Reconstruction era and times are clearly changing in Ole Miss. Mabus's narrow victory also reflected a reaction against his "high-profile efforts to promote efficiency and honesty in government

[which] ruffled some feathers in the courthouse cliques."[8] Mississippi politics in 1991 appear rather calm, with Mabus's reelection effort lacking the interesting twists of the Louisiana and Kentucky contests.

In 1988, when elections in the states coincided with a presidential election, there were legislative elections in most states but only twelve gubernatorial contests. The main message of the 1988 results in the states was stability.

For example, an all-time low of 16 percent of elected state legislators were "new," while the rest were incumbents being reelected. This low turnover suggests our state legislatures are starting to resemble the U.S. Congress, with its 8 to 15 percent turnover rate of recent decades.[9] In gubernatorial races, eight incumbents were able to retain their seats and only one incumbent, Arch Moore of West Virginia, was defeated in his attempt to stay in office. Moore later faced several criminal charges to which he plead guilty and went to prison. Only four new governors were elected: in Indiana, Montana, New Hampshire, and West Virginia. Presidential politics seemed to help the GOP, as seven of the twelve winners were Republican (58 percent) compared to zero in 1987 and seventeen of thirty-six in 1986 (47 percent).

In 1988, there were three states in which split-ticket voting was evident as voters elected a governor and a U.S. senator of opposite parties. Voters in Vermont returned Democratic incumbent Madeleine M. Kunin to office with 56 percent of the vote and elevated Republican representative James M. Jeffords to the U.S. Senate with 69 percent of the vote—a twenty-five point swing. In Indiana, Democratic secretary of state Evan Bayh was elected governor with 53 percent of the vote while Republican Richard G. Lugar was returned to the U.S. Senate with 68 percent of the vote—a swing of twenty-one points. In Washington state, Democratic incumbent governor Booth Gardner won with 63 percent of the vote while former Republican U.S. senator Slade Gorton claimed victory for a return to the Senate with a close 51 percent of the vote—a swing of fourteen points. Clearly, party-line voting was not the overriding rule guiding the voters in the 1988 statewide elections.[10]

In 1989, there were two states in which gubernatorial elections took place: New Jersey and Virginia. Voters in Virginia also were electing their legislators and New Jersey voters were electing members to their lower house, the General Assembly. The Democrats were victorious in both states: in the gubernatorial races, James J. Florio (N.J.) and L. Douglas Wilder (Va.) were elected, and in the legislative races, Democrats retained their hold over the Virginia legislature and recaptured the lower house in New Jersey.

But the focus in the 1989 elections was on abortion. In July 1989, midway through these campaigns, the U.S. Supreme Court announced a major decision on abortion.[11] In effect, the Court began the process of reversing the standard set in an earlier decision, *Roe v. Wade* (1973), which had provided women the right under the U.S. Constitution to choose an abortion within a certain time period. This earlier decision also had the effect of giving governors and "state legislators the opportunity not to choose sides in a wrenching political debate."[12]

The impact of the decision was almost immediate as candidates for office in the states were asked their positions on the issue: were they prolife or prochoice? The governor of Florida even called a special fall session of his legislature to tighten up that state's abortion laws. The legislators met, but decided not to act on the issue, much to the governor's embarrassment.

The abortion issue hurt the Republican candidates for governor in both New Jersey and Virginia since they held prolife views, in contrast to the more prochoice views of the Democratic candidates. But as the Republicans began to feel the heat of the rapidly growing ranks of the prochoice activists—even from within their own party—and as they saw the numbers in their polls rising against them, they waffled on the issue, moving away from their previous prolife stand. That strategy seemed to hurt them even more.

Virginia's gubernatorial race was significant for more than how abortion affected that state's politics. The Commonwealth's voters had the opportunity to elect the nation's first elected black governor, Lt. Governor L. Douglas Wilder (D). Wilder worked his way up through Virginia politics, winning a state senate seat in 1969, then lieutenant governorship in 1985.

There are two stunning messages from these 1989 elections: blacks can seek and win major offices as politicians instead of as civil rights warriors; and abortion is a major issue that can help or hurt candidates depending on their views and how they handle the abortion question on the campaign trail.

The Issues

In 1990, nineteen new governors were selected and seventeen incumbent governors reelected in the thirty-six states holding gubernatorial elections. Actually, three of the new governors weren't so new, as some old hands reappeared on the scene: Walter Hickel in Alaska, Bruce King in New Mexico, and Richard Snelling in Vermont. Democrats won nineteen of these contests, bringing their hold over statehouses to twenty-eight; Republicans won fifteen races, bringing their total to twenty statehouses. What was new about the 1990 elections was that two states elected independent candidates: Hickel and Lowell

Weicker in Connecticut. Both were former Republican office holders.

Democrats also fared well in legislative races, winning forty-three more seats across the states. But these were a very critical forty-three seats since the Democrats' control of state legislatures rose from twenty-nine to thirty states, while the Republicans dropped from controlling nine to only five state legislatures. This configuration of party wins and losses resulted in split political leadership in twenty-nine states, where the governor belongs to one party and one or both houses of the legislature are controlled by the opposing party. Split-ticket voting is very much alive and well across the states.

Again, some of the results in particular states demonstrate how wide an impact split-ticket voting can have on specific elections. Twenty-six states had contests for both their governorship and one of their U.S. Senate seats. In only eleven states were the winners of both contests from the same party; voters in fifteen states elected a governor from one party and a U.S. senator from the other.

For example, in Alaska, where the independent gubernatorial candidate Hickel won, Arliss Sturgulewski, the Republican candidate, received 26.2 percent of the vote while incumbent Republican U.S. senator Ted Stevens received 66.2 percent of the vote—a difference of forty points! In Idaho, incumbent Democratic governor Cecil Andrus won with 68.2 percent of the vote while Republican newcomer Larry Craig won the senate seat with 61.3 percent of the vote—a swing of nearly thirty points. In Wyoming, incumbent Democratic governor Mike Sullivan won with 65.4 percent of the vote; incumbent Republican U.S. senator Alan Simpson won his seat back with 63.9 percent of the vote—another swing of nearly 30 points.

As evidenced by the 1989 New Jersey and Virginia gubernatorial races, abortion can

be a very potent issue. Until 1989, issues in state campaigns varied considerably, not only from state to state but also among offices being contested. For example, campaigns for state legislative seats tended to focus on the individual candidate as he or she sought to achieve name recognition among the voters. Some candidates shied away from taking a position on specific issues, preferring instead to endorse economic development, reduction of crime, better education, and other broad issues. Others used specific issues such as antiabortion, tax repeal, or growth limits to achieve the name recognition they needed to win. On the whole, however, candidates preferred to take a position on broad issues rather than commit themselves to a specific issue that could alienate potential supporters. As *State Policy Reports* has pointed out,

> Campaigns rarely reveal candidate positions on the difficult questions of state policy. The easy question is whether candidates are for lower state and local taxes, better educational quality, higher teacher pay, and protecting the environment while stimulating economic growth. The candidates generally share these objectives. The hard question is what to do when these objectives collide as they often do.[13]

As a result, the average voter has a hard time discerning where the candidates stand on specific issues, and attempts to survey state legislative candidates on specific issues usually are not successful. One public interest organization in North Carolina does provide voters with information on how incumbents are rated by their peers, lobbyists, and the media covering the legislature in addition to information on the legislation they sponsored and their votes on key bills. However, no information of this kind can be provided on nonincumbent legislative candidates.[14]

Though the days of noncontroversial state campaigns were ended by the emergence of the abortion question, other controversial issues have intruded into state campaigns and begun to overshadow abortion as the principal issue. Not that the abortion issue wasn't important in some states; it was and made the difference in some campaigns. But, the state of the economy and especially individual state economies became the focus of many campaigns as did the question of the need for increased taxes. And with the 1990 U.S. census in hand, who controlled the governorship and the legislature became very important for the redistricting and reapportionment debates ahead.

The first article in this section is by Steve Henriksen of *Comparative State Politics* who reviews what went on in the thirty-six governors' races in 1990. Karen Hansen of *State Legislatures* examines the results of the 1990 state legislative races. Then there is a section on redistricting and reapportionment, the process stimulated by the 1990 census and certain to bedevil many state legislatures and governors. Here, Rhodes Cook of Congressional Quarterly lays out the nature of this unique political game in the states, indicating which states will have redistricting and reapportionment on their agendas and how the courts look at these questions.

Notes

1. Actually, one of the 1990 gubernatorial elections (Arizona) was not decided until February 1991 when there was a runoff between the Democratic and Republican candidates. Neither had received 50 percent of the vote in the November election so, by Arizona statute, there had to be a runoff. This statute was adopted after the 1988 impeachment of Governor Evan Mecham, who had won the 1986 election with only 40 percent of the total vote. In correcting for that problem, the Arizona legislature obviously created another problem.

2. "1987 Statewide Elected Women—44," *Women in State Government Newsletter*, December 1986, 4.

3. Meg Armstrong, "WSEG Campaign News," *Women in State Government Newsletter*, May 1986, 4.

4. Comments of Celinda Lake, Candidate Services Director of the Women's Campaign Fund, at a National Conference of State Legislatures seminar as reported by David Broder, "Hard-earned Credentials Give Female Candidates an Edge," [Raleigh] *News and Observer*, September 15, 1986, 13A.

5. Karen Hansen, "To the Democrats Go the Spoils," *State Legislatures* 16:11 (November/December 1990), 17.

6. Caroline Ashley, "History Is on the Side of the Democrats . . . in Kentucky's and Mississippi's Elections," *Congressional Quarterly Weekly Report*, October 31, 1987, 2689.

7. Bob Benenson, "The Edwards 'Hayride' Ends; Rep. Roemer to Be Governor," *Congressional Quarterly Weekly Report*, October 31, 1987, 2687.

8. Ashley, "History Is on the Side of the Democrats," 2688-2689, and "The Elections of 1987," *State Policy Reports* 5:21 (November 16, 1987), 26.

9. Karl T. Kurtz, "No Change—For a Change," *State Legislatures* 15:1 (January 1989), 29.

10. Adapted from Walter Dean Burnham, "Elections Dash GOP Dream of Realignment," *Wall Street Journal*, November 26, 1986.

11. *Webster v. Reproductive Health Services* (1989).

12. Wendy Kaminer, "From *Roe* to *Webster*: Court Hands Abortion to States," *State Government News* 32:11 (November 1989), 12.

13. *State Policy Reports* 2:20 (October 31, 1984): 11.

14. North Carolina Center for Public Policy Research, *Article II: A Guide to the N.C. Legislature*, (Raleigh, N.C.), published biennially.

The 1990 Gubernatorial Elections: Implications For Policy and Politics

by Steve Henriksen

After months of campaigning, millions of dollars, thousands of political commercials and more than a few scathing personal attacks, the races for the 36 governors' seats up in the 1990 election are finally over. For political analysts, pundits and political scientists, this is now the season for reviewing results and attempting to discern their meanings. (For voters, this time of year provides a respite before the next, if ever so quickly approaching, election cycle.)

Among the 36 states holding gubernatorial contests were the so-called "Big Eight": California, Florida, Illinois, Michigan, New York, Ohio, Pennsylvania and Texas. Collectively, these states have 48 percent of the nation's people, spend 50 percent of all state and local revenues and will elect nearly half (212) of all United States Congressmen in 1992. Each of these states will be the biggest winners and losers in the upcoming congressional reapportionment sweepstakes with California and Florida leading the beneficiaries and New York and Michigan heading the list of states forfeiting congressional seats. The governors elected on November 6 will play an important, perhaps even the deciding, role in determining the shape of the reapportionment maps within their respective jurisdictions.

Beyond the substantial specter of reapportionment lie considerable opportunities for the newly elected governors to influence public policy. Key decisions on education, taxes and abortion will be made at the state level over the next few years and, here again, our new state chief executives will bring their own preferences and personalities to bear on critical topics.

Going into the election, 20 of the seats being contested were held by Democrats and 16 by Republicans. Of the 36 officeholders, 23 had announced their intention to seek reelection. Among those choosing to retire from office, three were prohibited from seeking reelection (Celeste of Ohio, Carruthers of New Mexico and Harris of Georgia), others cited economic (leading to political) difficulties in their states (O'Neill of Connecticut and Kunin of Vermont), while the remaining few "just said no!" (Thompson of Illinois). Even if all incumbents running had been reelected, a substantial turnover (26%) in the gubernatorial ranks would have occurred simply

Steve Henriksen is the assistant to the director of the Illinois Legislative Studies Center at Sangamon State University. This article is reprinted with permission from *Comparative State Politics* 11:6 (December 1990): 1-9.

Governorships

Pre-1990 election		Post-1990 election*	
Democrats	29	Democrats	27
Republicans	21	Republicans	21
Independents	0	Independents	2

Democrats

Net loss	2
Incumbents re-elected	10
Incumbents defeated	2

Republicans

Net loss	0
Incumbents re-elected	7
Incumbents defeated	4

* These tallies were updated in May 1991. They reflect a resolution of the Arizona runoff in favor of J. "Fife" Symington (R) as well as the switch in party identification from Democrat to Republican of Louisiana governor Buddy Roemer. —Ed.

Source: Adapted from Holly Idelson, "Governors Find Re-Election A Trickier Proposition," *Congressional Quarterly Weekly Report,* November 10, 1990, 3838.

through attrition—constitutionally imposed, politically motivated or personally desired.

Prior to the election, a select number of gubernatorial races received the greatest amount of popular, academic and media attention. The obvious ones were the battles for the governorships of the "Big Eight" states. Both major political parties and their respective fundraising arms placed considerable emphasis on capturing gubernatorial contests in "Big Eight" states where incumbent governors were retiring: California, Illinois and Texas. Other contests which were the subjects of great interest in the political community (besides the "Big Eight") were Connecticut, Iowa, Massachusetts and Minnesota. Each of the gubernatorial races in these and other states will be discussed in a succeeding section as examples of one trend or phenomenon evident during this election year.

The returns from the 1990 gubernatorial elections are summarized below by relative party strength, changes in partisan control and the power of incumbency.

Democrats control [two] less statehouse[s] [27] than they did prior to the election. Republicans continue to hold [21] gubernatorial seats with independents in Connecticut and Alaska being elected to replace Democrats.[1] [After the November election failed to produce a winner in Arizona, voters returned to the polls in January and elected J. "Fife" Symington over former-Phoenix mayor Terry Goddard as the new governor. The November contest in the state was the closest in the country, and under Arizona law a candidate must receive a majority of votes to be elected.]

A further look at the gubernatorial results reveal a number of partisan changes. Democrats captured the governorships of seven states including Florida, Kansas, Nebraska, New Mexico, Oklahoma, Rhode Island and Texas. Republicans were successful in unseating Democrats in the states of Massachusetts, Michigan, Minnesota, Ohio and Vermont. The changes between parties reveal that the Democrats were unusually successful in the so-called "Sun Belt states" while the Republicans enjoyed triumphs in the "Snow Belt" region. This result counters recent trends demonstrating greater Democratic strength in northern states and improved competitiveness for Republicans in the South.

New governors were elected in [19] states across the country. This number of newcomers is in marked contrast to congressional results in which United States senators and representatives were returned to office at a rate of 97%. [Six] of the new governors defeated incumbents, including Lawton Chiles of Florida, Joan Finney of Kansas, John Engler of Michigan, Arne Carlson of Minnesota [, Ben Nelson of Nebraska] and Bruce Sundlun of Rhode Island.

More important than the actual results is their meaning for politics and policy across the country. While it is difficult to discern a single, consistent trend in the gubernatorial voting (many of the races turned on unique local issues and personalities), the results do suggest these possibilities.

Reapportionment: Twenty-one states are likely to be directly affected in their representation in Congress as a result of the 1990 census. Of those states likely to gain the greatest number of House seats, Democrats were successful in two (Texas and Florida) of the "Biggest Three". Wilson's triumph in California ensures the Republicans of some role in crafting a map accommodating that state's projected seven new House members. Among the states likely to lose the greatest number of congressional seats, the results were mixed with Republicans winning in Illinois, Michigan and Ohio and Democrats being seated in New York and Pennsylvania. However, combined with Democratic successes in maintaining overwhelming advantages at the state legislative level (the number of Democratically-controlled chambers increased as a result of the 1990 elections), it would appear that the Democrats are well-positioned to create a number of maps favorable to their interests.

Even in the states most affected by reapportionment considerations, newly elected Republicans will have to contend with state legislatures partly (Michigan and Ohio) or entirely controlled (California) by the opposite party. In contrast, the election of Richards and

Chiles means that the Democrats will have a free hand in reapportioning the states of Florida and Texas (Democratic governors plus Democratic legislatures equals Republican losses in the Congress for 1992).

In brief, the results from the gubernatorial races reenforce an already strong Democratic advantage in the reapportionment sweepstakes.

"Throw the Bums Out": The anti-incumbent mood of the electorate was extensively covered in pre-election analysis and actual results suggest that the nation's governors were the focus of this trend. It is not surprising that the predicted voter revolt failed to evidence itself at the national level where the advantages of campaign resources, constituency service and name recognition bolstered the campaigns of all but a few seeking reelection to the U.S. House and Senate. Governors, who are often highly visible in their states and forced to make controversial decisions about budgets, abortion and other volatile issues, were targets of voters unhappy with the present state of political and governmental affairs in the country. (In New Jersey, where the unpopular Governor Jim Florio was not on the ballot, voters chose the "next best candidate," incumbent U.S. Senator Bill Bradley, to send their message of discontentment.)

Voter anger was especially evident in races involving incumbent governors linked to recent tax increases. Among the [six] incumbents defeated, [three] (Martinez of Florida, Hayden of Kansas [and Orr of Nebraska]) were victims of popular discontentment with tax issues which are discussed later in this article. The remaining three losing governors were defeated for reasons other than taxes (DiPrete suffered for the state's economic woes, Perpich for his outspokenness and prolife stance, and Blanchard for his "dumping" of Martha Griffiths and length of service).

Newly elected governors successfully

Joan Finney: Simple Ideas in Complicated Times

Kansas has been producing populist politicians for more than 100 years, and it has produced just about every variety: angry ones, eloquent ones, avuncular ones, agitators on the left and demagogues on the right.

But it may never have elected a leader with a populist faith as simple and innocent as the one expressed by Joan Finney, the 65-year-old Democrat who took office as the state's 42nd chief executive. "I place my faith in people totally," Finney said during the campaign. "The people would be supreme in all things. I listen to the people."

How that translates into public policy for a state with big budget problems is the question of the year in Kansas politics. During her campaign against Republican Governor Mike Hayden, Finney did lay out a plan to provide property tax relief by extending the state sales tax to as many as 50 new goods and services. But she didn't always seem familiar with the nuances of her program, or articulate in talking about it, and she appeared more genuinely enthusiastic about some of her purely populist ideas, such as her plan to hold more public referenda and to insist on a state Board of Education that was subject to election by the voters.

Simple-minded as it seemed to her critics, Finney's message was the right one in a year when incumbents were, if anything, more suspect in Kansas than in most of the country. Hayden was unpopular with voters for mishandling a statewide property reassessment that ended up costing thousands of people unexpectedly large chunks of money. Finney defeated Hayden easily while being heavily outspent.

She did it by doing what she has been doing throughout her 16 years in the state treasurer's office: driving back and forth across dusty prairie roads, stopping voters at cafes and grocery stores, smiling warmly and grasping them with her trademark two-handed handshake. "I just have this compulsion," she says, "to touch them, to talk to them, to listen to them." It may be crucial to Kansas in the next four years that the people have something useful to say.

Source: Alan Ehrenhalt, "Joan Finney: Simple Ideas in Complicated Times," *Governing* 4:4 (January 1991): 14.

sought to paint themselves as "outsiders" or otherwise lacking any responsibility for the current state of affairs in their area. "Outsider" candidates in Connecticut (Weicker), Massachusetts (Weld) and Nebraska (Nelson) were particularly adept in this regard despite the fact that two of the three (Weicker and Weld) had considerable governmental experience. Gubernatorial candidates benefitting from poor economic conditions (the New England states of Rhode Island, Vermont and Massachusetts) and the unpopularity of their retiring predecessor (Oklahoma) were also in evidence during this election cycle.

Even some of the incumbent governors who were successful received approval by only a narrow margin. Governors McKernan of Maine and Hunt of Alabama were returned to office with less than spectacular majorities.

Finally, the election of independent candidates in Connecticut and Alaska suggests a willingness on part of the electorate in some areas to consider alternatives to the two party system. Combined with the victory of a socialist Congressional candidate in Vermont, the election of independents (real or self-proclaimed) represents a step forward for advocates of breaking the two-party monopoly.

Polling data and gubernatorial results indicate that American voters are increasingly dissatisfied with governmental institutions and policies. One issue in particular captured the public's attention and anger: taxes.

Taxes: One of the few policy preferences to emerge from a review of statewide, especially gubernatorial, results is significant opposition to state-level tax increases. In effect, voters adopted the often-repeated motto of the current President: "read our lips, no new taxes!"

Referenda across the country seeking to raise taxes or necessitating new public expenditures failed. The litany of losses included an Arizona referendum to raising state aid to education, "Big Green" in California and a proposed tax on liquor in the Golden State.

Some analysts claim that the results of state referenda suggest a more limited taxpayers' revolt, in other words, a popular desire to hold the line on spending. Citing the defeat of referenda in Massachusetts (Question 3), Colorado and Nebraska, these popular commentators capture only part of the message from the 1990 elections.

With the possible exception of Illinois (in which an antitax Democrat was beaten by racial divisions and low turnout in Chicago), voters chose gubernatorial candidates perceived to be or actually in opposition to new tax increases. Among governors who benefitted from an image of fiscal conservatism were Pete Wilson of California, William Weld of Massachusetts, Judd Gregg of New Hampshire and John Engler of Michigan.

Anti-tax sentiment was particularly acute in those states suffering from recessions. While much has been made of the three New England governors (Dukakis of Massachusetts, Kunin in Vermont and O'Neill in Connecticut) who wisely chose not to seek reelection due in large part to failing economies, gubernatorial candidates in other regions of the country rode a wave of economic distress and worry to victory. Governors in this category numbered Hickel of Alaska, Chiles of Florida and Walters of Oklahoma.

Abortion: Although the *New York Times* on the Sunday before the election proclaimed that abortion was not going to be the "silver bullet" of this election season, the issue played heavily in selected gubernatorial races. The pro-choice stance of candidates such as Arne Carlson of Minnesota, Barbara Roberts of Oregon and Ann Richards of Texas was an important reason for their wins. In addition, proclaiming oneself as being pro-life certainly did not hurt other gubernatorial candidates. Governors Bob Casey and John Engler proudly embraced the pro-life cause on their roads to victory.

An interesting sidelight to the debate over abortion was the switching of traditionally associated abortion positions between Democratic and Republican candidates for governor in some states. In Pennsylvania, Kansas and Minnesota, for example, the Democratic candidates were "pro-life" and the Republicans "pro-choice". Apparently some Republicans are taking quite seriously [the late] Lee Atwater's proclamation concerning the GOP's "big tent" on the abortion issue.

Education: After nearly a decade of "reform," one would think that the furor over and interest in public educational issues at the state level would be finally dissipating. Such is not the case after reviewing gubernatorial results.

Nearly every candidate released extensive proclamations and made promises to reform, revitalize or restructure (pick your "buzz word") their state's education system. Ironically, however, the one gubernatorial candidate with the most lengthy list of educational credentials, John Silber, fared poorly in a state (Massachusetts) with a great number of educational institutions and fellow Democratic Party identifiers. Several states featured gover-

Table 1 Gubernatorial Elections: 1977-1990

Year	Races	Democratic winner #	Democratic winner %	Eligible to run #	Eligible to run %	Number of incumbent governors Did run #	Did run %	Won #	Won %	Lost #	Lost %	Where lost Primary #	General election #
1977	2	1	50	1	50	1	100	1	100	—	—	—	—
1978	36	21	58	29	81	22	76	16	73	6	27	1[a]	5[b]
1979	3	2	67	0	0	—	—	—	—	—	—	—	—
1980	13	6	46	12	92	12	100	7	58	5	42	2[c]	3[d]
1981	2	1	50	0	0	—	—	—	—	—	—	—	—
1982	36	27	75	33	92	25	76	19	76	6	24	1[e]	5[f]
1983	3	3	100	0	0	—	—	—	—	—	—	—	—
1984	13	5	38	9	69	6	67	4	67	2	33	—	2[g]
1985	2	1	50	1	50	1	100	1	100	—	—	—	—
1986	36	19	53	24	67	18	75	15	83	3	18	1[h]	2[i]
1987	3	3	100	2	67	1	50	0	0	1	100	1[j]	—
1988	12	5	42	9	75	9	100	8	89	1	11	—	1[k]
1989	2	2	100	0	0	—	—	—	—	—	—	—	—
1990	36	19	53	33	92	23	70	17	74	6	26	—	6[l]
TOTALS	199	115	58	153	77	118	77	88	75	30	25	6 (20%)	24 (80%)

Source: Thad L. Beyle, "Gubernatorial Elections: 1977-1990," *Comparative State Politics* 12:2 (April 1991): 18-21. Reprinted with permission.

a Michael S. Dukakis, D-Mass.
b Robert F. Bennett, R-Kan; Rudolph G. Perpich, D-Minn.; Meldrim Thompson, R-N.H.; Robert Straub, D-Ore.; M. J. Schreiber, D-Wis.
c Thomas L. Judge, D-Mont.; Dixy Lee Ray, D-Wash.
d Bill Clinton, D-Ark.; Joseph P. Teasdale, D-Mo.; Arthur A. Link, D-N.D.
e Edward J. King, D-Mass.
f Frank D. White, R-Ark.; Charles Thone, R-Neb.; Robert F. List, R-Nev.; Hugh J. Gallen, D-N.H.; William P. Clements, Jr., R-Texas
g Allen I. Olson, R-N.D.; John D. Spellman, R-Wash.
h Bill Sheffield, D-Alaska
i Mark White, D-Texas; Anthony S. Earl, D-Wis.
j Edwin Edwards, D-La.
k Arch A. Moore, R-W.Va.
l Bob Martinez, R-Fla.; Mike Hayden, R-Kan.; James Blanchard, D-Mich.; Rudy Perpich, DFL-Minn.; Kay Orr, R-Neb.; Edward DiPrete, R-R.I.

nors' races in which education or the candidate's positions on the same were a primary determinant in the outcome. Ann Richards of Texas, Bill Clinton of Arkansas and Jim Edgar of Illinois all waged successful "pro-education" campaigns. Their opponents, Clayton Williams, Sheffield Nelson and Neil Hartigan, spoke extensively to educational questions, although, obviously not as successfully.

Among the issues drawing significant support among gubernatorial candidates were proposals for expanding early childhood educational opportunities, upgrading drug education and prevention programs, and controlling the costs of higher education. A general consensus also emerged among the candidates concerning the questionable quality of public education, linking improvements to other concerns such as economic competitiveness, amelioration of social ills, such as drug abuse and "quality of life" concerns.

Markedly absent from the debate were pledges to significantly boost resources for education (see previous "taxes" discussion) with many prospective governors noting the need to enhance opportunities within existing resources. In states where the adequacy or even constitutionality of their public school finance system was a generally recognized concern, candidates seemed to be anxious to avoid crafting specific promises. Instead, most (including Edgar of Illinois and Miller of Georgia) chose to describe the dimensions of the problem and offered little in the way of specific solutions. As Governor Florio of New Jersey quickly found out following his election in 1989, it is likely that several governors will be forced to address school finance during their terms.

In general, educational issues, while re-

ceiving the attention of many gubernatorial candidates, will be the "real test" of the winners' ability to respond to the public's concern regarding taxes and spending.

As these five possible trends suggest, the implications for politics and policy embedded in the 1990 gubernatorial results are enormous. The nation's governors will have a major role to play in determining congressional representation, tax questions and educational policy. Their ability to respond to a dissatisfied and increasingly skeptical public will test their administrations. Abortion, always a political wild card, is likely to explode on the political scene of some states.

With the addition of 19 new governors in 1990 and the prospects for change in the 1991 gubernatorial races (Kentucky, Louisiana, and Mississippi), the political climate for the next presidential election suggests a pro-tax, pro-life incumbent may be in for a rough time. To escape the volatility evident during the 1990 gubernatorial election cycle, the president and his Democratic opposition will have to craft campaigns addressing some of the trends and issues discussed here.

For the residents of the various states and political scientists, pundits and analysts, the election of 19 new governors promises changes in both electoral dynamics and policy decision—not to mention considerable entertainment opportunities for those citizens who watch the political process.

Notes

1. These tallies take into account the change in party identification from Democrat to Republican of Louisiana governor Buddy Roemer. — Ed.

To the Democrats Go the Spoils

by Karen Hansen

The long and arduous 1990 election campaign ended Nov. 6 with Democrats poised to solidify their control of the nation's legislatures and strengthen their grip on the U.S. House of Representatives.

A decade of unrelenting partisan combat waged to gain the power to reapportion the states ended by putting Democrats in control of 30 legislatures, up from 29 before Nov. 6 and edging toward their decade high of 34 legislatures in 1983. Republican control in nine legislatures going into the election shrank to five and with it their hopes for a fighting chance to regain and maintain majorities in a number of states in the '90s. Despite a long, costly and ambitious plan for developing more Republican muscle, the GOP is in a much weaker position today than it was 10 years ago. The day after Ronald Reagan was elected in 1980, Republicans held 15 state legislatures; today they are at their post-Watergate low of five, the same number they controlled in 1975 and 1977. In numbers of seats held, the percentage for Republicans is still about 40 percent, much the same as it has been for the last 30 years.

Still, the number of seats that changed partisan hands nationally is scant. Democrats won a net of only 43 state seats, but those seats gave them control of the Arizona Senate, the Indiana House, the Kansas House, and the Montana and Nevada Senates and tied the Idaho Senate, wresting four states from the Republican column, and adding to their own partisan numbers in several dozen more states. In addition, their victory in governors' races in Texas and Florida give them a complete lock on the reapportionment process in those states, which are expected to gain seven new congressional seats between them.

"We continue to control the state houses and now we've added governors in Florida and Texas. We're thrilled about that," said Jim Desler of the Democratic National Committee.

"The Republicans for the last six to eight years have been pointing to this election. This was their election where they were going to turn things around. This was their goal and they failed miserably in achieving their goal. We're still in control—Tuesday just validated the fact that the Democratic Party is controlling the reapportionment process."

Does 1990 bring any good news for the

Karen Hansen is editor of *State Legislatures*. This article is reprinted with permission from *State Legislatures* 16:11 (November/December 1990): 15-18. © 1990 by the National Conference of State Legislatures.

Republicans? Assuredly, yes. They won the Oregon House, tied the Vermont Senate, and held on to majorities in their target states of New York, Pennsylvania, Michigan and Ohio. They are within grasp of majorities in each of the chambers they lost as well as a handful of others. In numerous states Democratic domination is paper thin. In addition, Republicans continued their gradual inroads into the Democratic stronghold of the South. Since the 1988 elections, Republicans have gained a net of 11 seats in the southern states, either through party switches or electoral victories. Today, Republicans hold more seats in southern legislatures than at any time in this century.

The Democrats' gains this election were the second smallest in three decades—in 1988 they picked up only nine seats. And while Republicans won't be seated at the table when the maps are drawn in 16 states, they have actually enhanced their reapportionment position in several major states.

California is the big prize with an anticipated seven new congressional seats. Republican Governor . . . Pete Wilson [is] in a position to veto a plan unfair to Republicans. Democrats controlled both houses of the Legislature after the 1981 reapportionment, as well as the governorship. Led by the late Rep. Phil Burton, they drew a plan that increased the Democratic congressional margin from 22-21 to 28-17. Ever since then Republicans have unsuccessfully attempted to topple the plan, both through the courts and through initiatives on the June ballot to reform the reapportionment process. Wilson's victory is a big plum for Republicans.

Furthermore, in a surprise upset, Michigan Republican Senate Majority Leader John Engler beat two-term incumbent Governor James Blanchard, who several weeks before the election had a 25-point lead. Michigan Republicans also held on to their slim two-seat margin in the Senate, clearly giving them the

upper hand in the mapmaking in a state that could lose two to three congressional seats.

The Ohio governorship was another victory for the GOP, where they also increased their margin of control in the Senate and won the race for secretary of state, giving them control over reapportionment. In Illinois, Secretary of State Jim Edgar, a former state legislator, staved off Democratic Attorney General Neil Hartigan in a tough campaign with billboards proclaiming "No One for Governor." Republicans also increased their numbers in the New York Senate, which many thought would go Democrat. . . .

"These were the best results for Republicans in a mid-term election in 20 years," said Charles Black of the Republican National Committee. . . .

. . . Losses for legislative Republicans are . . . much less than the historical average for the president's party during mid-term elections. From 1962 through 1986, the president's party lost an average 347 seats in midterm elections. During the 1980s, the president's party lost an average of 150 seats in midterm elections. [In 1990] Republicans lost only 43 to the Democrats.

"Our goal at the start of this cycle was to get to the redistricting table in as many states as possible," said Norman Cummings, political director of the Republican National Committee. "That meant either a governor or a legislative chamber. We were in a posture of defense in legislative chambers—the New York, Pennsylvania and Michigan Senates, the Indiana and Arizona Legislatures. We tried to gain control of the Florida Senate and Oregon House. From our perspective we were extremely successful—beyond our best expectations considering the environment we had to work with.

"We did not lose in any state where we were at the table legislatively. In states where we held at least one chamber, we still hold one

Reflecting on Recent Election Trends in Order

The status of incumbents in the Kentucky legislature was somewhat . . . precarious. [In 1990] there were 17 incumbent senators and 99 incumbent representatives running for the 19 Senate and 100 House seats on the ballot. Four state senators and six representatives were defeated in the primary; and another four senators and seven representatives lost in the general election. This makes a total of 21 incumbents who were defeated . . . , 18 percent of the total who were running, well above the average of 11 percent of incumbents losing in elections during the 1980s.

Obviously the most important question about the Kentucky legislative races is how much the large tax increase enacted by the 1990 legislature contributed to the defeat of incumbents. Exactly two-thirds of the 21 legislators who lost in the primary or the general election voted for the tax increase. Surprisingly, all eight senators who were defeated (all but one of them Democrats) voted for the tax increase, but only six of the 13 representatives who lost had supported the tax, three of them Democrats and three of them Republicans.

We can speculate that the stand taken by senators on the tax issue attracted more attention, or the Republican party was more successful in finding and supporting strong challengers in the Senate races. But there is no firm evidence to support any of these theories.

We should remember that legislative races are individual contests, and each is different. In some districts, there seemed to be little concern about the tax issue, or both candidates took the same position on it. There was also great variation in the vigor and skill with which challengers used the tax issue. . . .

It seems obvious that support for the tax increase played some role in the defeat of most of the 14 supporters who lost. But it is fair to conclude that most of those incumbents who were beaten, including the tax supporters, had other weaknesses or liabilities that were not connected to the tax issue.

Three or four who lost in the general election were running in districts usually controlled by the other party. Several others had been in office for long periods, and may have become complacent. . . . Several were not particularly effective legislators or politicians.

One factor in the defeat of eight Democratic incumbents in the general election was the unusually active role played by the state Republican party. The party made a much greater effort than usual to recruit candidates and, consequently, more Republicans were running than at any time since [1967-71]. Moreover, the party raised a quarter of a million dollars to assist Republican candidates, and presumably distributed these funds to those candidates with the best chance of winning.

This was an ideal time for the Republicans to make such an effort because the tax increase offered them a potent issue, and most Republican legislators had opposed the tax increase. Given all these factors, it is somewhat surprising that the Republican party made a net gain of only three seats in each chamber of the legislature; among the incumbents running, it gained eight and lost three.

Bill Straub, the *Kentucky Post* columnist, reviewed the Republican effort and concluded: "It resulted in a gain of six measly seats. Some revolution." It is hardly a revolution; whether it is the start of an evolution depends on whether the Republican Party can continue this practice of recruiting and supporting more candidates—and of course whether the Democratic Party will decide that it has some responsibility to help its legislative candidates.

If both of these things were to happen, we might have many more seriously contested legislative races—giving more voters some real choice at the polls.

Source: Malcolm Jewell, "Reflecting on Recent Election Trends in Order," *The Kentucky Journal* 2:9 (December 1990): 11. Malcolm Jewell is professor of political science at the University of Kentucky and editor of *The Kentucky Journal.*

chamber." In fact, Republicans lost their majority in the Montana Senate, giving Democrats control of both chambers. But, after a close race and a recount, they held on to their one-seat margin in the Washington Senate.

Only once in the past 30 years have so few seats changed in the legislatures. In 1988, George Bush was the first president in U.S. history to win while his party did not make any gains in the state legislatures, governorships, U.S. House or Senate. That year Democrats won nine state legislative seats.

The DNC's Desler explains the Democrats' low gains this way: "Well, we're starting at an historic high. Normal off-year projections aren't accurate when George Bush's coattails in 1988 were non-existent. So we came in—not only in congressional seats but in state elections—with very comfortable majorities, and any additional gains beyond that are just icing on the cake."

The 1990 election was clouded by a strong anti-incumbent sentiment symbolized in California, Colorado and Oklahoma by term limitation initiatives. All three states passed term limits, although Californians defeated one of two initiatives on their ballot and passed the other by the slimmest of margins. And, in fact, the voters did not "throw the rascals out" at the polls. Preliminary analysis of 25 state house races indicates that only 9 percent of the incumbents standing for re-election were defeated.

But in some states the numbers were much larger. In Massachusetts, a state wracked by fiscal uncertainty and an immensely unpopular governor, five incumbent senators and 11 House members were defeated. In Nevada, where an unpopular increase in lawmakers' pensions became a hot issue, eight House members and three senators lost their reelection bid. Pennsylvania voters defeated 15 members of the House and two senators, and in Tennessee, 10 incumbents,

including three House committee chairmen, lost. In Maryland where abortion was a top issue, eight House members and two senators won't be coming back. And in Kansas, voters turned out their governor and 15 House incumbents, and handed over control to Democrats in the House. . . .

What does it all mean?

"It's not an election with a message," said Curtis Gans, director of the Committee for the Study of the American Electorate. "It's not anti-tax—tax cutting initiatives didn't pass. It's not anti-incumbent. It's only marginally anti-Republican, but very marginally. It's not a referendum on Bush. There wasn't any national message."

Democrats disagree.

"The '90s are going to be a Democratic decade. All the way through," says Jim Desler of the DNC.

He might be right, says political analyst Norman Ornstein of the American Enterprise Institute, if Republicans can't recruit "good vigorous candidates."

"Democrats just have a natural advantage in this regard and Republicans have a worrisome problem. They're going to have to do something, which includes finding a much more positive side to conservatism, a sense of purpose, and also finding incentives to get people into public life, not just [government] bashing.

"If they don't change, they're not going to do any better. They're not going to fade away to nothingness at the state and local level, but they're going to continue to have poor results—even when you have a public that's in sympathy with their general point of view.

"They're not going to become a majority party across the country unless they start to do something from the ground up."

To the winners goes the last word: "A Democratic decade, all the way through, and we're thrilled with what happened on Nov. 6," says Jim Desler.

Map-Drawers Must Toe the Line In Upcoming Redistricting

by Rhodes Cook

As the myriad players in the coming round of redistricting dust off their maps, plug in their computers and pore over 1990 population figures, they will also have to acquaint themselves with a legal landscape substantially altered since 1980.

For most of the nation's political community, the process of redrawing congressional district lines is a once-in-a-decade activity. But for the courts, it is an ongoing preoccupation. Judges have become the not-so-silent partners of the redistricting process.

In the past decade, the courts have underscored the "one-person, one-vote" doctrine by which states must divide their population equally among districts.

They have sharply increased the pressure on state mapmakers to assure minority representation, even to the brink of mandating the election of minorities.

Moreover, the Supreme Court has opened the door to suits alleging partisan gerrymandering — the politically one-sided, often tortured, line drawing that clearly gives one party an advantage over the other.

And weaving through the issues of population, race and political partisanship in the 1990s are questions regarding the accuracy of the 1990 census itself.

A new legal debate now focuses on whether the tally should be statistically adjusted to compensate for an anticipated minority undercount.

For anyone contemplating a congressional candidacy — or interested in the composition of Congress in the 1990s — these issues are far from academic concerns.

Uncertainties Abound

After any redistricting process, the first election spells electoral opportunity for parties and individuals waiting to make their move.

The stakes are even higher if such an election coincides with a presidential campaign, as in 1992.

The exact shape and composition of each district dictates candidates' strategy and tactics. So it can be excruciating enough for office-seekers to wait on legislatures and governors to work out their redistricting differences. The added round of recourse to the courts means, at minimum, a longer wait. Such extended uncertainty becomes one more obstacle for would-be candidates.

Rhodes Cook is a staff writer for the *Congressional Quarterly Weekly Report*. This article appeared September 1, 1990, 2786-2793.

Minority candidates, for example, may begin a campaign by appealing across racial lines, only to learn that the district they are seeking will consist almost entirely of minority voters.

In many states, candidates may go well into the election year itself still wondering whether a given district will be hospitable to them — or even whether it will continue to exist.

No one is quite sure at this point how the courts will approach redistricting litigation in the 1990s. After a quarter-century of Supreme Court involvement in the issues of population equality and minority representation, the court would seem to be unable to disengage itself — even if it wanted to.

At the same time, the high court may be less eager than in the past to break new ground, particularly with the recent retirement of Justice William J. Brennan Jr.

Probably more than any other member, Brennan pushed the court into what Justice Felix Frankfurter (1939-62) warned was the "political thicket" of reapportionment and re-districting.

Brennan wrote the majority opinion in *Baker v. Carr*, the landmark 1962 case that brought the court into redistricting, as well as several other cases that subsequently estab-lished and tightened the interpretation of the one-person, one-vote doctrine.

His rulings were controversial, since they often forced states to split historical geographic entities such as cities and counties between districts in order to achieve the strict popula-tion equality the court now requires.

Yet even before Brennan announced his retirement in July 1990, there were signs the Supreme Court was becoming more. selective in the cases it would hear, to the point of being described as a "take your problems elsewhere" court.

But that does not necessarily imply less

legal action elsewhere. It could mean more running room for state and lower federal courts. And it may even provide an opening for Congress, if it wants one, to address aspects of redistricting law.

Population Equality

For most of its history, the court viewed redistricting as a political act that was essen-tially none of its business.

That attitude only gradually began to change in the 1950s as an activist court headed by former California Gov. Earl Warren began to take shape. By the early 1960s, it was clear that redistricting could be a ripe area for legal involvement.

By then, wide population disparity among congressional districts could no longer be ignored. Louisiana had not redrawn its district lines since 1912. Georgia, Wisconsin, Colorado and South Carolina had not done so since the early 1930s.

Rural areas generally benefited from the population disparity. In Florida, the most populous district was nearly three times as large as the least populated one. In both California and Illinois, the most populous district was nearly twice as large.

And by 1960, not a single state legislative body existed in which there was not at least a 2-to-1 population disparity between the most and least populous districts. In many legisla-tures the disparity was huge: 223 to 1 in the Nevada Senate, 422 to 1 in the California Senate and 1,480 to 1 in the Vermont House.

In California, three mountain counties with a combined 1960 population of less than 15,000 had one state senator; so did Los Angeles County, with more than 6 million residents.

It was against this backdrop that a group of urban plaintiffs from Tennessee challenged the apportionment of their state legislature. While the Supreme Court did not rule on the merits of the case, the court did decide by a 6-to-2 vote in *Baker v. Carr* that the plaintiffs had raised a justiciable issue.

Bandwagon Rolls

In short order, other decisions followed. *Gray v. Sanders* in 1963 established the one-person, one-vote standard. *Wesberry v. Sanders* in 1964 extended the one-person, one-vote principle to congressional districts.

Had it acted, Congress might have slowed, if not stopped, the court's headlong march toward rigid population equality at this point.

Throughout the 1950s and early 1960s, House Judiciary Committee Chairman Emanuel Celler (D-N.Y., 1923-73) regularly introduced a bill to permit state lawmakers some flexibility regarding population in designing districts.

Celler's legislation went nowhere until after *Wesberry*. But in 1965, a version passed the House. It established 15 percent as the maximum percentage by which a congressional district's population might deviate from the average population of the state's districts.

There was little doubt that a major reason for House approval of Celler's bill was a fear that the courts would impose even more rigid criteria. But the measure died in the Senate without coming to a floor vote.

It stalled, in part, because it was overshadowed by the spirited reaction to another 1964 Supreme Court decision, *Reynolds v. Sims*. Applying the one-person, one-vote dictum to state legislative line drawing, the court ruled in *Reynolds* that legislative districts must be of substantially equal population.

Critics viewed the *Reynolds* decision as an invasion of states' rights. In Congress, Republicans and Southern Democrats joined forces. In both 1965 and 1966, Senate Minority Leader Everett McKinley Dirksen (R-Ill., House 1933-49, Senate 1951-69), pushed proposals for a constitutional amendment to allow states to apportion at least one house of their state legislature on a non-population basis.

In both years, Dirksen won a substantial majority for his proposal, but each time fell a few votes short of the two-thirds majority required for a proposed constitutional amendment.

The "substantially equal" standard of *Reynolds* led the court to accept state legislative plans with a population range of up to 10 percent.

Zero Tolerance

But after *Wesberry*, the population-equality standard for congressional districts was quantified and steadily tightened. In 1967, the court sent back Indiana and Missouri congressional redistricting plans that had allowed for as much as 20 percent deviation from the average district population.

Two years later, Missouri's revised plan returned to the court for full review (*Kirkpatrick v. Preisler*). It allowed a range of approximately 6 percent between the most and least populous districts. By a 6-3 vote, it was rejected.

The judicial rulings of the 1960s had their effect. A total of 385 of the 435 House members elected in 1972 were chosen from districts that varied less than 1 percent from their state's average congressional district population. The average variance from the ideal district size was less than 0.5 percent for the 93rd Congress (1973-75), compared with 17 percent for the 88th Congress (1963-65).

Any doubts in the political community about the courts' obsession with population equality were dispelled by the early 1980s, when a court-imposed map in Michigan created 16 districts with exactly equal population — 514,560. The state's other two districts listed a population just one person less — 514,559.

"Will we be faced with that kind of potential absurdity this time?" asks Kimball Brace, a Washington-based redistricting consultant. "I don't know."

Brace speculates that the court might be ready to take a more lenient view on population equality, particularly since the accuracy of the 1990 census has become a subject of controversy.

But Bruce Cain, a University of California-Berkeley political scientist, warns that no state should count on a change in the court's attitude in drawing new districts. "It's clear you have to get as close to zero as you can get," he says.

Any state that does not do so could find itself hauled into court. Plaintiffs with any number of agendas will know that population disparity gets the court's attention.

The late Democratic Rep. Phillip Burton (1964-83) also realized that in crafting a congressional district map for his home state of California in the early 1980s.

Partisan Gerrymandering

Burton's now-famous creation featured a number of odd-shaped districts that were drawn neither compactly nor with respect to community boundaries. But Burton could brag that his map was loyal to the court's edict: The average variance in population between districts was only 67 people.

To the national GOP's delight, the Supreme Court in 1986 decided that the entire area of partisan gerrymandering was open to legal challenge — even if the disputed districts met the one-person, one-vote test.

Ironically the court's decision, in *Davis v. Bandemer*, resulted from a challenge by Indiana Democrats, who complained that the legislature's GOP majority unconstitutionally gerrymandered them out of legislative seats following the 1980 census. In 1984, a divided lower court agreed and voided the plan. Indi-

ana Republicans appealed to the Supreme Court.

Two separate decisions followed in June 1986. The court first had to rule on whether partisan gerrymanders should be subject to constitutional review. Six justices declared they were.

But the court rejected, by a 7-2 vote, the specific challenge by the Indiana Democrats. Left unclear were what standards the court would find necessary to prove a legally unacceptable partisan gerrymander.

National Republicans expressed delight with the *Bandemer* decision. The GOP had long held that Democratic control over most state legislatures had allowed them to draw congressional and legislative districts to their partisan advantage. In finding that partisan gerrymanders are open to constitutional challenge, the court gave the GOP a chance to fight those plans outside the electoral arena.

In particular, Republicans expressed confidence that the *Bandemer* decision lay the groundwork for overturning the Democratic-drawn congressional district map in California — a map, Republicans argued, that was as close to a classic partisan gerrymander as the political world can produce.

With the Burton creation in place for the 1982 election, the California congressional delegation went from a 22-21 Democratic edge to a 28-17 Democratic majority.

The map was redrawn slightly in 1983, after Republicans managed to get rid of the first version in a statewide referendum. In 1984, the GOP gained one seat. That was the only change in the delegation's party balance for the rest of the decade.

A Pattern of Exclusion?

The GOP's lawsuit against the Democratic plan was filed in federal district court in San Francisco by Rep. Robert E. Badham (1977-89) in 1983. The district court held a

Table 1 Key Redistricting States

Seat Change in 1992	State	1990 Elections Party Holding			Comments
		State House	State Senate	Gov.	
+7	Calif.	D	D	R	GOP gubernatorial win is likely to prevent a repeat of the partisan Democratic remap approved by legislature in the last redistricting round.
+4	Fla.	D	D	D	Gubernatorial takeover plus Senate hold gives Democrats complete remap control. But influx of Republican voters probably ensures GOP a share of the new seats.
+3	Texas	D	D	D	Democrats take governorship, but legislative alliance between Republicans and conservative Democrats as well as GOP growth in state may help GOP in remapping.
+1	Ariz.	R	D	R	Democrats take over Senate, but lose the governorship, clouding the picture.
+1	Ga.	D	D	D	Democrats will decide shape of new district.
+1	N.C.	D	D	R	GOP Gov. Martin has no veto, and Democratic gains in House may weaken GOP role in deciding how to draw new district.
+1	Va.	NA	NA	NA	No elections held. Democrats have control.
+1	Wash.	D	D	D	Democrats pick up Senate, but that has no impact on remapping, which is done by a bipartisan commission with broad powers.
−3	N.Y.	D	R	D	Lackluster showing by Gov. Cuomo helps Republicans hold off Democrats challenging GOP Senate control. Seat loss likely to hit both parties.
−2	Ill.	D	D	R	Democrats protect slim Senate lead but cannot wrest governorship from GOP, so both parties may take a hit in remapping.
−2	Mich.	D	R	R	A Republican advance here, with a gubernatorial pickup and a narrow Senate hold making Democrats skittish.
−2	Ohio	D	R	R	Republicans hold governorship and Senate. Seat loss could hit both parties.
−2	Pa.	D	R	D	Chambers remain closely divided and split between parties, so both parties may have to yield a seat in remap.
−1	Iowa	D	D	R	Maps drawn by nonpartisan agency, but Democratic legislature retains veto.
−1	Kan.	D	R	D	Democrats gain here, taking over governorship and state House. GOP newcomer Dick Nichols may see his 5th District disappear in remap.
−1	La.	D	D	R	Party switch by governor from Democrat to Republican has confused the issue.
−1	Mass.	D	D	R	Republicans still have little say in the legislature but pick up the governorship.
−1	Ky.; N.J.; W.Va.				In each of these states, Democrats control the governorship and both legislative chambers.

Source: "Key Redistricting States," *Congressional Quarterly Weekly Report,* November 10, 1990, 3844.

hearing on *Badham v. Eu* in the wake of the *Bandemer* decision but dismissed the Republican claim by a 2-1 vote.

Essentially, the district court ruled that a party seeking to overturn a remap must show a general pattern of exclusion from the political process, which the California GOP — in control of the governorship, a Senate seat and 40 percent of the House delegation — could not do.

The Republicans appealed to the Supreme Court, but the court refused to become involved, finally voting 6-3 in 1989 to reaffirm the lower court's decision without comment.

"I think the courts have shown they're cowards, and it's a cowardice I applaud," says Cain. In his opinion, "they have shown themselves wary of intervening and have set a threshold as high as possible without saying partisan gerrymandering is outside their jurisdiction" so that they will not get pulled into every politically charged case.

Jeffrey M. Wice, the counsel for the Democratic State Legislative Leaders Association, basically agrees: "The kind of proof that you have to show . . . is that the political party has been wiped off the face of the state's politics. That's a tough nut to crack."

Many in the political community believe that it would take distorted results from not one but several elections to make the case for partisan gerrymandering.

Even Republicans acknowledge that partisan gerrymandering is not easy to prove. "There is no doubt that the political gerrymandering claim is probably the most difficult of all redistricting claims to make," says Michael Hess, the deputy chief counsel for the Republican National Committee (RNC).

But Hess hopes the Supreme Court's refusal to hear GOP arguments in the *Badham* case was merely a matter of timing; the case reached the court at the end of the decade, shortly before lines were to be redrawn.

"What the RNC will be doing and what we'll be encouraging Republican lawyers around the country to be doing," Hess says, "is to be aware that [partisan gerrymandering] is still a valid cause of action. The Supreme Court doesn't find that things are justiciable just for the heck of it."

Encouraging to Republicans is the fact that three members of the court were ready to hear arguments on *Badham*, one short of the number needed. All three — Chief Justice William H. Rehnquist and Justices Anthony M. Kennedy and John Paul Stevens — are still serving.

"If the court gives any sign of going to the Republican interpretation," predicts Cain, "you would see a flood of litigation at all levels. If it holds to *[Badham]*, there will probably be some cases to test the water and then they would fritter away."

Minority Representation

No aspect of redistricting law has changed more dramatically over the last decade than minority representation.

Ten years ago, the burden of proof was on minorities to show that lines were being drawn to dilute their voting strength. Now, the burden of proof has been shifted to the lawmakers to show that they have done all they can to maximize minority voting strength.

"We've gone from, 'Can you do something affirmative?' to 'Can you afford to avoid race?' " says Cain. "That's gone a long way in 10 years."

The cornerstone of minority representation cases is the Voting Rights Act of 1965, extended in 1970, 1975 and 1982. It bans redistricting plans that dilute the voting strength of minorities.

Originally aimed at those Southern states where blacks had long been targets of discrimination, the law was subsequently extended to other minorities, including Hispanics, Asian-

Americans, American Indians and native Alaskans.

In 1980, the Supreme Court for the first time narrowed the reach of the Voting Rights Act in the case of *Mobile v. Bolden*, a challenge to the Alabama city of Mobile's at-large system of electing city commissioners.

By a vote of 6-3, the court ruled that proof of discriminatory intent by the commissioners was necessary before a violation could be found; the fact that no black had ever been elected under the challenged system was not proof enough.

The *Mobile* decision set off an immediate reaction on Capitol Hill. In extending the Voting Rights Act in 1982, Congress amended it to outlaw any practice that has the effect of discriminating against blacks or other minorities — regardless of the lawmakers' intent.

The congressional mandate in the Voting Rights Act is so specific, says Cain, that the court would find it virtually impossible to reverse direction even if it wanted to. "I think Congress tied their hands," he says.

Expanding Results Test

The Justice Department later adopted a similar "results test" for another part of the act (Section 5), which requires certain states and localities with a history of discrimination to have their electoral plans "pre-cleared" by the department.

In 1986 the court applied this test in *Thornburg v. Gingles*, ruling that six of North Carolina's multimember legislative districts impermissibly diluted black voting strength.

Sharply departing from *Mobile*, the court held that since very few blacks had been elected from these districts, the system must be in violation of the law.

The court also used the *Thornburg* decision to develop three criteria that, if met, should lead to the creation of a minority

legislative district: The minority group must be large and geographically compact enough to constitute a majority in a single-member electoral district, the group must be politically cohesive, and the white majority must vote as a bloc to the degree that it usually can defeat candidates preferred by the minority.

Legal action since *Thornburg* has increased the pressure for fuller minority representation.

In June 1990, Los Angeles Federal District Judge David V. Kenyon ruled in *Garza v. County of Los Angeles* that the Los Angeles County Board of Supervisors had violated the Voting Rights Act by gerrymandering its districts to dilute the Hispanic vote.

No Hispanic has ever held a seat on the five-member governing board of the nation's most populous county (which has an estimated 8.7 million residents), even though the county is about one-third Hispanic. In August 1990, Kenyon ordered the creation of a majority Hispanic district.

Also, the Justice Department in August filed a lawsuit against the Georgia election runoff system on the grounds that it discriminates against minority voters.

Runoffs are almost exclusively a feature of Southern politics. Civil rights activists have long argued that they dilute minority voting power because even if a black finishes first in a primary, he usually falls to united white opposition in the runoff.

Assistant Attorney General John R. Dunne, the head of Justice's Civil Rights Division, which enforces the Voting Rights Act, had signaled such a move in a speech to a National Conference of State Legislatures' redistricting conference in June.

"Our staff serves as watchdogs of minority voting rights," he said, and its basic approach to redistricting could be summed up in the words: "Read my lips: No minority dilution."

But Dunne has not tipped his hand as to how far his office might go in requiring the creation of minority districts.

A 24-year veteran of the New York Senate, Dunne has expressed appreciation for the rough and tumble nature of the redistricting process, and he has said that incumbent protection is not impermissible as long as it does not impair minority voting strength.

Justice's responsibility "is to call them as we see them," he says. "There are so many variables that go into making this sausage."

Many observers expect minority representation cases to be the most active area of redistricting litigation in the 1990s, and not just because minority plaintiffs have an improved chance of winning.

Minority groups have traditionally viewed the courts as their prime avenue of redress. "The courts brought me to the table, not the parties," says Tony Harrison, the project director of voter participation for the Southern Regional Council.

Harrison speaks from personal experience. He was elected to the Alabama Legislature in 1974, he says, from a court-drawn district that the Legislature had refused to create.

Other litigation is inevitable because the legal landscape surrounding minority representation is still being defined.

One case that was watched closely is *Armour v. Ohio,* which focused on the issue of whether "minority influenced" districts should be created in areas where a district with a majority of minorities cannot be drawn.

The plaintiffs asked that black populations that are split between two state legislative districts be combined into one district to maximize their political influence — even though the black population (which is 11 percent in one district and 25 percent in the other) would not constitute a majority in the new district. [The 6th U.S. Circuit Court of Appeals in

Cincinnati reversed and remanded the case on February 15, 1991.]

Still a Hot Button

The courts may also revisit the question of how large a proportion of a district's population must be of a particular minority group to give that minority a fair chance of winning the seat. For years, the rule of thumb has been that the minority population of a district needs to be at least 65 percent to compensate for lower rates of minority voter registration and turnout.

But it is possible that so high a minority population is not needed. In 1990, 16 of the 17 House districts with a 1980 population at least 50 percent black had black representatives — the exception having been the New Orleans-based Louisiana 2nd, where retiring Democrat Lindy (Mrs. Hale) Boggs held the seat.

And eight of the nine majority Hispanic districts had Hispanic representatives in 1990—the exception having been Democrat Ronald D. Coleman in the El Paso-based Texas 16th. . . .

Efforts to increase minority representation have spawned talk of enlarging the size of a variety of legislative bodies. A possible solution advanced by one of the plaintiffs in the *Garza* case, for instance, was to expand the number of seats on the Los Angeles County Board of Supervisors.

Expansion, they argued, is a way to promote racial and ethnic diversity on the board and shrink the size of districts in a huge jurisdiction such as Los Angeles County, where a single supervisorial district is as populous as three congressional districts.

It is a prospective solution that is also being voiced by some state legislators, who must apply new minority-representation rules in drawing their own state legislative lines. Many of them see expansion of legislative bodies as a relatively painless way to allow incumbents to retain their seats while facilitating minority representation.

Proposals have even been made to expand the U.S. House, which has had 435 seats for nearly 80 years, but which can change its size by statute.

Population Undercount

The building block of the whole redistricting process is the census count, and concern about the accuracy of the 1990 tally has already been the subject of litigation.

The core issue is whether the count should be left as is or be statistically adjusted to compensate for a population undercount. No such adjustment has been made in previous censuses.

An undercount is nothing new. In 1980 the Census Bureau estimated that it counted about 99 percent of the white population but only about 94 percent of blacks. The 1990 count, it is estimated, may fall even further short.

Calls for an adjusted count are not new either. Several cities with large minority populations sought but failed to win adjustment of the 1980 census count.

The latest debate began in 1987, when the Commerce Department (which includes the Census Bureau) announced that it would not adjust the 1990 count.

That fueled charges that the Republican administration was undercounting a Democratic constituency. And it was not long before a lawsuit was brought by New York City (along with other cities, states and civil rights organizations), calling on the Census Bureau to make a statistical adjustment of the tally to account for people who were missed.

In response to the lawsuit, the Commerce Department agreed to defer a final judgment on the adjustment question until as late as mid-July 1991.

This concession did not mollify Commerce critics, who see that scenario as opening the door to chaos. It is estimated that by mid-July 1991 the deadlines for finishing the redistricting process will have passed in close to 20 states. And if states were given two sets of population figures — one adjusted, one not — that could lead to innumerable logistical, political and legal headaches in the redistricting process.

Early in 1990, the plaintiffs in the New York City case reopened their lawsuit in an effort to get the Commerce Department to draft new guidelines that would require the department to adjust the count in 1991, unless it could demonstrate that a statistical change would not be more accurate than the actual tally.

In something of a split decision, a federal district court in New York ruled in June of that year that an adjustment would be constitutional and that the Commerce Department would "clearly incur a heavier burden" to explain an anti-adjustment decision in 1991. But it also ruled that the Commerce Department's guidelines on the matter were not inadequate or biased.

Meanwhile, an avalanche of litigation on the question seems inevitable. There has to be some form of adjustment and relief, says Harrison, and relief "has to come from the judiciary."

The Courts Warily Find Their Way Into the 'Political Thicket'

by Rhodes Cook

While the federal judiciary has in recent years become a prominent, if somewhat unpredictable, player in the congressional redistricting process, for most of the nation's history the courts were content to be spectators, letting Congress set the ground rules for how district lines were drawn.

In the words of Justice Felix Frankfurter, congressional redistricting was a "political thicket" that the courts should avoid. It was not until the early 1960s that dramatic population shifts combined with a mood of judicial activism to shift the court's philosophy.

Over the course of the previous century, Congress did pass several pieces of legislation urging states to create districts of equal population, as well as of compact size and contiguous shape. But the prevailing attitude on Capitol Hill was that these standards were to serve as guidelines and were not binding on the states.

By the early 20th century, large population disparities had developed between lightly populated rural districts and heavily populated urban districts. But rural-dominated state legislatures often were reluctant to redraw the lines, and the courts provided no impetus for change. The Supreme Court maintained a hands-off attitude toward redistricting until well after World War II.

1932 — *Wood v. Broom* — In the first significant congressional redistricting case to reach the Supreme Court, a Mississippi law that had created congressional districts of unequal population is upheld. Four justices underscore the court's hands-off attitude by suggesting that it does not have jurisdiction over redistricting.

1946 — *Colegrove v. Green* — Supreme Court reaffirms its laissez faire attitude to redistricting in a case involving a challenge to the unequal population of Illinois districts (they ranged in size from barely 100,000 residents to more than 900,000). Justice Frankfurter warns that redistricting is a "political thicket" that courts should avoid. But the vote in *Colegrove* is only 4-3, and the dissenters argue that the court does have jurisdiction over redistricting.

1960 — *Gomillion v. Lightfoot* — Supreme Court strikes down the Alabama Legislature's attempt to redraw the city boundaries of Tuskegee to exclude virtually all black

Rhodes Cook is a staff writer for the *Congressional Quarterly Weekly Report*. This article appeared September 1, 1990, 2789-2790.

voters. This is one of a series of civil rights cases that begins to lay the groundwork for the Supreme Court's change of attitude. A commentator later describes the decision as amounting to a "dragon" in the "political thicket" of *Colegrove.*

1962 — *Baker v. Carr* — In a landmark 6-2 decision, the Supreme Court abandons its non-interventionist attitude by ruling in a case involving the apportionment of the Tennessee General Assembly that legislative redistricting (and by implication, congressional redistricting) is within its jurisdiction.

Justice William J. Brennan Jr. writes the majority opinion, emphasizing that the federal judiciary has the power to review the apportionment of state legislatures under the 14th Amendment's equal-protection clause.

Now in the minority, Justice Frankfurter writes that the decision is "a massive repudiation of the experience of our whole past" and is an assertion of "destructively novel judicial power."

1963 — *Gray v. Sanders* — The "one-person, one-vote" concept is enunciated by Justice William O. Douglas in this Supreme Court case striking down Georgia's weighted county unit system of voting in primary elections.

1964 — *Wesberry v. Sanders* — The Supreme Court applies the one-person, one-vote standard to congressional districts, striking down a Georgia map that has not been changed since 1931 and features a population disparity of 550,000 between the most and least populous districts.

In defending its decision, the court cites Article I, Section 2 of the Constitution, which states that "representatives shall be apportioned among the states according to their respective numbers" and be "chosen by the people of the several states." This language, the court states, means that "as nearly as is practicable," one person's vote in a congressional election is to be worth as much as another's.

The impact of *Wesberry* is sweeping: Nearly every state redraws its congressional district lines over the rest of the decade — sometimes more than once. By the end of the 1960s, 39 of the 45 states with more than one representative make adjustments.

1969 — *Kirkpatrick v. Preisler* — By a 6-3 vote, the Supreme Court reaffirms the strict application of one-person, one-vote to congressional redistricting, rejecting a Missouri plan that calls for a disparity of approximately 6 percent between the most and least populous districts. The court decides that minor deviations from strict population equality are to be permitted only when the state provides substantial evidence that the variation was unavoidable.

1969 — *Wells v. Rockefeller* — Supreme Court rules as unacceptable a New York redistricting plan that had created congressional districts of nearly equal population within regions of the state, but not of equal population throughout the state.

1973 — *White v. Weiser* — Supreme Court continues to tighten its interpretation of the one-person, one-vote doctrine, rejecting a Texas congressional district map that calls for a disparity between the most and least populous districts of roughly 5 percent. The court rejects the argument that the disparity is an acceptable result of an attempt to avoid splitting political subdivisions.

1980 — *Mobile v. Bolden* — The reach of the 1965 Voting Rights Act is narrowed by this case concerning the city of Mobile's at-large system of electing city commissioners. Even though no black had been elected under the system, the Supreme Court rules that it does not violate the Voting Rights Act. It is not enough to find a voting system discriminatory in effect, the court says, unless there is also evidence that it was created with the intent to be discriminatory.

1982 — Reacting to the *Mobile* decision, Congress amends the Voting Rights Act to loosen the burden of proof in discriminatory vote cases. The new language states that discriminatory results are sufficient to demonstrate that a minority had been wronged.

1983 — *Karcher v. Daggett* — By a 5-4 vote, the Supreme Court rejects a New Jersey congressional district map that calls for a variation between the most and least populous districts of 0.7 percent. The court emphasizes that there is no uniform level of population disparity that is so small as to be acceptable, and that variations are permissible only if a state can prove that they are necessary to achieve some legitimate goal.

1986 — *Thornburg v. Gingles* — In a test of the 1982 Voting Rights Act, the Supreme Court agrees that a voting system that has the effect of discriminating against minorities is in violation of the law regardless of the lawmakers' intent. Specifically, the court rules that six multimember legislative districts in North Carolina violate the Voting Rights Act because they impermissibly dilute the strength of black voters. The decision is seen by many in the political community as a warning to states to create minority districts wherever possible.

1986 — *Davis v. Bandemer* — Supreme Court declares for the first time that partisan gerrymanders (line-drawing that blatantly

gives one party an advantage over another) are subject to legal challenge. But the court decides that the specific case before it, involving a GOP-drawn legislative map in Indiana, does not constitute a partisan gerrymander.

1987 — Responding to charges that the 1990 census would undercount urban minorities, the Commerce Department announces that it will not make a statistical adjustment in the 1990 tally. Although no previous census count has been adjusted, the ruling fuels lawsuits and charges that the Republican administration is "playing politics" with the census.

January 1989 — *Badham v. Eu* — Supreme Court rules without comment that a Democratic-drawn congressional district map in California, long recognized as aggressively partisan, does not constitute an unacceptable partisan gerrymander. The court leaves unclear the question of what would be unacceptable. The vote to dismiss the Republican challenge is 6-3; three justices agree to hear the case, but the approval of four is needed.

July 1989 — Responding to a lawsuit brought by New York City (along with other cities, states and civil rights organizations), the Commerce Department agrees to keep the adjustment question open until July 1991. Other lawsuits are filed seeking to require Commerce to statistically adjust the census, or at least to make a final determination on the issue before mid-1991.

April 1990 — The nationwide census count begins. An initially low response rate heightens debate on the possibility of a serious undercount and the need for adjustment.

June 1990 — *Garza v. County of Los Angeles* — A federal district court judge in Los Angeles gives further impetus to the minority representation issue. He rules that the Los Angeles County Board of Supervisors had violated the Voting Rights Act by gerrymandering its districts to dilute the large Hispanic vote. In August, the judge approves a new map that creates a majority Hispanic supervisorial district in the nation's most populous county.

August 1990 — The U.S. Justice Department files suit against Georgia's "second primary" or election runoff system on the grounds that it discriminates against minority voters. The action is seen as an indicator that Justice may be an active ally of minority groups in redistricting cases.

II. POLITICS: DIRECT DEMOCRACY

Repeal the Seventeenth!

52

Voters in some states do more than choose candidates for state offices; they also vote directly on particular issues. Rather than have their elected representatives make the policy decisions, the voters themselves decide. This is called *direct democracy*. The concept of direct democracy has had a long history in the Midwest and West and at the local level in New England communities, where citizens and leaders often assemble in town meetings to determine the town budget as well as other policy issues.

There are three specific vehicles for citizens to use in states with direct democracy: *initiative, referendum,* and *recall.* In seventeen states, citizens may change the state constitution by initiating constitutional amendments to be voted on in a statewide referendum. In twenty-one states, an initiative provision allows proposed laws to be placed on a state ballot by citizen petition; the proposal is then enacted or rejected by a statewide vote. Thirty-seven states have a referendum provision in their constitutions that refers acts passed by the state legislature to the voters for their concurrence before they become law. Most amendments to state constitutions are referred to the voters for approval. In fifteen states, a recall provision allows voters to remove a state elected official from office through a recall election.[1]

The provisions for the initiative vary among the states, the most important difference being the role of the legislature. In fourteen states the initiative process is direct: no legislative action is required to place the proposal on the ballot once the requisite number of signatures on the petition is secured. In 1988, South Dakota voters ratified an amendment to their state constitution removing the legislature as part of the initiative process. In four other states the process is more indirect:

the petition with the necessary signatures is submitted to the legislature, which then can (1) enact the proposal directly without a vote of the electorate, (2) alter the proposal before placing it on the ballot, or (3) place it on the ballot as submitted. Three states provide for both types of initiative—direct and indirect. Another important difference is the number of signatures required on the petition for an initiative to be considered.[2]

Like the initiative, provisions for a referendum on state legislation vary from state to state. In nineteen states, a referendum is required on certain types of bills, usually those related to state debt authorization (bond issues). In twenty-four states, a citizen petition can place an issue on the ballot for a vote by the electorate to approve or disapprove. In practice, this usually proves to be an attempt to reject an act already passed by the legislature, although many states restrict the type of legislation that can fall under this provision. Finally, fourteen states allow their legislatures to voluntarily submit laws to the voters for their concurrence or rejection.[3]

Provisions for the recall of all elected officials are included in only fifteen state constitutions. Eight states have provisions allowing the removal of all officials, six exclude judicial officials, and Montana includes all public officials, elected or appointed. Considerably more signatures are required for a recall to be placed on the ballot than for an initiative or a referendum.[4] The success of recent recall efforts indicates that this vehicle for direct democracy can be more than the "loaded shotgun behind the door" to keep elected officials on their toes. In 1983, two Michigan legislators were recalled after voting for a tax increase during the state's severe recession, and in 1977, a Wisconsin judge was recalled for his insensitive remarks during a rape trial.

The importance of the voters' right to recall an elected official was recently demonstrated in Arizona. The words and actions of Governor Evan Mecham, elected in 1986, angered many Arizonans sufficiently so that a recall petition was circulated to remove him from office. Their drive was successful and was part of the series of events that led to Mecham's removal from office in April 1988, after having served only seventeen months in office. Mecham had won a three-candidate race by gaining only 40 percent of the general election vote. As mentioned in note 1 of Section I, this situation led to voter approval of a 1988 constitutional amendment calling for a runoff election should no candidate receive a majority vote in the general election—that is, no more plurality vote governors. However, the 1988 Arizona legislature failed to adopt the so-called "Dracula clause" in that state's constitution that would have barred Mecham, as an impeached official, from ever seeking or holding office again. He did seek the governorship in 1990 and drew enough votes in a third place finish to force the top two vote getters into a February 1991 runoff.

Immediate Effects

The effects of direct democracy can be far reaching, affecting not only the state that has the initiative, referendum, or recall provision, but also other states and the broader political milieu in which state government operates.

When California voters adopted Proposition 13 in 1978, they sent a message to elected officials across the country. This successful initiative put the brakes on state and local governments in California by restricting their ability to fund governmental programs and services. Property taxes were reduced to 1 percent of property value rate (a 57 percent cut in property tax revenues); future assessments were limited to an annual increase of only 2 percent; and a two-thirds vote of the

state legislature was required for the enactment of any new state taxes.

The voters' message to state and local governments was clear: "We have had enough! We want less government, fewer programs, and greatly reduced taxes. You have become our problem because of the tax burden we must shoulder. We have asked you to do something about this; nothing has been done, so we are restricting the amount of money you can raise through taxes and placing this restriction in the constitution where you will not be able to tamper with it." This message— from what had been considered the most progressive electorate and state government among the fifty—prompted a widespread reevaluation of the goals of state and local governments. To what extent should elected officials expect the taxpayers to pay to achieve these goals?

There were other signals besides Proposition 13 for decision makers to consider. Opinion polls at the beginning of the 1980s reported that more than 70 percent of the public felt that income taxes were "too high"; only 45 percent felt this way in 1962. Those who felt that "the government wastes taxpayers' money" rose from 45 percent in 1956 to 80 percent in 1980,[5] and dropped to only 76 percent in 1986.[6] In some states, elected officials heeded their electorates' call to reduce taxes; in others, tax increases for governmental services and programs were postponed. Although Proposition 13 did not spark a nationwide tax revolt, it set the possibility of such an occurrence high enough on state policy agendas to get the attention of politically concerned policy makers.

State elected officials might be wary of a "ripple-effect" of the successful recall effort conducted against Arizona Governor Mecham. Will voters in those fourteen other states with a recall provision in their constitutions take a more critical view of their elected officials and be willing to recall them from office for cause? Will there be efforts in the other thirty-five states to add recall provisions to their constitutions? So far there have been none.

Politically, this would be difficult as most states require the legislature to place constitutional amendments on the ballot, and legislators may be unwilling to provide voters with an additional means of removing them from office. There are sixteen states, however, in which an amendment to the constitution can be brought before the voters by the initiative, so that the legislatures in those states could be circumvented politically. Nine of these states do not have a recall provision.[7]

Pragmatic Decisions

Initiatives are now being placed on state ballots and voted on at the highest rate since World War II. In 1986, there were 226 referenda on the November ballots in forty-three states, in 1988 there were 230 on the ballots in forty-one states, and in November 1990 the voters decided 214 initiatives. The initiative and referenda processes are not only becoming more prevalent in the states but more complex and expensive as well. One estimate of the cost of fighting for and against the twenty-nine referenda on the 1988 general election ballot in California was $100 million, or $4 per capita![8] Initiative and referenda politics are becoming big business.

In a study of 199 initiatives acted on between 1977 and 1984, *Initiative News Report* found that the vehicle was being used by interests at both ends of the ideological spectrum. Seventy-nine initiatives were backed by those on the liberal side of the political spectrum, seventy-four by those on the conservative side, and forty-six were not classifiable in ideological terms (usually because the initiatives concerned narrow, business-related issues). The approval rates for both the liberal and the conservative initiatives were about the

same, 44 percent and 45 percent, respectively. Two-thirds of the initiatives between 1980 and 1984 qualified for the ballot through volunteer efforts alone; the others used "paid petition circulators" in addition to volunteers. The importance of using only volunteer or grassroots support was clear: 51 percent of these initiatives passed.[9]

The referenda considered in 1988 indicate just how varied these questions can be across the states. Lotteries were approved in four states (Idaho, Indiana, Kentucky, Minnesota), English was adopted as the official state language in three states (Arizona, Colorado, Florida), taxpayer-funded abortions were banned in two states (Arkansas, Michigan), and tax revolt initiatives failed in three states (Colorado, South Dakota, Utah). Maine voters made their state constitution gender neutral, Arizonans voted to remove a constitutional requirement that constitutional officers be male, while Oregonians revoked their governor's executive order protecting state employees from sexual discrimination.[10]

Several state electorates took aim at their state legislatures. Voters adopted referenda shortening legislative sessions in Colorado and Missouri while Montana voters refused to let the legislature meet annually—all actions directed at maintaining part-time citizen legislatures. Colorado voters approved the GAVEL (Give A Vote to Every Legislator) initiative that directs how bills are processed by committees and reduces the power of committee chairs.[11] And voters in Arizona and Massachusetts voted down legislative pay raises.[12]

In 1989 there were at least twenty-one referenda votes conducted in six states; eleven passed and ten failed. West Virginia's governor lost in his attempt to change the political topography of that state when the voters soundly rejected his proposals to eliminate the statewide elective offices of secretary of state,

state treasurer, and agricultural commissioner, as well as eliminate the state board of education and state superintendent of education as constitutional offices, all in favor of more gubernatorial appointments.[13] Voters in West Virginia also rejected the governor's proposal to give more autonomy to local units of government.[14]

The legislature fared poorly in Texas when the voters rejected proposals to give legislators a raise in salary and expense allowances. Maine voters turned aside an attempt to limit the spending in gubernatorial campaigns.[15]

Bond issues were approved in Maine (juvenile corrections), in Rhode Island (environment and mental health), in Texas (water, corrections, and mental health), in Utah (planning for hosting the Winter Olympics), but one failed in Maine (adult corrections). Two proposed options for a sales tax increase were defeated in Michigan, and the governor of Washington was unable to convince voters in his state to support a major tax increase for education. Rights of crime victims were the subject of two successful referenda in Texas and Washington state.[16]

In 1990, the voters across the states sent several messages to state officials. Surprisingly, one of the messages was rejecting a series of major environmental referenda. A second was in the adoption by voters in three states of term limitations on some state and local officials.[17] Since the power of incumbency seems to be insurmountable in many states, the way to beat incumbents is not to allow them to serve more than a set number of terms or years. This particular trend will be watched carefully by officials in all states.

In this section, Jeffrey Katz of Congressional Quarterly looks at the new efforts to restrict state legislative tenure through the passage of term limitation referenda. Thomas Parrish from *The Kentucky Journal* discusses

just how up to date that state's constitution is. Larry Sabato of the University of Virginia reviews how that state's voters reacted to four constitutional amendments in 1990. Finally, Ronald Peters from the Carl Albert Center at the University of Oklahoma makes the case for reforming how U.S. senators are chosen—to go back to the way set out in the U.S. Constitution by having the state legislatures choose them!

Notes

1. *The Book of the States, 1988-89* (Lexington, Ky.: The Council of State Governments, 1988), 17, 217-220.
2. Ibid., 217.
3. Ibid., 218-219.
4. Ibid., 220.
5. Susan Hansen, "Extraction: The Politics of State Taxation," in *Politics in the American States: A Comparative Analysis*, 4th ed., ed. Virginia Gray, Herbert Jacob, and Kenneth N. Vines (Boston: Little, Brown, 1983), 441-442.
6. Survey by the *New York Times*, December 14-18, 1985, reported in *Public Opinion* 9:6 (March-April 1987), 27.
7. *The Book of the States, 1988-89*, 17, 220.
8. "The Long Ballot in California," *State Policy Reports* 6:15 (August 1988), 27-28.
9. Reported in "Liberals, Conservatives Share Initiative Success," *Public Administration Times* 8:4 (February 15, 1985), 1, 12.
10. Elaine S. Knapp, "Voters Like Lotteries, Reject Tax Cuts," *State Government News* 31:12 (December 1988), 26.
11. Sandra Singer, "Voters Dabble with Legislative Details," *State Legislatures* 15:1 (January 1989), 30.
12. Knapp, 27.
13. "West Virginia Setbacks," *State Policy Reports* 7:18 (September 1989), 23-24.
14. Ibid., 23.
15. "Election USA: 1989," *USA Today*, November 9, 1989, 6A-7A.
16. Ibid.
17. Rae Tyson, "Environmentalists Take a Drubbing," *USA/Today* (November 8, 1990), 4A.

The Uncharted Realm of Term Limitation

by Jeffrey L. Katz

It's swearing-in day at the Colorado House of Representatives, a cold January morning in Denver, early in the next century. The 65 legislators are greeting each other and sorting themselves into little clusters, corresponding to the four classes that make up the institution. About half are either just taking office or preparing to leave; all are allowed only four two-year terms under the law approved by voters back in 1990.

Each of the legislative classes is behaving about as those who watch the institution have come to expect. The freshmen are gaping at the ornate chambers and wandering the hallways, trying to reassure themselves that they aren't the first ones to have gotten lost. The second-termers, the sophomores, are relieved that much of the hazing is finally over, but still deferential to upperclassmen and realistic enough not to expect the best committee assignments.

Those with a couple of terms under their belts, the juniors, are swiveling in the chairs in their new, well-located offices, musing that these may be the best, most carefree days of their legislative careers before they grapple seriously with the burdens of earning a living outside the Capitol walls. And then there are the seniors, the lame ducks, who by tradition

are just now settling into the most valued leadership and committee positions. Obsessed with their plans for after legislative graduation day, they will spend a disproportionate amount of time maneuvering for jobs on the outside.

Other seniors will be debating the sort of legislative gift they should bestow on the public as their class legacy. Some of them want to leave behind a new environmental program; others prefer a tax cut. All of them want to be remembered as a class that accomplished something before moving together into the cold world beyond. Many of them will find it difficult to concentrate on their legislative chores.

Is this what we can expect from term limitation? Is it possible that a movement launched last year with the idealism of a grass roots demand for good government will merely turn our legislatures into institutions plagued by all the depressing rigidities of high school? Could a law designed in part to control the evils of seniority actually end up magnifying them?

Perhaps. The preceding is one of many

Jeffrey L. Katz is a staff writer for *Governing*. This article appeared in *Governing* 4:4 (January 1991): 34-39.

plausible scenarios that can be spun about the consequences of placing limits on legislative terms. But the very ease of constructing those scenarios raises questions about the full impact of the reform. When it comes to term limitation, the possible side effects are endless and just as likely to come true as the movement's ultimate goal: a corps of public-spirited citizen-legislators eager to do the public's business untainted by the careerist virus.

One thing seems certain. We are going to find out how it works. California, Colorado and Oklahoma have already adopted citizen initiatives to limit state legislative terms. In Colorado, the limit on consecutive service will be four two-year terms in the House, two four-year terms in the Senate. In Oklahoma, it will be a total of 12 years in either chamber. California's new law will be the most restrictive: State senators will be able to serve a maximum of two four-year terms, but members of the Assembly, the legislature's lower house, will be allowed just three two-year terms.

The movement has been fueled, of course, by the growing public awareness of the extraordinary re-election rate in most legislatures. Nearly all the term-reformers cite the high costs of campaigning, the overwhelming incumbent fund-raising advantage and the staff support that challengers cannot match. The result, they say, is a crew of life-tenured legislators out of touch with the way the public lives and thinks. The solution is to cut through the assurance of re-election, create more opportunities for candidates who are not career politicians and force the commonsense values of ordinary American people into the corridors of public office.

Ed Crane, president of the Cato Institute, a libertarian think tank, says turnover will be valuable in itself, almost regardless of who comes in. "I literally think," Crane says, "that you'd have a better legislature with a lottery."

Lloyd Noble II, the Tulsa oilman who led the fight for Oklahoma's new law, envisions a broad cross section of citizens cycling in and out of legislatures, encouraged both by their chances of winning and of getting things done in a more dynamic institution. A legislative career, Noble says, "ought to be like serving on jury duty."

But is that realistic? Most juries serve for a few days or weeks. Twelve years is a long time; so, for that matter, is eight. Would people who are reluctant to break off their private careers to run for office under the current system be inclined to do so just because they could count on being back home in eight years?

"This notion that you're going to get citizen-legislators is silly," says Gary C. Jacobson, a political science professor at the University of California at San Diego. "You're going to get those people who can afford to interrupt their careers for a few years, and that precludes people who have a normal job or family life. It includes people who are wealthy or on pensions, retired people in general, and political fanatics or zealots who are willing to make that sacrifice for whatever they believe in."

In the larger states, particularly, it seems likely that the experienced political activists who make the strongest candidates now would also perform best in a term-limited world. Being motivated enough to run for and win a legislative seat will require certain skills and sacrifices no matter how often the seats come open. Candidates will still face financial disclosure, intense public and media scrutiny, door-to-door campaigning, a steady diet of speech-making and the burden of pleading for money from friends and strangers.

So even if term limitations do usher in more legislative newcomers, there is no assurance that they will be much different in background or outlook from the current crop.

This is the argument made by Jeffrey A. Neubauer, chairman of the Wisconsin Democratic Party and a former legislator himself. "The person who wanders in and says, 'I'm middle-aged, raised a family, own a home and paid property taxes and you ought to vote for me because I'm a good guy or woman'—they lose. They lose to younger, more aggressive people, well connected to the interest groups through their work as legislative aides." In Neubauer's opinion, a term limitation is not going to change that.

Cleta Deatheridge Mitchell knows all about those problems, having spent eight years in the Oklahoma House. But she believes that term limits will be worth it for the sheer turnover they will create, even if the same sorts of people are elected. She is a member of the board of Americans to Limit Congressional Terms, which is pressing its case upon the legislatures as well as Congress. "It takes a certain amount of ego," Mitchell agrees, "to take the risk and abuse and be foolhardy enough to believe you can run and win and make a difference. That's not going to change. But hopefully there will be more opportunities."

Or will there? A state that limits legislators to six two-year terms will be able to assume, on the average, a biennial turnover of 16 percent, plus whatever changes are brought about by the retirement or defeat of members who have not reached the 12-year limit. This means that the legislature can count on a big crop of newcomers every time—IF a reasonable number do retire or lose before their terms are up.

But some commentators argue that there will be very little competition within the 12-year tenure period, that once members have been in a term or two, challengers will be inclined to avoid taking them on, waiting for the seat to open up at the 12-year point. "Why take a risk trying to knock off an incumbent," Jacobson asks, when you know the seat will soon be vacant anyway? If that attitude takes hold, there might be less turnover with limits than without them.

In fact, there is currently quite a bit of turnover. According to a study published by the National Conference of State Legislatures, the lower houses of California, Colorado and Oklahoma all experienced membership turnover of 89 percent or more in the 12-year period from 1977 to 1989. Three-quarters or more of the Senate seats in Colorado and Oklahoma changed hands in that period, as did two-thirds of the Senate seats in California. In 1988 alone, there was a turnover of 24 percent of both houses in Colorado and 30 percent in Oklahoma. If competition in term-limit states dries up except when the seat is vacant, Cleta Mitchell's dream will be difficult to realize.

Some reformers see value not only in frequent membership changes, but in party changes as well. They argue that with no limits on tenure, one party can keep its majority almost indefinitely on the basis of incumbency alone. It is not only the individual challengers who have trouble being heard, it is the challenging party. No matter how good its platform or its talent may be, the minority party falls victim every two years to an avalanche of public relations gimmicks launched by the majority officeholders to keep their jobs.

Term limitation, its advocates say, would help even the score. "It strengthens whichever party has the better idea, better candidates, better resources," says Republican Terry Considine, a three-year veteran of the Colorado Senate and main author of that state's term limitation measure. Term limitation will be harmful, Considine believes, to the party that has the most to lose.

Perhaps. But the necessity of filling more open seats will put a premium on the parties' ability to recruit and assist a bigger crop of candidates. That could exaggerate the importance of the very qualities that gave a party the edge in a legislature in the first place. Paul Schauer, a Republican and 12-year veteran of the Colorado House who opposes term limits, says they would benefit "whichever party has the best trainers, has the more permanent party structure that can recruit candidates and influence candidate input and, once they're elected, keep them more in line with the party." In other words, the party that knows how to find 20 good candidates each election year might have an even greater advantage at finding 30—regardless of what the hot issues of the moment happened to be.

Whichever party predominates in a term-limited legislature, the members will have to conduct business in the absence of the 15- and 20-year veterans who have made many of the important decisions in the past. How would such an institution behave? Peter Schrag of the Sacramento Bee argues that the state's limitation law will turn the California legislature into "something that looks like an airport waiting room—inchoate, without organization or leadership, where most of the occupants are either just arriving or just preparing to go."

That is not what the reformers have in mind at all. As they see it, a legislature purged of its most senior members will finally be able to select leaders on a rational basis, choosing the people with the most ability, not people who have simply been there the longest, or who take orders from those who have. There will be more competition for leadership posts and key committees. Ideology will count for more, as will specific public policy stands and styles of governing. "You would see a much more substantial style of campaigning for those positions," says Jim Weber, director of Americans to Limit Congressional Terms.

That remains to be proven, however. If nobody in a legislature has more than a few terms of seniority, then seniority might be more precious, not less. Awarding key positions on an automatic basis to the least inexperienced people might be hard to avoid. If nothing else, it would guarantee everybody a slice of power in the brief time before they were mustered out.

If term limits promise a change in the way legislatures organize themselves, they promise an equal change in the way legislatures interact with the rest of the political system. And that is exactly what many of the reformers would like. They believe that familiarity breeds coziness, and ultimately cronyism—between legislators and the lobbyists and bureaucrats they should be dealing with on an arm's-length basis.

In the term-limited legislature Jim Weber envisions, so many members would be rotating in and out that it would be much harder for lobbyists to do business on a buddy system. As Weber sees it, lobbyists would be forced to stop patting backs and start talking more about the merits of legislation. "It ought not to be a wink and a nod and a campaign contribution," Weber says.

Henry McMaster, who ran unsuccessfully for lieutenant governor of South Carolina last year on the issue of term limits, makes the same point. He concedes that a term-limited legislature might be more dependent upon lobbyists for information than an experienced legislature is now. But he thinks that, with the right sort of members, that wouldn't be anything to worry about. "If you have good people running," McMaster insists, "going to a lobbyist for information is like going to a library for information.

You have to sort out the good information from the bad." He is confident that clear-headed newcomers arriving fresh from the outside world would, if anything, be better able to do that than the current bunch.

It should come as no surprise that today's senior legislators disagree with this idea. Political scientists generally disagree with it as well. Many argue that the typical legislative freshman—short of experience and information, frequently burdened with a large campaign debt that has to be retired—is the most susceptible to trickery by lobbyists.

"That's when a member feels especially beholden," says Thomas E. Mann, director of governmental studies at the Brookings Institution. "Over time you acquire some independence and confidence." Under term limits, Mann says, legislators would acquire those traits just as they were nearing their final terms and thinking about jobs in the outside world. In some cases, the jobs they were applying for would be lobbying jobs. It does not sound like a recipe for creating McMaster's world, in which lobbyists are used solely for purposes of information.

Cleta Mitchell worries about legislators being soft on bureaucrats. She says those who stay in office term after term become ineffective watchdogs of the bureaucracy they're supposed to be overseeing. "People get familiar with executive agencies," she says. "They get familiar with personnel and programs, and they become unwilling to challenge them because they become their friends." During her tenure in Oklahoma, Mitchell watched legislators pal around with bureaucrats, increase agency appropriations in order to get jobs for their cronies and generally take the edge off what she believes should be an adversarial relationship.

Imposing term limits may be a good way to re-establish an adversarial attitude toward the bureaucracy. What is not so clear is whether a legislature loaded with junior members would know enough about the system to be a competent adversary. "The bureaucrats are going to be here forever," says Ted Strickland, president of the Colorado Senate. "Their experience in dealing with legislators is going to be much greater than that of the legislators who will be dealing with the bureaucrats." Strickland thinks a legislature full of short-termers will get outsmarted time after time. He warns of agencies that will wait until after the year's legislative session and then embark on new programs or initiatives that don't have legislative approval.

"It takes a while to have a good understanding of the budget, and a budget is the lifeblood of any agency," says Wayne Goode, a 28-year veteran of the Missouri Senate. "When you don't have people there who understand it, the bureaucrats are going to have a better opportunity to build empires, hide items in the budget and build the size of the bureaucracy around them, because people are going to quickly forget what they got a couple of years ago."

To term-limit activists, of course, that is merely the special pleading of incumbents who don't want to be forced from office. "I happen to believe that new, enthusiastic, interested lawmakers as they go through their learning curve can test and keep an eye on the bureaucrats," says Los Angeles County Supervisor Pete Schabarum. He is a prime sponsor of the new California law that limits Assembly members to six years and state senators to eight.

If state bureaucrats have reason to be happy about term limits, governors may have more reason. Although some who favor the limits say their goal is to make legislatures more creative and dynamic, others acknowledge that a less experienced legislature without a continuing core of veteran members would wield less clout when jousting with the chief executive. As they rotate from office, legislative leaders would have less leverage to strike a deal with the governor and probably less instinct for what sort of deal to strike. The senior legislators who exercise personal power over large areas of public policy would gradually become extinct.

California's John Garamendi:
Insurance Commissioner for Life?

In the pantheon of statewide offices, the post of insurance commissioner doesn't set most politicians' hearts aflutter. With no guarantee of political benefit, it entails mastering a staggering amount of arcana and handling complex issues that don't easily lend themselves to 30-second sound bites.

Even so, John Garamendi, who took over as California's first elected insurance commissioner, may find himself the subject of some envious glances. The same day that Garamendi won his post in November 1990, California's voters slapped state politicians with a term limitation law that's almost punitive in its scope. In addition to limiting members of the Assembly to six years in office and state senators to eight, it keeps statewide officeholders from serving more than two terms in any one office—except, it turns out, for the insurance commissioner.

Although the post was made elective in a 1988 initiative, last year's term limitation measure did not mention it. Should the measure survive the expected court challenge, Garamendi will be California's only elected state official who does not have a deadline bearing down on him.

That it should be Garamendi who finds himself in that position is a bit ironic. He was considered one of the state's most promising young politicians after he won a Senate seat in 1976. But after a failed gubernatorial bid in 1982, an attempt to unseat Senate President Pro Tem David Roberti and an unsuccessful try for state controller, a consensus developed in Sacramento that Garamendi's ambition exceeded his grasp.

No longer, it appears. Auto insurance rates have been a seething topic in the state, and Garamendi should have no trouble keeping himself in the public eye. As he says, "The public is still very unhappy with their insurance situation. They have every reason to be disturbed." He vows a complete restructuring of the insurance department to make it more receptive to consumers' concerns, and has also said that it is his goal "that every Californian at the end of my four-year term have health insurance."

With a U.S. Senate contest and a gubernatorial race set for 1994, the betting in Sacramento is that Garamendi probably won't take advantage of the breathing room that the 1990 term limitation measure left him.

Source: Rob Gurwitt, "California's John Garamendi: Insurance Commissioner for Life?" *Governing* 4:4 (January 1991): 13.

This is seen by some reformers as a blessing. Ed Crane, of the Cato Institute, longs for less aggressive legislatures. He claims that veteran lawmakers get indoctrinated in the political culture of a state capitol and end up spending too much money and adopting too many regulations. Similarly, Henry McMaster figures less experienced legislators would be more willing to take sensible direction from a chief executive who has the welfare of the entire state in mind. "I think the legislature ought to be weaker in its interaction with the governor," he says.

Alan Rosenthal, the Rutgers University political scientist who has studied governors and legislatures for 20 years, believes that sapping legislative authority may make states overly dependent on governors in a system that is supposed to feature separation of powers. Under term limits, he says, "it will be up to the governor to advance a program, provide the experience and pull the legislature together even to a greater extent than they do today. The legislature will be a weak branch of government." He does not want to go back to the rubber-stamp legislatures that predominated in many American states a generation ago; it is an open question whether most term-limit reformers, if they remembered the old days of arbitrary gubernatorial power, would want to go back to them either.

In the end, it is not turnover or partisan change or competition that reformers mainly seem to want. It is courage. They believe they can generate a new breed of legislator willing to make the right decisions on the basis of facts and common sense regardless of the political repercussions. Pete Schabarum, the Los Angeles County supervisor, believes term limits will gradually attract people who will take risks that the incumbents currently fear. He doesn't mind that this might mean going against the majority's wishes. "On some occasions," he says, "that isn't all bad."

If Schabarum is right that term limits are a formula for creating the political courage that today's legislatures often lack, then there probably is no good argument against them. But one has to take that on faith. It isn't just a swarm of special interests that block the enactment of sound public policy, it's also the absence of any public consensus on major issues. Term limitations wouldn't change that. The same forces that make legislators reluctant to take unpopular or controversial stands now are likely to temper term-limited legislatures in the same way.

Or so concludes Joe Clarke, a 21-year veteran of the Kentucky House. Clarke says he has spent years trying to persuade lame-duck legislators to vote their consciences, and finding that the prospect of retirement doesn't make them any more courageous. Not long ago, Clarke reminded a lame-duck colleague that he needn't worry about political retribution, since he wasn't seeking re-election. "No," the man told him, "but I'm going to be living back there."

Kentucky's Fourth Constitution a Product of Its 1890 Times

by Thomas Parrish

In 1890 the automobile was just being invented and the airplane was still a dream, space flight was the fantasy of romancers like Jules Verne, and the world of miracle drugs, television and computers lay many decades in the future. The United States as a whole was highly parochial behind its ocean barriers, and one of its most parochial corners was the Commonwealth of Kentucky, a state almost totally rural and little concerned about what went on in other states, let alone foreign countries. At that time, as Judge J. William Howerton has observed, foreign trade for Kentucky involved shipping a barrel of bourbon across the state line.

When, in that same year, a convention came together to draft what would be Kentucky's fourth constitution, the members saw unscrupulous behavior by giant corporations as the great threat to individual freedom. Railroads in particular had long displayed the arrogance of power and money, buying and controlling state legislatures; the Kentucky legislature itself was busily passing special legislation of various kinds and handing out favors. Nobody sent to Frankfort, the constitution makers seemed to feel, could be trusted to serve the public interest unless he had no other choice. The way to deprive the legislators of

choice, the framers decided, was to bind them to a constitution that would be as specific as a statue book, even in such matters as executive-branch salaries (to be limited to $5,000) and the level of allowable state debt (to be limited to $500,000); inflation concerned the framers no more than did the economic life of faraway places like Japan and Germany. One delegate summed up the feelings of most of his fellows: "The principal, if not the sole, purpose of this constitution which we are here to frame, is to restrain the legislature's will and restrict its authority."

Another delegate, one A. J. Auxier, took a longer view of history. With commendable foresight he predicted that "before another constitution convention shall be assembled in this hall, men will be navigating the air instead of traveling in railroad coaches; that instead of going thirty or forty miles an hour, they will go two hundred miles an hour, and hundreds of thousands of unthought things will be brought into existence." These wonders, he said, would require "new systems of government, or modifications, at least," and therefore

Thomas Parrish is an author from Berea, Kentucky. This article is reprinted from *The Kentucky Journal* 3:1 (January 1991): 5-6.

the framers of 1890 should make it easy for future generations to adapt the new constitution to their needs. But Auxier found himself in a distinct minority; the convention rejected his plea for a simple and direct method of amending the constitution. As a forecaster, actually, Auxier proved to be conservative: since his day men (and women) have left the earth at speeds not of 200 miles an hour but of almost 25,000, and still no new constitutional convention has assembled in any Kentucky hall.

The 1890-91 constitution has proved to be by far the most durable of the state's four charters (though it owes its relative longevity principally to the fact that the first three constitutions—1792, 1799, 1849—lack any amendment clause and hence could be changed only by being written in conventions), but during its century of life the courts have performed what have been called "spectacular legal gymnastics" to render it workable through the changing times foreseen by A. J. Auxier. One of the most important of these feats has been the adoption in 1962 of the "rubber dollar" theory, which has allowed salaries to be adjusted upward as long as they are based on comparable 1949 values (that being the year when the salary limit was finally raised, through amendment, from $5,000 to $12,000). In another bit of judicial gymnastics, the courts in 1948 declared Louisville's occupational tax valid as a license tax; that is, even though the tax is based on income, it is officially not an income tax. In the 1987 Toyota case, the courts went to remarkable lengths to salvage the efforts of the governor and the legislature to promote industrial development, though a dissenting Supreme Court justice felt bound to declare that five "disemboweled sections" of the constitution "lie scattered about us."

On the other hand, this judicial elasticity has not always been predictable. Sometimes, as

in the 1965 decision requiring enforcement of property assessments at 100 percent of current value, the courts moved toward strict interpretation of the constitution. In a current controversy, the plaintiff is calling on the courts to declare unconstitutional a $600 million road-bond issue approved by the 1990 legislature; the plan is said to violate the constitutional restriction on general obligations. What will the courts say? Judge Howerton has noted that, as matters stand, "we live with the debt limit through the use of more costly revenue bonds." But no one can be sure what the courts will decide in such cases. [At presstime the issue had not been resolved. - Ed.]

Clearly, the constitution of Kentucky, if not completely a strait-jacket, has proved through the years to be an extremely tight-fitting suit. Even though no new convention has been assembled in the last hundred years, the discomfort felt by the body politic has expressed itself in numerous efforts to convene a convention.

But the voters, however their feelings about legislators may have evolved, have repeatedly made it plain that they look on members of possible constitutional conventions with deep suspicion. Accordingly, the constitutional changes that have come about in the past century have resulted from individual amendments, of which 29 have been adopted out of 62 proposed by the legislature. The procedure, which until 1980 allowed only two proposals to be offered in any one election, has been slow and difficult, and the limited success of such proposals has generally made the legislature reluctant to offer them to the voters (although Sheryl Snyder has observed that the figures are somewhat misleading, since a number of the defeated amendments were ultimately passed in altered forms and others embodied views we would find abhorrent today—one would have abolished the secret ballot, another would have given us a poll tax). Even though the legislature for the past 10 years has had the authority to put as many as four proposals on the ballot at one time, the lawmakers never ventured beyond the old limit of two until 1991.

The 1990 Elections in Virginia: The Constitutional Amendments

by Larry Sabato

Rarely does an electorate split 80 percent to 20 percent on any ballot proposition. But in 1990 such was the approximate proportion on all four constitutional amendment referenda. Furthermore, two of these ballot issues secured the *approval* of eight in ten voters, while the other pair were *rejected* by close to the same margin. (See Table 1.)

The two constitutional amendments that won overwhelming backing were centered, naturally enough, on "motherhood and apple pie" issues: authorizing lower tax rates on personal property for the elderly and disabled (81.6 percent approval), and using drug offenders' assets for law enforcement purposes (a "yes" vote of 79.1 percent). The other two were far more controversial, since they asked voters to authorize "pledge bonds"—a new category of state and local debt to be used for transportation improvements. The debt was to be secured by "pledged" state and local tax receipts. Most importantly, the debt authorization would *not* require voter approval.

Proponents argued that Virginia's overloaded transportation system was in crisis, and that pledge bonds permitted a faster resolution. Under the state's existing "pay-as-you-go" arrangement, 70 percent of the cost of a transportation project was required to be in

hand before construction could begin. Imagine, the pledge bond advocates said, if the average person had to buy a house under a similar stricture. The bonds would permit "pay-as-you-drive," greatly speeding up the state's efforts to break the gridlock existing in most urban areas. While pledge bonds were originally advocated by Governor Gerald Baliles (D, 1986-90) during his transportation-oriented term, current Governor L. Douglas Wilder (D) made a "yes" vote on bonds his own goal, and set up a campaign organization headed by Lieutenant Governor Douglas Beyer, Attorney General Mary Sue Terry (both Democrats), and former 1985 Republican gubernatorial candidate Wyatt Durrett. The campaign staff was commanded by a Wilder veteran, Dwight Holton, son of former GOP governor Linwood Holton.

The opponents took a very different view: pledge bonds are a wolf in sheep's clothing, they said. Such bonds will lead to substantially increased state and local debt, endanger the

Larry Sabato is professor of government at the University of Virginia. This article is excerpted from "The 1990 'Election' in Virginia: Noncompetition and the Parties' Shame," unpublished analysis, Department of Political Science, University of Virginia, 1990.

Table 1 Statewide Election Results, 1990 Constitutional Amendment Ballot Questions in Virginia

Question	Vote (%)		Percent voters voting[1]
	Pro	Con	
Lower Tax Rates for Elderly and Disabled[2]	81.6	18.4	92.2
Drug Profits Seizures Used for Law Enforcement[3]	79.1	20.9	90.4
Local Pledge Bonds[4]	23.9	76.1	87.8
State Pledge Bonds[5]	21.3	78.7	87.5

1. Percent of those voting in 1990 who voted on the question.
2. Question: Shall the Constitution of Virginia be amended to authorize lower tax rates on personal property belonging to persons sixty-five and older, or permanently and totally disabled, in defined cases?
3. Question: Shall provision in the Constitution of Virginia pertaining to the Literary Fund be amended so that proceeds from property seized and forfeited to the Commonwealth for drug law violations can be used to promote law enforcement?
4. Question: Shall the Constitution of Virginia be amended to authorize a new category of local debt for transportation purposes which would be secured by pledged local tax revenues, subject to limits on the amount of the debt, and exempt from county voter approval requirements and municipal debt limits?
5. Question: Shall the Constitution of Virginia be amended to authorize a new category of state debt for transportation purposes which would be secured by pledged tax revenues, subject to limits on the amount of the debt, and not require voter approval?

state's triple-A bond rating, and inevitably lead to new taxes as debt mounts. An "Old Virginia" coalition led by former U.S. Senator Harry F. Byrd, Jr., former Governor Mills E. Godwin, Jr., and former House of Delegates Appropriations Committee chairman Roy Smith[1] warned Virginians against following the wayward example of Congress and urged citizens to adhere to time-honored, fiscally conservative principles. This group spent approximately $39,000 to spread the old-time gospel; to little apparent effect, bond advocates spent much more (about $145,000), most of it raised from developers, investment bankers, and lawyers, many of whom would have had a stake in the construction boom that bonds could have generated.

In light of Washington's deficit crisis and the federal budget impasse that dominated the autumn headlines, Virginians found the opponents' arguments more persuasive. These arguments found reinforcement in the inartful wording of the referenda themselves. The legislative language was confusing enough, but certain key words and phrases were memora-

ble and damning: "tax revenues," "debt," and "not require voter approval," among them. (See the notes to Table 1.) A considerable proportion of voters enter the polling booth undecided or completely uninitiated about ballot referenda. Their impressions, and indeed their voting decisions, are instantaneous, reached as a result of a quick reading of the questions. The pledge bond wordings probably encouraged a "no" vote, thus swelling the already substantial opposition.[2]

Whatever the reasons, the "no" vote was a tidal wave that engulfed even localities where transportation problems were greatest. Neither of the pledge bond referenda won a single city or county in Northern Virginia, for instance. In fact, not a single locality in the state could be found in the "yes" column on either referenda. Overall, 76.1 percent of the voters statewide opposed the local bonds and an even greater 78.7 percent turned thumbs down on state bonds. In only the Tidewater and Northern Virginia congressional districts—the locus of rush-hour gridlock—did the bonds manage to accumulate even as much as a quarter of the

California's Presidential Primary

The California legislature ended its [1990] session without fulfilling predictions that it would adopt a March Presidential primary to give the state's voters a larger role in the selection process. The problem was the interaction of primary dates and California's many voter initiatives. Republicans feared that the separate March primary would, at least in 1992, result in a large Democratic turnout for an exciting primary contrasted with a small one for a dull Republican contest. So the fear was that the many "liberal" ballot initiatives would gain an advantage. The converse fear was that with no Presidential vote in the statewide June primary, the many "conservative" ballot initiatives would gain an advantage. The result: no change.

Source: State Policy Reports 8:19 (October 1990): 25.

of suburbanites voted no. Even central city residents were against pledge bonds by nearly a two-to-one margin, but thanks primarily to black voters, pledge bonds drew a favorable response in the central cities that exceeded a third of the votes cast.

The overwhelming rejection of the pledge bond referenda is a reminder of the limits of voter tolerance. The so-called New Dominion is undeniably more progressive and tolerant in some respects than its predecessor, but Virginians still wish to preserve constructive aspects of their heritage and traditions. Thus, while social attitudes on many matters have evolved, fiscal conservatism continues to be a mainstay of the state's politics. In the matter of pledge bonds, the New Dominion was reintroduced to the Old in 1990, and the trip back to the future was conducted by an electorate bent on sending an old message about debt and taxes to a new generation of leaders.

Notes

1. This coalition was strengthened toward the end of the campaign by indications of pledge bond opposition from U.S. Senators John Warner and Charles Robb as well as a gaggle of state legislators (including several former supporters of pledge bonds). The *Richmond Times-Dispatch* and *News Leader* also vociferously editorialized against pledge bonds.
2. For an earlier example of question wording's effect on a Virginia ballot referendum, see Larry Sabato, *Virginia Votes 1979-1982* (Charlottesville: Va. Center for Public Service, 1983), 145-150.

vote. Support sank to as low as 12.5 percent in the Richmond Third district, where the *Times-Dispatch* and *News-Leader* had editorially crusaded against the bonds.

Demographically, rural Virginia was most strongly opposed to the bonds, with 88.3 percent of rural voters casting a "no" ballot on state pledge bonds. Suburban residents closely mirrored the statewide results, as 78.4 percent

Repeal the Seventeenth!

by Ronald M. Peters, Jr.

The reform of the Congress is a topic that is never out of vogue. Amidst current concern about the general incapacity of the national legislature to govern, the questionable activities of some of its members, and rising protest against a campaign financing system that was itself a product of an earlier reform impulse, suggestions for more radical change might seem particularly appropriate. Generally, proposals for the reform of Congress lie within a safe boundary of political acceptability, and in consequence usually don't offer much change. Yet occasionally more fundamental reform is undertaken, the most noteworthy example of which was the adoption of the seventeenth amendment to the Constitution in 1913, which provided for the direct election of senators. As we observe the far-reaching changes that are now taking place in Eastern Europe, we may be reminded of the fact that fundamental regime change is possible. One such change that ought to be considered in the United States is the repeal of the seventeenth!

This notion will fall upon at least 100 sets of deaf ears among senatorial incumbents, but it is our welfare, and not theirs, that is at stake. The case for repealing the seventeenth amendment grows upon one the more one thinks about it; whether one eventually out-grows it, is for the reader to decide.

There were five main reasons why the country amended the Constitution to take the election of United States senators out of the hands of the state legislatures and give it to the people of the several states. (1) It was argued that the principle of equality demanded it. Interestingly this argument . . . was not the major force behind the seventeenth amendment. For a hundred years senators were selected by state legislatures with little public outcry. It was only at the end of the nineteenth century that progressives and populists pushed the case for direct election, and even then the main arguments were not based on political equality.

(2) More often, it was alleged that the Senate was corrupted as a result of influence peddling in the states. The "millionaires club" of the nineteenth century won its name from the alleged influence of corporate interests in influencing senatorial appointments. (3) Occasionally, state legislatures would deadlock over

Ronald M. Peters, Jr., is director of the Carl Albert Congressional Research and Studies Center, University of Oklahoma. Reprinted by permission from *Extensions*, Spring 1990, a copyrighted publication of the Carl Albert Congressional Research and Studies Center, University of Oklahoma.

the choice, in some instances causing the state to be without representation for an entire congress. This was more likely to occur when the state legislature was under split party control or when the governor was of a different party from the legislative majority. (4) Due to the malapportionment of the state legislatures, senatorial nominations were often the product of factional rather than majority choice. (5) Finally, the task of nominating senators took up considerable legislative time, and the struggles often contributed to a souring of the legislative environment. It is not surprising, therefore, that it took the state legislatures less than a year to ratify the seventeenth amendment after the Congress submitted it to them.

This list of objections to the election of U.S. senators by the state legislators is formidable, but also considerably contextual. There can be little doubt that the repeal of the seventeenth amendment would lead to conflict at the state level, occasional paralysis, and a good deal of influence peddling. Yet the scope and degree of conflict would likely be a good deal less in today's equally apportioned and modernized state legislatures than was the case a century ago. Today it would not be possible for minority factions to control senatorial nominations, and the professional ethos of most state legislatures would dampen partisan conflict. It also seems less likely that states today would permit legislative deadlock to deny the state senatorial representation. There is now too much at stake. There always remains, of course, the normative argument. The progress of democracy shows few instances in which a polity has chosen to constrain democratic choice once it has been extended. Egalitarians will always favor direct rather than indirect popular choice. The value to be placed on democratic choice should, however, be weighed against the value of the alternative, and a consideration of the alternative is interesting.

What would be the consequences of repealing the seventeenth amendment? In the first instance, the states would be greatly empowered in the national government, as the Founders intended that they should. Students of state government recognize the extent to which states have become dependent upon federal policy. State governors commonly cavil at their lack of influence over federal policy. In every state the reason is clear. The United States senators are independently elected political entrepreneurs who are often in competition with their state's governors for influence in the state. The common pattern of state governors jumping to the United States Senate is a sufficient indication of where the power and influence has come to reside.

The empowerment of the states is, however, only the first and most direct benefit that would accrue to a repeal of the seventeenth. Consider next the pattern of recruitment. When state legislatures chose United States senators they selected from within the legislative body half of the time. This had two effects. On the one hand, it ensured that United States senators had experience as legislators and in dealing with state problems. On the other hand, it required that those who would serve in the United States Senate start their careers at the state level. A return to state control over senatorial selection would make the state legislatures the beneficiaries of the lure of the Senate. Furthermore, it would not be sufficient for a prospective senator to simply serve in the state legislature. He or she would have to win the confidence of peers and public alike. The public would pay more attention to state elections with more at stake, and it would be necessary for senatorial aspirants to establish and maintain a political constituency among state elites. This would tie the senators closely to the power structure of the states, as the Founders intended.

The repeal of the seventeenth would have

the happy effect of reducing the membership of the new millionaires club. It is ironic that the old millionaires club that was the object of so much complaint never exceeded twenty percent of the Senate. The percentage of millionaires in the Senate today is much higher. The reason is obvious. When it costs vast amounts to get elected, the rich are very much favored. The rich could still prey upon state legislators by sprinkling campaign contributions around, but it is less likely that they could simply buy a senatorial election. There will be far more persons of ordinary means in state legislatures than in federal service, and this would over time lead to a democratization of the Senate.

The effect on federal campaigns would be even more significant. The main object of big-dollar campaigns would be removed from contemplation. Money would no doubt flow where it could make a difference, i.e. to the state level. This would create both problems and opportunities for state governments. One likely result would be state laws prohibiting out-of-state contributions in state election campaigns. While passthrough money would remain a problem, it is likely that state legislative campaigns can be made at least as clean as are federal campaigns now. In the meantime, the greater attention and visibility that would be given to state elections would enhance the vitality of state government. Likewise, state political parties would be greatly strengthened. Our political parties have always lived, when alive at all, at the state level. Recent decades have seen the atrophy of state party organization. If control over the state legislatures meant control over United States Senate nominations, then the national parties would have a strong incentive to strengthen state party organization. Grass-roots democracy would be much enhanced.

The final argument in favor of repealing the seventeenth amendment is also the most significant. The seventeenth was adopted during the era of nationalization of American politics. The focal point of public policy shifted from the state to the federal level during the half century from 1880 to the 1930s. The role of the federal government continued to grow in the half century thereafter. We have now arrived at the apex of this historical cycle. The decades ahead will witness the revival of the states as the main seat of policy-making initiative. The federal government will defend the nation, pay interest on its imprudent debt, and transfer wealth; the state governments will do the rest. As the states assume more and more of the obligation of governance, it is fitting that their role in the federal system be strengthened. In an era in which state governments are promoting creative policies and making hard budgetary choices, they should be protected against preemptive federal policies. In order to protect their interests (more and more of which will be in common), they need to have a greater say in federal policy making. The best way to ensure this is the first way. Repeal the seventeenth amendment. . . .

III. POLITICS: PARTIES, INTEREST GROUPS, AND PACS

Politics in the American states is changing. Political parties, once the backbone of the U.S. political system and the chief force in state government, are becoming less influential, or so say many observers. As Malcolm Jewell and David Olson point out, "It has become a truism that party organizations are declining in importance, and there is no reason to anticipate a reversal of that trend." [1]

But what are political parties? This question must be addressed before the reasons for their "decline" can be understood. Are they the organizations from precinct to national convention—*the party in organization?* Are they the individuals who run, win, and control government under a party label—*the party in office?* Or are they the voters themselves, who identify more with a particular party and vote accordingly—*the party in the electorate?* Political parties are all three, diverse in definition, and ever changing in their impact on state government.

Perhaps the clearest signal that parties sway voters less than they once did is the rise of split-ticket voting. In state and local elections in 1956, only 28 percent of the voters who identified themselves as either Democrats or Republicans did not vote the straight party line but split their ticket by voting for candidates of both parties; in 1980, 51 percent split their ticket. [2] In 1986, 20 percent of those identifying themselves as Democrats and 17 percent of those identifying themselves as Republicans voted for the U.S. Senate candidate of the opposing party. [3] This divided party voting and its impact is discussed in further detail in the introduction to Part I.

What's Happened to the Parties?

Various explanations have been offered for the decline of political parties. Direct primaries—the means by which party voters can participate directly in the nomination process rather than have party leaders select candidates—certainly have curtailed the influence of party organizations. By 1920 most of the states had adopted the direct primary. [4] No longer could party organizations or party bosses rule the nominating process with an iron hand, dominate the election campaign, and distribute patronage positions and benefits at will. The ability to circumvent official party channels and appeal directly to the electorate greatly increased the power of individual candidates. A candidate's personality has taken on new importance as party affiliation has become less influential in determining voting behavior.

In the political environment of the 1990s, parties are challenged by the mass media, interest groups, independent political consultants, and political action committees—vehicles that perform many of the historic functions of the political party. Public opinion polls, rather than party ward and precinct organizations, survey the "faithful." Today,

> ... [P]olitical consultants, answerable only to their client candidates and independent of the political parties, have inflicted severe damage upon the party system and masterminded the modern triumph of personality cults over party politics in the United States. [5]

One analyst argues, however, that the rise of the political consultant has opened up the political process through the use of polls and other techniques. Now candidates can talk about the issues voters are concerned about without the "party communications filter." [6]

Changes in government itself are another explanation for party decline. Social welfare programs at the federal, state, and local levels of government have replaced the welfare role once played by party organizations. Those in need now turn to government agencies rather than to ward and precinct party leaders, even though domestic cutbacks during the Reagan-Bush years, and projected future cutbacks, have reduced the ability of government agencies at all levels to meet those needs.

To most citizens, parties are important only during the election season. Our system is unlike that of most European countries, where there are rigid election schedules in which campaigning is limited to a specific time period. The American state and local government election season is generally thought to start around Labor Day in early September and run until election day in early November. Cynics believe that this is too long, and that in most voters' minds, the season really begins at the end of the World Series in late October. Of course, the candidates have been at work for months, even years, getting ready for this unofficial election season, but the impact of other events, such as the World Series, often conspires to distract the electorate.[7]

Alan Ehrenhalt of *Governing* makes another intriguing observation on the fate of the major political parties in the minds of the citizens. He argues that "solutionists" have become our new majority party. Those with "fuzzy optimism" promise that we can solve any of our problems and that "everything is possible" if we set our minds on a solution. "Voters, who are routinely informed by candidates that their problems can and will be solved, have a right to turn cynical when the same problems are still on the table . . . years later."[8] Such cynicism quickly turns to apathy and nonparticipation in politics, regardless of party affiliation.

Signs of Party Resurgence

Yet not everyone is ready to declare the parties moribund. The party process is still the means of selecting candidates for national, state, and, in some cases, local office. Control of state legislatures is determined by which

party has the majority, with the sole exception of Nebraska. Appointments to state government positions usually go to the party colleagues of state legislators or of the governor.

Although party in organization and party in the electorate are weaker than they once were, party in office may be gaining strength, argues Alan Rosenthal of the Eagleton Institute of Politics at Rutgers University. Legislators are increasingly preoccupied with winning reelection. The "art of politicking" may be superseding the "art of legislating."[9] Party caucuses have begun to play an important role in selecting the legislative leadership, assigning committee and other responsibilities, and establishing positions on issues. In fact, the party in organization may not be as weak as many think. Since the 1960s, budgets and staffs have grown in size, staffs have become more professional, party services and activities have increased, and elected leaders may be even more involved in party affairs.[10]

Regional Differences in Party Politics

Of course, party politics differ in each state. As Samuel C. Patterson writes, "In some places parties are strong and vigorous; in other places, they are sluggish; in yet others, moribund. But, on balance, the state parties appear remarkably vibrant."[11]

New York appears to be content with its four-party structure of Conservative, Republican, Democratic, and Liberal parties; Nebraska operates on a nonpartisan basis for many of its elections; Wisconsin still has deep ties to populism; and California, once represented by a liberal northern half and conservative southern half, is expanding to include the strengthening Hispanic and Asian minorities. The political growth and impact of these minorities are increasing as they learn how to play the game of politics by American rules.

Today, few states are consistently dominated by one party. This is true even in the

South, which for many years was the Democrats' stronghold. Southern states now see growth around urban centers shaking up old party lines as "yuppies," northern corporate executives, and retirees join the "Bubbas" and presidential Republicans of old to create more competitive two-party systems.

At one time, being a Democrat was practically a necessity to vote and hold office in southern states. Party primaries decided who would be elected; general elections were simply ratifying events. But the old one-party dominance is fast eroding as is the role of the primary in determining who will govern.

For example, between 1987 and 1990, when the last full round of state elections was held in the southern states, Republicans won the governorship in five states, Democrats in twelve; however, one of the Democrats recently switched his party registration to Republican.[12] After the 1990 state legislative elections, nearly 24 percent of the state senators and 29 percent of the state house representatives were Republican, continuing a trend of increasing Republican party strength in these bodies.[13] However, the Republicans are only able to control one of the thirty-four houses in the seventeen states (Delaware's House of Representatives by five votes). The state legislative redistricting that results from the 1990 census should give the Republicans a boost in the number of state legislators they are able to elect in the 1990s since much of the growth in the southern states is in metropolitan areas, and especially in the suburbs, which is Republican territory.

While still a political minority, the Republicans' winning trend is causing southern Democrats to question the political "sanity" of continuing to hold divisive party primaries in which Democrats battle with each other when seeking the party nomination, only to have their Republican challengers use these same arguments to defeat them in the general election. In effect, the primaries expose weaknesses in the Democratic candidates that the Republicans exploit. In fact, the North Carolina legislature recently reduced the percent of the vote needed to win in the first primary from 50 percent to 40 percent in an attempt to forestall divisive second primaries.

Not all of these Republican wins are beneficial to the party: in February 1989, the former grand wizard of the Ku Klux Klan and organizer of the National Association for the Advancement of White People, David Duke ("the Duke"), won a seat in the Louisiana legislature as a Republican. In a bitter and often racist campaign, Duke defeated John Treen, a longtime Republican party functionary and brother of the first Republican governor of Louisiana in this century. Treen had the strong support of newly elected president George Bush and former president Ronald Reagan—an unprecedented national-level intrusion into a local race. Within three months, the Duke not only had become a folk hero for many Louisianans, but his "avowed racism in an area that's racially polarized" intensified the state's problems.[14]

Duke challenged Democratic U.S. senator J. Bennett Johnston and received over 40 percent of the vote in Louisiana's unique "you'all come" primary in which everyone runs in the same primary for the nomination and election. In 1991, Duke is running for the governorship, thereby keeping his name and issues before the voters. Republicans—both national and state level—prevailed upon Democratic governor Buddy Roemer to switch his party affiliation in order to draw Republican voters to him and away from Duke. It is the contest to watch in the states in 1991.

Interest Group Politics

Are interest groups an evil that must be endured or are they a necessary part of the governing process? Is their impact on state government primarily beneficial or harmful? Perhaps most importantly, do the interests that groups seek to advance or protect benefit the whole state or only of the lobbies themselves? State officials, pressured by a myriad of interest groups, wrestle with these questions and reach different answers.

Interest groups' influence on the political process varies from state to state. Business groups are by far the most predominant; the influence of labor groups pales in comparison. Thus, the interest group structure of most states is business oriented and conservative. Lately, however, groups representing government employees, local government officials, and the public interest (for example, Common Cause and environmental protection groups) have increased their visibility and effectiveness in state politics. According to Sarah Morehouse, there are twenty-two states in which interest groups are very strong, eighteen in which they are moderately strong, and ten in which they are weak.[15]

An interest group's effectiveness depends on the representatives it sends to the state legislature and executive branch agencies—the so-called professional lobbyists. Who are these people? Usually they have served in government and are already known to those they seek to influence. Their ranks include agency heads, former legislators, and even former governors in private law practice who have clients with special interests. Some of the most effective lobbyists represent several interests.

The relationship between political parties and interest groups in the states tends to follow a discernible pattern: the more competitive the party system, the weaker the interest group system. Of the twenty-two states in which interest groups have been classified as strong, sixteen are one-party or modified one-party states; of the eighteen states in which interest groups have been classified as moderately

strong, thirteen are competitive two-party states.[16]

This apparently symbiotic relationship between parties and interest groups largely determines who controls state government. Theoretically, in a competitive, two-party state, the stakes are more likely to be out in the open as one party fights the other for control. Conversely, in the noncompetitive, one-party state, the stakes are less easy to see as interest groups do battle with each other to maintain or change the status quo. Again, in theory, the power of the party flows from the voters through their elected representatives; the power of interest groups is derived from their numbers, money, and lobbying skill. But in practice the relationship is not as clear as this explanation would suggest. In fact, once the parties organize state government, state politics usually become the special quarry of interest groups—except, of course, on distinctive, party-line issues (such as selecting the leadership).

The Role of State Governments

State governments have two main roles vis-à-vis the other actors in state politics: they set the "rules of the game" in which parties and interest groups operate, and then they regulate their financial activities. The rules govern the nomination and election processes and the ways in which interests are allowed to press their demands. However, the rules change at a glacial pace because those who know how to play the game fear that change will upset the balance of power—or at least their spot in the power system. In fact, it often takes a lawsuit by someone outside that power system to change the rules or a scandal to tighten financial reporting requirements.

For example, the federal courts continue to support challenges to at-large voting schemes on the grounds that they dilute a minority group's voting strength.[17] At-large voting schemes allow voters to select several representatives at one time from a larger geographical area rather than just one representative from a smaller geographical area. For example, the Maryland U.S. congressional delegation consists of six Democrats and two Republicans selected from eight individual districts. Had that delegation been selected by a statewide (at-large) vote in 1988, the Democratic candidates, who had just under one million votes, would hold all eight congressional seats since the Republican candidates garnered only 624,021 votes.

Recently, portions of Mississippi's electoral laws were successfully challenged in federal courts. In 1987, a federal district court ruled that Mississippi's dual registration voting laws were in violation of the federal Voting Rights Act. The Mississippi laws required voters to register twice: once in the county courthouse for federal, state, and county elections and again at the local courthouse for local elections.[18] In 1988, a federal district court ruled that the state's judicial election procedures were discriminatory under the Voting Rights Act. This ruling led to changes to concentrate minority voting power. The numbers proved the case: although blacks made up 35 percent of the state's population, of 111 judges in the state, only 3 were black (less than 3 percent).[19]

Laws regulating campaign finance have been on the books for almost one-hundred years. In 1892, New York and Massachusetts adopted laws in reaction to the corruption of the day requiring candidates to report how they spent their campaign money. Other states followed with a variety of "publicity laws," restrictions on corporate contributions, and limits on campaign expenditures. By 1925, a majority of states had some restrictions on their books, but these often were not enforced.[20]

Recently, the states have adopted policies that increase their regulatory role regarding political parties. Public disclosure and campaign finance laws are more strict, and political action committees (PACs) are monitored with a more watchful eye due to their increased activity.

The number of PACs has grown rapidly in the American political scene. At the national level, they increased from 608 in December 1974 to 4,165 in December 1987, a 685 percent increase.[21] The number of PACs in New York nearly quadrupled from 84 in 1978 to 325 in 1984. Special interests financed 60 percent of the campaign costs for an assembly seat in the 1984 contests in California, and they contributed 40 percent of the money raised by Illinois legislators in 1984-85, leading one observer to protest, "What we have now is government of the PACs, by the PACs, and for the PACs."[22] In the 1987 elections in Louisiana, more than 600 PACs registered with the state's campaign finance office.[23] PAC spending for statewide offices and state legislatures across the country was $95 million in 1972, $120 million in 1976, $265 million in 1980, and a whopping $400 million in 1984.[24]

Part III provides some insight into politics at the state level. Susan Biemesderfer of *State Legislatures* takes a look at the recent style of campaigning in the states and wonders whether the states are up to controlling it, while Herbert Alexander from *State Government News* explores what the real costs of campaign reform are. Finally, Michel Burgess in *Empire State Report* shows what the people as an interest group can do in a state's politics.

Notes

1. Malcolm Jewell and David Olson, *American State Political Parties and Elections* (Homewood, Ill.: Dorsey Press, 1982), 280.
2. David E. Price, *Bringing Back the Parties*

(Washington, D.C.: CQ Press, 1984), 15.

3. Survey by ABC News, November 4, 1986, reported in *Public Opinion* 9:4 (January-February 1987): 34.

4. Price, *Bringing Back the Parties*, 32.

5. Larry Sabato, *The Rise of Political Consultants: New Ways of Winning Elections* (New York: Basic Books, 1981), 3.

6. Walter DeVries, "American Campaign Consulting: Trends and Concerns," *PS: Political Science and Politics* 12:1 (March 1989): 24.

7. Rick Sinding, "Politics," *New Jersey Reporter* 17:3 (September 1987): 300.

8. Alan Ehrenhalt, " 'Solutionists': America's Majority Party," *Congressional Quarterly Weekly Report*, September 20, 1986, 2251.

9. Alan Rosenthal, "If the Party's Over, Where's All That Noise Coming From?" *State Government* 57:2 (Summer 1984): 50, 54.

10. Timothy Conlan, Ann Martino, and Robert Dilger, "State Parties in the 1980s: Adaptation, Resurgence, and Continuing Constraints," *Intergovernmental Perspective* 20:4 (Fall 1984): 23.

11. Samuel C. Patterson, "The Persistence of State Parties," in *State of the States*, ed. Carl E. Van Horn, (Washington, D.C.: CQ Press, 1989), 169.

12. The Republicans won Delaware, Missouri, and North Carolina in 1988, and Alabama and South Carolina in 1990. The Democrats won Kentucky, Louisiana, and Mississippi in 1987, West Virginia in 1988, Virginia in 1989, and Arkansas, Florida, Georgia, Maryland, Oklahoma, Tennessee and Texas in 1990. Buddy Roemer of Louisiana is the governor recently switching his party loyalty from Democrat to Republican as he prepared to seek reelection in 1991.

13. "1990 Election Results," *State Legislatures* 16:11 (November/December 1990): 20.

14. Associated Press, "Former KKK Head Wins La. Election," [Raleigh] *News and Observer,* February 19, 1989, 1A. Jason Berry, "In Louisiana, the Hazards of Duke," *Washington Post National Weekly Edition,* May 22-28, 1989, 25.

15. Sarah McCally Morehouse, *State Politics, Parties, and Policy* (New York: Holt, Rinehart & Winston, 1981), 107-112.

16. L. Harmon Zeigler, "Interest Groups in the States," in *Politics in the American States: A Comparative Analysis*, 4th ed., ed. Virginia Gray, Herbert Jacob, and Kenneth N. Vines (Boston: Little, Brown, 1983), 116.

17. "Newsbriefs: At-Large Voting under Attack," *Governing* 1:2 (November 1987): 8.

18. "Justice: Mississippi Voter Registration Laws Struck Down," *State Government News* 31:2 (February 1988): 29.

19. Ronald Smothers, "Ruling Spurs Change in Racial Makeup of Mississippi Judiciary," New York Times News Service, in [Raleigh] *News and Observer,* June 3, 1989, 4A.

20. Kim Kebschull, et al., *Campaign Disclosure Laws* (Raleigh, N.C.: North Carolina Center for Public Policy Research, 1990), 20.

21. Findings of Citizen's Research Foundation as reported by Jeffrey Stinson in "PAC Money Follows Power to the States," *USA Today* March 26, 1986, 8A.

22. Harold W. Stanley and Richard G. Niemi, *Vital Statistics on American Politics* (Washington, D.C.: CQ Press, 1988), 143.

23. Citizen's Research Foundation, "PAC Money Follows Power," 8A.

24. "PAR Analysis: Campaign Finances in the 1987 Governor's Race" (Baton Rouge, La.: Public Affairs Research Council of Louisiana, May 1988), 7.

Campaigning Ad Nauseam

by Susan Biemesderfer

"Campaigns should be to inform the public, not nauseate them."

This may be U.S. Senator John Danforth's opinion about campaigns, but strategists in [1989 and 1990 were more] worried about losing votes than sickening voters. Danforth ... introduced a bill aimed at curbing political attack ads, but its passage [was] less likely than the continued proliferation of negative campaign ads at the federal, state and local levels.

If 1989's nastiest races were any indication, the ... political season promises to bloom with more controversy. For example:

● New Jersey's gubernatorial race [in 1989] turned into a fierce match of television jabs thrown by Congressmen Jim Florio and Jim Courter. Now-Governor Florio's initial attack depicted Courter with a Pinocchio-like nose, alleging he had misrepresented his legislative record; Courter's response charged that Florio took money from corrupt unions and showed Florio's nose growing while Courter's nose simultaneously shrank;

● In Virginia, newly elected Governor Douglas Wilder held on to a diminishing lead over an opponent who ran television ads that showed a woman weeping as the announcer talked about a bill introduced by Wilder that allowed for the questioning of rape victims about their private lives;

● David Dinkins defeated Ed Koch for the New York City mayor's seat despite Koch's charges that Dinkins engaged in shady financial dealings; and

● In Cleveland, Senator Michael White won a tight mayor's race in which he was labeled a "slumlord" and called his opponent a "master of sleaze."

[The 1990] state primaries sustained the negative ad trend. Texas gubernatorial candidate Ann Richards ... wrestled with allegations from other Democrats that she used illegal drugs; in California's Democratic primary, Dianne Feinstein emerged as the party's candidate for governor in a race where, as reported by *Newsweek,* "a single 30-second spot" could "move 10 percent of the vote."

It seems that in the age of the political sound bite, the emphasis is on the word "bite"—a slick, 30-second attack ad can irreversibly wound a reputation that took years,

Susan Biemesderfer specialized in election issues for the National Conference of State Legislatures. This article is reprinted with permission from *State Legislatures* 16:8 (September 1990): 24-26 © 1990 by the National Conference of State Legislatures.

even decades to develop. And it's the kind of damage, say public relations experts, that can't be remedied by any amount of public appearances, knocking on doors or other traditional campaign practices. Some observers say traditional tactics have been overshadowed by a new conventional wisdom—nasty ads are effective.

"If you don't respond to a negative ad with an ad of your own, the public tends to think that the attack is true," says Ken Bode, former NBC reporter and media consultant to the 1988 Michael Dukakis presidential campaign, who believes that noble silence is not an effective response. Bode claims Dukakis learned the hard way that turning the other cheek is not sufficient damage control for a candidate who has been attacked in a negative radio or television ad.

In fact, many observers trace the turning point of the 1988 race to the Bush campaign's controversial "revolving door" ads, masterminded by media consultant Roger Ailes. The spots showed inmates walking through fictional revolving doors of Massachusetts prisons, depicting Dukakis as a governor who endorsed the furlough of repeat offenders such as rapist Willie Horton. Dukakis hesitated before responding with ads of his own and, by the time he did, Bush's ratings in the polls had soared.

"Quite simply, negative campaign advertising works," says Julian Kanter, a political science professor at Oklahoma University. He explains that the American voter has a natural "suspicion and cynicism regarding political candidates." Ron Walters of Howard University concurs: "In a close race, a candidate will grab at almost anything to tip the balance, and that's where you find the most negative campaigning."

Less questionable than the effectiveness of negative campaign advertising is the reality that certain groups of voters and elected officials find such ads repugnant. According to

Curtis Gans, director of the Committee for the Study of the American Electorate in Washington, D.C., negative campaign ads "are at best over-simplified and misleading, at worst and often, distorted and downright dishonest." Gans argues that "they work for only 50 percent of the consultants and candidates who win while 100 percent of the public who view these ads become the losers."

One result, if you agree with Gans and other opponents of negative campaigning, is that these ads have jaded the American electorate—not necessarily because the ads are so scurrilous, but because they are so common. "Negative ads are not a new phenomenon, nor are they all that much more outrageous than in previous years," asserts Gans. "What's different is not the type but the volume. Attack ads were once limited to the occasional campaign and were typically received with outrage, but now they're a staple of most campaigns." Ohio Congressman William Batchelder agrees: "Voters get desensitized and it's understandable."

According to Batchelder, it all started with the 1964 television commercial that depicted a little girl holding a daisy, then a nuclear explosion and a mushroom-shaped cloud. The ad was produced by the presidential campaign in which Lyndon Johnson trounced Senator Barry Goldwater and, says Batchelder, "Set the stage for all of the negative campaigning that ensued."

As these ads have proliferated, so have their effects on the public which, according to some observers, go beyond sickening or desensitizing voters. In his testimony [in] summer [1989] before the U.S. Senate Subcommittee on Commerce, Science and Transportation, Gans theorized that negative campaign ads contribute to "the increasing demagoguery and trivialization of our politics" to an extent that "makes the perceived stakes not worth the effort to participate."

Gans' list of public ailments attributable to negative ads encompasses more than the nationwide decline in voter participation. It includes:

● Spiraling campaign costs, linked to the increased use of television advertising in general;

● A disproportionate allocation of 90 percent of campaign funds to media advertising, leaving less than 10 percent of those funds for activities that "involve the citizenry";

● A drop in taxpayer check-off contributions to state funds for public financing of candidates, presumably linked to distaste for the negative ads on which these funds might be spent; and

● Restricted political choice—based on the notion that potential leaders may now choose not to run for office because they fear that something they once said or did may be taken out of context in a negative ad.

Even so, dealing with the phenomenon of negative campaigning, whatever its roots or true impact on voters, has proven tricky. The First Amendment's guarantee of freedom of speech applies to politicians, too, and laws designed to squelch negative ads have not fared well in the courts. For example, in Ohio a state law prohibiting false campaign statements was overturned on constitutional grounds. Until the appeal of that 1987 decision is decided, similar legislative efforts in Ohio are likely to be stymied.

Of the 22 state laws that have been enacted to prohibit false campaign statements, one—passed by the Nebraska Legislature— has been repealed following a successful constitutional challenge, and two—those in Louisiana and Ohio—have been struck down as unconstitutional and are now the subjects of appeals. The laws remaining on 21 states' books are similar in verbiage—typified by Wisconsin's prohibition against "knowingly" making or publishing a false representation tending "to affect voting at an election"—but differ in their scope and implementation. For example, statutes in seven states apply only to written false statements. And in California, misrepresentation of party support is the only type of false statement prohibited; in Michigan and Nevada, these prohibitions apply only to candidates who falsely represent themselves as incumbents.

More significant, as well as more difficult to document, is the degree to which these laws are enforced from state to state. During the course of the 50-state telephone survey conducted to collect data for this article, contacts from at least half a dozen states were confident in their assessments that, although a prohibition against false campaign statements existed, it was not actively enforced.

"Enforcing these laws," explains Fred Hermann, executive director of the New Jersey Election Law Enforcement Commission, "means risking a lawsuit that could lead to the repeal of the statute." New Jersey's Legislature hasn't enacted such a law, but Herrmann observes that recent New Jersey proposals designed to discourage negative campaigning have "eventually died." He traces the lack of legislative support to lawmakers' skepticism about the legality of such measures.

Some of that skepticism is rooted in legislators' knowledge of a 1975 ruling that struck down New York's prohibition against campaign misrepresentations. In *Vanasco vs. Schwartz*, a case that went all the way to the U.S. Supreme Court, sections of the New York election code were found to be "repugnant to the right of freedom of speech."

The *Vanasco* case stemmed from complaints filed against two candidates for the New York Assembly in 1974. Roy Vanasco, an unsuccessful Republican candidate, had distributed campaign literature that allegedly misrepresented his party affiliation as "Republican-Liberal" and falsely implied he was an incumbent. A successful Democratic-Liberal candidate in another Assembly district, Joe Ferris, was accused that same fall of misrepresenting his opponents' voting record. Under the authority of New York's statutory prohibition against distributing false campaign literature, the New York Board of Elections ordered both candidates to surrender their campaign literature. The two candidates joined forces to file suit against the Board. The court's decision in their favor held that any state regulation of campaign speech must be premised on the "actual malice" standard applicable to public figures since the U.S. Supreme Court's landmark libel ruling in *New York Times vs. Sullivan*

"It is that standard—the requirement that false campaign information be of libelous, malicious nature—that makes our state law such a challenge to enforce," says Graham Johnson, executive director for the Washington State Public Disclosure Commission. The commission has been charged with the delicate task of discerning where "actual malice" may be the root of false statements made in the heat of campaign combat. Washington's prohibition against false campaign statements has been amended in light of the *Vanasco* ruling, making it, in Johnson's opinion, "all but impossible to prove a violation has occurred. It hasn't happened yet with a state legislative race. The circumstances of campaigns are unique and not well documented, and proving malicious intent on the part of a candidate is an almost insurmountable task."

An alternative approach to dealing with negative ads is the use of "fair campaign practices" codes. These codes are on the books in seven states and are generally signed voluntarily by candidates. Typically, fair campaign codes include language similar to that found in Washington's provision, wherein candidates vow not to participate in "personal vilification, defamation and other attacks on any opposing candidate or party." And while such codes have at least occasionally raised the consciousness of candidates and voters, they are generally regarded as good-faith but meager attempts to temper negative ads.

"The options we're left with, then," says New Jersey Assemblyman Bob Franks," are either ignoring the problem or doing our best to pass a law that will survive the courts' scrutiny." Franks ... introduced a bill that would require a candidate to appear in any campaign ad that mentions the opposing candidate; in a print ad referencing another candidate, the attacking candidate's photograph would have to appear. Because the bill doesn't require that any judgment be made about the ad producer's intent and imposes an affirmative act on the part of the candidate—rather than restricting the content of the candidate's speech—proponents are optimistic about its chances to get around constitutional hurdles. A similar bill [was] introduced in the Florida House of Representatives.

Both the Florida and New Jersey bills resemble the legislation proposed in Congress by Senators John Danforth and Ernest Hollings. "If a candidate wants to sling mud at his opponent," says Danforth, "the public should be able to see the candidate's dirty hands." Media consultant Roger Ailes counters Danforth with claims that the bill violates the First Amendment. "If we're going to start with censorship in this country," Ailes argues, "We ought to start with child pornography and political commercials ought to be far down the list."

[Measures such as these,] if passed, are certain to face the scrutiny of judges with watchful eyes on constitutional freedoms. Still, some legislators persist in their efforts to tone down negative campaign ads. "The sentiment of the American people today when they look at politics," insists Danforth, "is nausea."

Hidden Costs of Campaign Reform

by Herbert E. Alexander

The skyrocketing costs of political campaigns have prompted concern that the need for money is jeopardizing the ethics of candidates.

Reformers wish political costs were not so high, fund-raising demands on candidates were fewer and political money was easier to raise. Before adopting reforms, we need to understand why costs are high, to put those costs in perspective and to recognize political fundraising imperatives.

Electing our leaders demands adequate money to carry out the public debate of politics. Political money is a scarce resource and must be raised in a manner that does not heavily influence government decisions. And the fund-raising process must be seen as fair and trustworthy.

Interest Groups, PACs and Lobbies

Many who want election reform assume that special interests and large donors seek undue influence through their contributions. The implication is that lawmakers sell their votes for contributions. In most cases, the facts belie that theory. Most campaign contributions are not bribery or payments for services rendered. Yet the popular perception, magnified by the media, is that campaign contributions are unduly influential.

With high campaign costs and low contribution limits in many states and localities, it is unreasonable to suppose that elected officials "sell out" for a $1,000 or $5,000 donation to a campaign costing scores of thousands of dollars.

Social science has yet to perfect tools that measure influence. Analyses that correlate campaign contributions with roll-call votes fail to evaluate the impact of committee hearings, floor debate and procedural motions and agenda setting. Most research finds special interest contributions are far less important than party loyalty, constituent interests, a legislator's ideological leanings and a bill's anticipated longterm effects on society.

Many people today focus on political action committees as the corrupting factor in government. No doubt PAC contributions play a role in issues of low visibility and turn a vote at times. But on major issues such as education

Herbert E. Alexander is professor of political science and director of the Citizens' Research Foundation at the University of Southern California. This article is reprinted with permission from *State Government News* 33:4 (April 1990): 16-18. © 1990 by the Council of State Governments.

New Jersey

New Jersey has a good law covering gubernatorial races, which combines partial public financing with limitations on the size of contributions. But despite a reasonably effective disclosure law for all other contests, special-interest money is pouring into legislative races, where there are no contribution limits. Spending on these races has escalated at an alarming rate, with increases of 80 percent and more from one election to the next during the past decade. The size of individual contributions is also spiraling upwards.

Furthermore, disclosure alone is not an effective deterrent to campaign finance abuses. Political races that can be won with large campaign expenditures are much more common than those lost because of the disclosure of an embarrassing source of money or shocking excess in the total amount spent.

Source: Bill Schluter, "Contributions Don't Affect Votes? Don't You Believe It," *Governing* 3:11 (August 1990): 98. Bill Schluter is a Republican member of the New Jersey Assembly.

---

and public welfare, the impact of PAC or lobby contributions is minimal. On specific issues with no clear partisan or ideological content and no clear relevance for a lawmaker's constituents, PAC contributions may tip the lawmaker's vote in the special interest's favor. As with individual contributors, however, there is much diversity among givers. There are varied motives, some non-economic, for giving; and the more givers, the more diffused the impact of contributions.

Contributions of campaign money clearly do not assure special interest groups the legislative outcomes they seek. Special interest more often have enough votes to block legisla-

tion they oppose rather than obtain legislation they support.

If the role of PACs was diminished, more corporate and labor money would move into lobbying. Those with sophisticated lobbying operations would then have an advantage over those without savvy lobbyists. So would those groups—including single-issue groups—that are able to mobilize, or threaten to mobilize, voters.

Debates over campaign finance often get bogged down in moralistic hand-wringing and charges of undue influence. It might be better to focus on the dependency on interest group dollars. Alternative acceptable sources of funds might include public financing, tax incentives for political contributions or political party funds. The infusion of any of these could create new dependencies and diminish old ones.

High Campaign Costs

Many critics charge that campaign costs are too high. But just as there are no reliable measures of influence, no credible research exists documenting how much campaign spending is too much. To argue that campaigns cost too much is to suggest that campaign spending should be limited, which means restrictions on political speech. Elections are improved by well-financed candidates able to wage competitive campaigns, not by stifling political dialogue. If we want to place blame for the escalating costs of electioneering and the need for large sums of money, then the growth of technology and the reliance in statewide campaigns on television advertising are better places to start. These pose new questions about how money is spent and why, not just how much.

The role of political consultants—whom former California Treasurer Jess Unruh called "modern-day Hessians"—is a major factor in rising political costs. The profes-

sionalization of politics began when contribution limits shifted the emphasis away from big
individual donors. Forced to broaden and up-
grade their donor base, campaigns hired professional computer and direct mail experts.
With television a primary medium for direct
communication with voters, paid political advertising consumes budgets of candidates who
run for major offices.

The role of media consultants has grown
accordingly. These image experts groom the
candidate's presentations. They decide where,
when and what their political ads will do, say,
play and for whom.

A candidate's success in hiring high-
powered consultants often confers credibility
on the campaign. Most candidates for major
office are obliged to employ a professional
campaign manager, a pollster, media specialists, computer experts, and lawyers and accountants to navigate the complexities of election laws. The professionalization of politics
creates one class of candidate with access to
high-tech services, and another class without
the funds to buy them in abundance. That
results in some candidates—mostly incumbents
or the wealthy—as the technological "haves,"
while others—usually challengers—are the
"have-nots." That lack of balance too often
diminishes the challengers' chance to win. As
costs inevitably continue to rise, some candidates are not able to keep pace.

The more we regulate, the less flexibility
we experience at the campaign level. Whatever
changes we make, the electoral process always
has to deal with the classic conflict between the
democratic ideal of full public disclosure in
free elections and the demands of a free
economic system. Money is essentially symbolic. It represents a profound competition for
power, prestige, deference and other transcen-
dent values. In that scene, money is merely the
exchange medium—the green power—that individuals use to advance their aims and ambi-

tions. But money also is needed to amplify free
speech so it can be heard by the electorate.

Ideally, the challenge of election reform is
to reconcile the principle "one person, one
vote"—should we add one dollar?—with the
reality that a free society assumes unequal
distribution of money to pay for the political
campaigns. Proposed changes in campaign
finance are not free of pitfalls.

For example, how do we improve political dialogue, attract better informed and more
responsive citizens, stimulate volunteers, contributions and voters—while reducing the
dominance of big money, promoting fairness in
media coverage and encouraging our most
qualified people to become candidates? How
can we apply democratic principles to a campaign climate that emphasizes media over-
simplification, 10-second sound bites and 30-
second television spots, fueled by huge dollar
expenditures—and still bring about the desired recognition of constitutional guarantees?

Before submitting to pressure from the
media and reform groups and rushing to
change the system, care should be taken to
make sure that changes will make things better
instead of worse. This could happen if changes
are made without improving the process or
raising public confidence. Strict expenditure
limits also can enhance the power of the
media.

The moral dimensions of election reform
are not easy to discern. Is it moral to permit
unlimited spending, considering the possible
obligations that may be incurred in raising the
money? On the other hand, is it moral to
restrict spending by a challenger who needs
more exposure to get sufficient name recognition to compete against a better-known incumbent?

It is important not to confuse differences
in values with differing ethical postures. Elections serve their purposes best when promoting
differing values. Election reform proposals

A Question of Purpose

Was the Committee for a Clean and Safe America created to resolve long standing environmental problems or to help Jim Florio get elected governor of New Jersey in 1989? Chemical industry lobbyists give one answer. Committee records suggest the other.

The committee's name evokes soothing images of clean skies and waters, as would befit Florio, a strong supporter of environmental legislation while he was in the House and an author of the Superfund toxic waste cleanup law. Incorporated as a non-profit organization in New Jersey in March 1987, the committee raised $481,674 and spent $420,715 through March 31, 1989, four days before Florio officially announced for governor. Of some 630 contributions, half came from corporations and other businesses: many would be illegal if made to a candidate's campaign committee.

The committee's early contributors included five eyebrow-raisers: chemical companies American Cyanamid, Ciba-Geigy, GAF Chemical Corp., Merck and Co., and Dow Chemical. Florio's record made him an enemy of the chemical industry or, at best, "a fact of life," as one industry lobbyist says. But in 1987 the companies kicked in a total of $6,000 when his back-pocket PAC solicited money. . . .

As two industry lobbyists perceived it, Florio formed the committee to help environmental activists and industry leaders find common ground. Clair Tweedie, the Washington government affairs director for American Cyanamid, says, "He organized this group to develop programs which would bring environmental, business and public groups together." Tweedie recalls a technical seminar and other events sponsored by the committee. "There was a kick-off meeting on that at the Democratic Club [on Capitol Hill]," he says. "There must have been 150 people there."

At the time, Florio was chair of a House commerce and consumer protection subcommittee, wielding regulatory power over the chemical industry. Tweedie asks rhetorically of his decision to donate: "How do you ascribe motives?"

Never, the lobbyists protest, did they suspect that their money was supporting a political operation. But expenditures listed by the back-pocket PAC suggest the opposite. In 1987 and 1988 it paid a political and fundraising consultant more than $100,000. It threw a golf outing to raise money, sent five of its employees and consultants to the 1988 Democratic National Convention in Atlanta, paid $3,600 for a reception at the convention and donated $5,000 to two South Jersey Democratic organizations.

Florio strategists eventually decided that convention costs and some other expenses should have been paid by the gubernatorial campaign, according to [David A.] Luthman [treasurer of the committee]. In 1989 the campaign reimbursed the PAC more than $61,000. Pains were taken to separate the PAC from the gubernatorial effort, Luthman says, adding, "I don't think that anyone was misled."

But the PAC's biggest outlay—less than a month after Florio was elected governor—was purely political. It turned over $50,000, most of its treasury, to the state Democratic committee to pay off debts from Florio's 1981 gubernatorial bid.

Ciba-Geigy lobbyist William T. Lyons seemed surprised when told of the PAC's overtly political activities. Company officials willingly supported an attempt to solve environmental problems by consensus, he says, but would have reacted differently had they known the committee was a PAC. "I was under the impression that this was incorporated as a foundation of some sort," Lyons says. Tweedie's final comment: "If we had thought that that was a campaign financing organization, you would not have seen a penny from American Cyanamid in there."

Source: Peter Overby, "Back-Pocket PACs: New Ways to Skirt the Law," *Common Cause Magazine* 16:4 (July/August 1990): 26-28. © 1990 by *Common Cause Magazine*, Washington, D.C.

bring out different values about the proper role of government, political parties, and the free market place. Election reform also triggers partisanship. Democrats, for example, often advocate public funding. On the other hand, expenditure limitations proposed with public financing are unacceptable to many Republicans. Republicans believe they will be relegated to permanent minority status in Congress and many state legislatures unless they are able to spend freely in marginal districts and states, or against vulnerable incumbent Democrats.

Bacteria Needed for Growth

Politics is about people, ideas, interests and aspirations. Since people seek political fulfillment partly through groups, groups cannot be excluded from political participation. Politics without the influence of interest groups or PACs or lobbies is not realistic or desirable. Too many ideas and interests of value to society would get lost without the organized participation of groups in electoral politics.

Some groups with few members participate mainly through their wealth. Conflict occurs because people and groups differ. But conflict takes place in a political arena in which government sets the rules and the players are expected to abide by them. The govern-

ment, however, also is a player. The only fail-safe guarantee against government dominance lies in the ability of special interest groups to articulate their demands and to oppose government policies with whatever resources—including money—they command.

I would suggest two danger signs associated with campaign reform measures: (1) High campaign costs as well as excessive regulation may work to keep qualified candidates out of the process; (2) Political parties should not be slighted but have their roles enhanced as legitimate political actors. Parties represent a broadly based alternative to financing from narrowly focused interest groups.

And I would ask these questions:

When moral passions are at their peak, do they cleanse and purge society? Or do they merely reinforce negative perceptions about government and politics? When moral passions subside, do they leave in their wake stronger or weaker processes and institutions?

The challenge is to use such passions constructively, and that is not always done.

While politics and political financing can be improved, it probably cannot and certainly should not be sterilized and purified to the degree that many reformers seek. Former Sen. Eugene McCarthy has reminded us that water lilies do not grow without a bacteria count.

When Citizens Take to the Streets Politicians Eventually Listen

by Michael Burgess

The 1990s had barely dawned when the New York state Capitol was besieged by nearly 1,000 militant AIDS demonstrators who wrapped the building in red tape in March and then in June more than 10,000 hospital union workers and consumers encircled it in the largest protest Albany [had] seen in decades. More and more, the state capital is turning into a stage for citizens groups.

Besides the marches and mass rallies, more polite "lobby days" have been bringing thousands of people to Albany to represent senior citizens, hospitals, day care workers, tenants, religious federations, family planning and pro-life activists and many others. More than one group has even congregated outside the offices of Senate Majority Leader Ralph Marino demanding to see him for an explanation of why the Senate hadn't moved their bills.

Tour buses from every corner of the state roll into town on Tuesdays and Wednesdays during session. In the maze of marble buildings that houses state government, citizens join staffers coping with jammed elevators and long lines at hotdog carts. Such has become life in this era of budget deficits as more citizens groups realize how their daily lives are affected by the business in Albany.

Reasons for the increasing demonstration of people power in Albany go beyond just problems in the Empire State. To many, it is federal inactivity and the transfer of responsibility to the state government for important programs like social services and issues like abortion. Assembly Majority Leader Jim Tallon, whose office has been turned into an "emergency room" for the victims of government retrenchment, notes, "on domestic policy, Congress has been in paralysis or on the margins."

To Libby Post, co-chair of the Empire State Pride Agenda, it was the "whole resurgence of the radical right" which threatened the gay community. "With the advent of Ronald Reagan, we realized we were no longer protected by the people who held the reins and we had to do it for ourselves because no one was going to do it for us."

The Reagan program of block grants and new federalism which sought to decentralize bureaucracy and government responsibility has altered the political landscape in Albany. But a whole spate of converging forces com-

Michael Burgess is executive director of the Non-Profit Resource Center. This article is reprinted from *Empire State Report* 16:10 (October 1990): 35-37.

bined to make 1990 the year of the biggest demonstrations in Albany since the Vietnam era.

Richard Kirsch, director of Citizen Action's New York chapter, believes that people tend to seek responses more from "those levels of government which are closest to home." His organization has joined with others in a campaign for a state program of universal health care, not waiting for national health insurance which was the only focus of many labor-citizen coalitions for decades. With federal paralysis, activists like those in Citizen Action have seen more opportunities for success at the state level.

The emergence and re-emergence of critical issues like abortion, AIDS and the environment has spawned an activism from those who feel personally affected or threatened by what the state does. Prior to the July 1989 Supreme Court Webster decision, the states had been battlegrounds over Medicaid funding for abortion, parental consent and other efforts to regulate abortion.

The Webster decision shifted the burden of abortion policy to the states, and state capitals became the stomping ground for both pro-choice and pro-life organizations. Albany saw numerous protests on this issue [in 1990]. ... With the retirement of Supreme Court Justice William Brennan, it appears very possible that the court will overturn Roe v. Wade and let the states decide the very legality of abortion.

Since Earth Day in 1970, traditional environmental groups have become more vocal and attracted larger numbers of activists. During the 1980s, the movement solidified its presence in Albany, taking on state government on numerous occasions. Ten years ago, the Environmental Planning Lobby had less than two full time staff persons. Today, they have ten. The Adirondack Council and the Adirondack Mountain Club also have their own lobbyists now.

... Local outrage over the Shoreham nuclear power plant on Long Island, the siting of coal plants in the Capital District, low-level nuclear waste in Central New York and the growing solid waste crisis have prompted local activists to trek to Albany to demand action. In early May [1990], more than 1,000 people took part in a rally against the incineration of solid waste. In the Adirondacks, some residents ... initiated traffic slowdowns on the Northway in an attempt to stop further restrictions on development as proposed by the Governor's Commission on the Adirondacks in the 21st Century. All of these grassroots groups have become increasingly aware of how to shake things up at the capital and are able to use the media to focus attention on their issues.

Ten years ago, AIDS was not even an issue. Now, not only is it a growing health problem, but the gay community, already very politically cohesive on the issue, has risen up. Those personally affected by AIDS, many with their lives at stake, have nothing to lose by taking on state government. The aggressive group ACT UP has resorted to militant 1960s-style civil disobedience tactics. On March 28 [1990], 80 people were arrested and had to be bodily removed from the Capitol after a sit-in outside Senate chambers. The day before, they got into the Chamber and disrupted [the] session.

The root of all the commotion, however, is the state budget. As the state's fiscal condition worsens over the years, the stakes become higher for interest groups, who in turn, become more vocal in protection of their programs.

For many health care and social services programs, state budget deficits have come on top of years of federal deficits and funding cuts. The state deficits have prompted increasing calls to reduce Medicaid spending. The resulting crisis in New York City hospitals led to efforts to organize the two largest demonstrations in Albany in recent years. On June 13 [1990], over 10,000 persons were organized by a union-led coalition and joined by Jesse Jackson to demand universal health care and increased state subsidy of hospital costs.

Assemblyman Richard Gottfried, chairman of the Health Committee, observes that New York City residents "have been very well aware of Washington and City Hall, but regard Albany as some sort of strange, alien place that occasionally interferes with their lives." Gottfried believes that this attitude lets "Albany off the hook" to some extent but that the focus on Albany is growing because people do realize Albany impacts them as much if not more than City Hall and Washington.

The number of professional lobbyists in Albany has risen dramatically. The Temporary State Commission on Lobbying reported . . . that there were 1699 registered lobbyists in 1989 and lobbying expenses rose to $26.6 million . . . , up from $5.5 million ten years earlier.

Grassroots organizations founded on a shoestring by citizens have also become more sophisticated in recent years. Ten years ago, groups like Citizen Action, the Hunger Action Network, ACT UP and others did not exist. Others are moving their offices to the state capital. Such is the case of the New York Statewide Senior Action Council and the League of Women Voters. Many of these groups are led and staffed by "thirtysomethings" whose college years and early political development were shaped by the political activism of the late 1960s and early 1970s. They decided to pursue their political interests in the form of community organizing and local and statewide advocacy.

Another factor in the increasing activism by citizens groups is simply the presence of Mario Cuomo. Cuomo's national prominence and the extensive press coverage he receives state- and nationwide makes him a target for activity. Advocates want to get his attention because of his power to respond to their protests.

[One] frequent administration critic . . . notes that advocates often get very frustrated with a commissioner and "need to go right to his boss (Cuomo) and alert him to how his agency is consistently screwing up."

More and more, demonstrations are not just planned for the Capitol, but for the Executive Mansion's front lawn on Eagle Street. Cuomo, the politician and conciliator, has often walked out to talk to demonstrators when he was home.

Since he took office, Cuomo has tried to be closer to the people. He has encouraged them to participate in the process and has praised activists for using the system. The rallying cry for ACT UP in March [of 1990] was "Time's Up," a response to a statement Cuomo made a year earlier inviting them to protest at the Capitol if state government didn't respond to their needs.

"Very often, groups feel the one way to get the governor's attention is to hang out and be loud," observes Gottfried. "In previous administrations, you might have felt the governor would act negatively. The Cuomo administration has reacted positively."

Cuomo's administration has sent not-so-subtle messages to advocates that the squeaky wheel will get greased. Common knowledge now is that an issue has to generate a lot of public attention if it is to move up the priority scale. Indeed, it seems that top staff often gauge the importance of issues based on how much public uproar and media pressure organizations can generate. Indeed, groups that engage in demonstrations and draw media attention often garner more attention than policy papers issued by groups specializing in think-tank research.

The bottom line of course is whether

people power really works. Assembly Majority Leader Jim Tallon says the impact is clear. "Some fairly well organized, citizen-oriented groups have a real impact on the system. Everyone understands it doesn't take enormous numbers of people to look like a crowd, an organized constituency of 500 spread across the state appearing to act in concert and speaking for a larger group can emerge in leadership roles on issues because the playing field is still not enormous."

To be sure, in a media-conscious capital city, the ability of organizations to go public with rallies and capture media attention is something watched very closely. In a place that thrives on control, the threat of civil disobedience by ACT UP seemed to even immobilize the Capitol because people didn't know what the group's tactics were going to be that day.

Gottfried suggests that aggressive style might be a necessity for groups on limited budgets. The groups that don't demonstrate or disrupt "tend to be well established groups with large lobbying budgets and large campaign contributions and I think that's too bad." Like Tallon, Gottfried also notes that the aggressive groups often serve to strengthen the hand of their moderate allies who then are dealt with more seriously because they are open to negotiating compromises.

But while people power does not necessarily gain money for an issue or program in deficit years, the Cuomo administration has been trying to incorporate advocates' viewpoints in state policy. Cuomo advisers have begun to negotiate state policy on low-level radioactive waste with citizen activists, for example.

And people power puts issues on the agenda, and helps take programs off the budget chopping block. Political leaders get backed into a corner because they know they have to respond to the protest. Democrat Tallon calls the split control of state government a "divided

government paradigm" that has existed since his party took control of the executive in 1974. "This means that rarely does one side vanquish the other. The way of government since 1974 is that progress is made over time with some compromise from a polar position."

To Tallon, the key role of more potent citizens advocacy organizations is that "they validate the compromises from the polar positions. The Legislature on its own has a hard time doing that." Tallon notes how [in an earlier session] senior citizens organizations "signed off" on a compromise on legislation restricting doctors charges for services for the federal Medicare program. Senior organizations had lobbied for their pure position of an absolute ban on overcharges and whipped up their constituencies into an uncompromising mood. In the end, their leaders accepted restrictions phased in over a few years with incentives to doctors based on their rate of acceptance of Medicare rates as full payment.

Legislators who before may have been shocked at protests are getting used to commotion in the capital. But as always, the bottom line is in the voting booth. Lawmakers are primarily concerned with those organizations able not only to mount a one-shot rally, but able to keep up the pressure back home and at the voting booth. Clearly, the pro-choice and pro-life movements are powerful, as well as labor and teachers unions. And the environmental movement recently established its own political action committee, the League of Conservation Voters, to enhance its clout.

Some groups are feared not so much because of their ability to donate campaign money and deliver votes. Legislators are also sensitive to the "embarrassment power" of such groups, like senior citizens and their ability to influence public opinion.

Post, of the Pride Agenda, believes that large demonstrations are only "stop-gap" measures, effective only if there is a long-term lobbying strategy in Albany and in the districts. "You have to make sure if you're going to have demonstrations that they are not your only strategy; you have to have grassroots organizing and education going on. You've got to work it from the inside and the outside."

The irony is that while the number of citizen activists and lobbyists has multiplied, voter apathy has surged. As the number of voters is at an all-time low, activists most influential at the polls will play a bigger role in deciding what happens in Albany. . . .

IV. MEDIA AND
THE STATES

A Barrage of Campaign Ads for State
and Local Office: Just Around the
Corner—On Cable TV?

102

The media—in all forms—have become important actors in state politics and government. This is especially true given the changes that have been occurring in politics, such as the decline of political parties and the rise of individual, media-oriented campaigns. Every candidate for statewide office and many candidates for local offices now have to count a media consultant among the consultants they must hire. The rapidly increasing costs state and local political candidates incur are, in great part, tied to the rapidly escalating costs of running media-oriented campaigns.

But this is only part of the reason that the media are important in the states. With the demise of the old political organizations and machines, the means of government-citizen communication have changed. In many cases, it is the media that carry the messages between government and citizens.

The media have no formal powers per se, but they are protected by the First Amendment's free speech clause. This allows a certain freedom of action for the media; they cannot be constrained by governmental action. However, part of the media is regulated by the federal government through the licensing of radio and television stations. Among the components of granting a license are the equal time and public service provisions.

The equal time provision protects an individual or a group by assuring them an opportunity to respond to attacks or critiques; it is sort of a "letters to the editor" space required of radio and television. This provision is especially important for political campaigns because it may affect what will be allowed on the air. The public service provision calls on the licensee to devote a certain amount of air time to public affairs.

Types of Media

"The media" is a broad term that needs to be broken into its components for us to better understand how the media operate in the states. There are the print media, the daily and weekly newspapers we read; the television stations, which provide local and national news; the radio stations, which offer a large variety of formats; and the wire services, which provide the backbone of news stories and other information to the other media.

In fact, it is the wire services and the daily newspapers that set the agenda for television and radio, although TV and radio stations pick and choose what they want to cover. Look at your state's or city's major morning paper and compare the main stories on the front page with what you hear on the early morning radio news. Go into any radio or television station and watch how closely they follow and use the information coming over the AP or UPI wire services. A recent study indicates that state elected officials find newspapers and the wire services the two most politically significant media in the states. This is in contrast to the general perception that newspapers and TV are the most important media at the national level.[1]

There are assets and liabilities to each medium. For example, the newspapers can cover a broad range of items and concerns, making them attractive to many readers. In fact, some critics argue that the newspapers may be covering too many types of stories and may be losing their focus and concern over larger public issues. Television is a "hot" medium because stories are expressed through pictures, which is an easier way for most people to absorb the news. However, TV is limited by its own technology since it depends on pictures to carry the message; how does one take a picture of taxes? A study conducted in the mid-1970s of forty-four newspapers and television stations in ten cities found that newspapers allocated more space to stories on state government than did television stations. Newspapers also gave stories on state government greater prominence (front page location) than did the television stations (lead story status).[2] But Bill Gormley, the study's author, argued that even with this newspaper coverage, "few give it [state government] the kind of coverage it needs."[3]

Gormley cited the comments of others who had misgivings about the media's coverage of the states. Political scientist V. O. Key, Jr. argued in 1961 that the media "may dig to find the facts about individual acts of corruption but the grand problems of the political system by and large escape their critical attention."[4] Former North Carolina governor Terry Sanford (D, 1961-65) questioned, "Who, in some 40 states or more, can say he begins to understand state government by what he reads in the newspapers?"[5]

State Media Structures

There is great variety in the media structures across the states just as there is great variety in population size, population centers, and economic complexity. For example, New Jersey sits within two major media markets—the northern part of the state receives broadcasts from the New York City metropolitan area, and the southern part receives broadcasts from the greater Philadelphia metropolitan area. Radio, TV, and cable stations emanating from those major markets dominate what is seen or heard in New Jersey, and there are no strong New Jersey-based media outlets to combat this. News about New Jersey must fight for a spot in these media outlets.

West Virginia also faces this problem: much of the state is served by media markets in Cincinnati, Pittsburgh, and Washington,

D.C. West Virginia lacks its own major media outlet because its terrain makes it impossible for any station to reach all parts of the state. In his 1980 reelection bid, Governor John D. "Jay" Rockefeller IV (D, 1977-85) spent a lot of money on outlets in these large cities in order to reach potential voters in remote areas of the state. There were stories of voters in Washington, D.C., going to the polls to vote for Rockefeller because they had seen his ads on TV so often.

Then there are states that have many media markets within the state's own boundaries. California clearly is the leader in media markets because there are so many large communities to be served in the state, ranging from San Francisco and Sacramento in the northern part of the state to Los Angeles and San Diego in the southern part. And there are many other markets in between. Texas also has many media markets, as does Florida, New York, and North Carolina.

At the other extreme are states with only one major media market that dominates the state. Examples are Colorado with the Denver media market, Georgia with Atlanta, and Massachusetts with Boston. In fact, the Boston media market spreads well into Rhode Island, southern New Hampshire and southwestern Maine, making it difficult for residents there to get a clear understanding of what is happening in their own states. When one such market or major city dominates the state, there is little chance for those in the remainder of the state to voice their own particular interests. A rural-urban or rural-suburban rift in the state's media coverage is the rule.

Some comparative figures also indicate the wide variation between the states in media markets. In 1988, there were 1,642 daily newspapers in the United States, or an average of 33 per state, but they were not distributed equally. There were 120 daily newspapers in California, but only 3 in Delaware. Texas had

106, whereas Hawaii and Utah had 6 each. The other states ranged between these extremes.[6]

This means some states' residents have a greater opportunity to read local newspapers than do residents of other states. In 1987, the daily newspaper circulation per one-hundred residents was forty-four in New York and forty-two in Virginia, compared to fifteen each in Maryland and Mississippi. The rate was thirty-six in Massachusetts and thirty in both Nebraska and Rhode Island, compared to seventeen in Utah and eighteen each in Alabama, Georgia, Kentucky, and Louisiana.[7]

The number of television stations also varies by state, although with the expansion of cable systems across the United States the actual number of stations available to a household through cable may be in the twenty-five to forty range. But even among those cable systems and their many channels, there is considerable variation in the number of local stations available. In 1985, there were 1,167 television stations in the United States, or an average of 23 per state, but again they were not distributed equally. Texas had seventy-nine and California had seventy-six stations, compared with Delaware with two and Rhode Island with four. Florida had fifty-two stations and Ohio had forty-five, Utah and Vermont had seven each, and New Hampshire and Wyoming had eight each.[8]

Radio is a considerably more ubiquitous form of media; in 1985 there were 9,521 stations in the United States. If the stations were distributed equally across the states, there would have been an average of 190 stations per state. In actuality, there were 594 radio stations in Texas and 564 in California, compared with 20 in Delaware and 28 in Rhode Island. Pennsylvania had 384, New York had 376, and Florida had 366, whereas Hawaii had 41, Vermont had 49, and Nevada had 50.[9]

Much of the variation in the data noted above is tied to the size of the state in terms of land area and population. But some of the variation is related to population diversity: some newspapers and radio stations target specific populations.

How the Media Work in the States

There is almost a definite pattern in how the media cover state politics and state government. During political campaigns, when candidates are vying for nominations and election to office, the media are involved selectively. Being involved can mean several things. First, the media cover some of the campaigns on a day-to-day or week-to-week basis, especially those campaigns with the greatest appeal in terms of what the media feel will sell papers or draw listeners and viewers.

Second, the media have become the major vehicle for political messages—the paid fifteen- or thirty-second campaign ads that we see on TV and hear on the radio and the printed advertisements we see in newspapers.

Third, some of the media become part of campaigns when they conduct public opinion polls, which delineate the important issues in the race and show which candidate is ahead. The media also become part of campaigns when they sponsor debates between the candidates and endorse candidates through editorials. A new role some newspapers have adopted is that of a monitor or critic of political campaign ads, especially those shown on television. In monitoring the ads, the papers have a reporter present the text of the political ad (often negative in tone and style), then match that with the facts of the situation. Then there is an analysis of the differences, if any.

For their part, candidates and their campaign organizations develop ways to obtain "unpaid media"—getting candidates and their names on TV or in print to increase their name recognition. Knowing when the major

TV stations must have their tapes "in the can" for the nightly news can determine when a candidate makes an appearance or holds a press conference.

Fourth, the media become a part of the calculus by which decisions are made and actions are taken in politics and government. The best example of this is the pervasive influence that the *Manchester Union Leader* has on New Hampshire government and politics. This newspaper runs very conservative editorials on the front page for all to see. An observer of the state wrote in the 1960s that "[m]any state officials said they feared personal and vindictive editorial reprisal on the front page if they took exception to one of the paper's policies." [10] These officials felt "the paper has created an emotionally charged, reactionary atmosphere where new ideas are frequently not only rejected but fail to appear in print for public discussion." [11] This may or may not be an exception to how most papers operate. Sometimes such an atmosphere or situation can be created in more subtle ways than front page editorial attacks but exist nonetheless.

Other media organizations have acted in a more responsible manner over the years. These organizations have worked with those in government and politics to help their readers understand what is happening. For years, the *Louisville Courier-Journal* did this for Kentucky and for parts of adjoining states.[12] As one newsman argued, "Publishers have a responsibility to the public to do more. Call it public service, if you will ... but the press has the responsibility to enlighten and serve." [13]

A second pattern to media coverage and activity in the states has to do with the timing of state legislative sessions. There is an adage that when the legislature is in town, no one is safe. More to the point, when the legislature is in town, so are the media of the state. Not only do the capital press and media corps regulars cover general legislative activity, but specific newspapers and TV stations send reporters to cover the representatives from their city or county. Also, if there is some legislation that will have an impact on a particular section of the state, there most certainly will be media from that section to monitor what is happening.

This leads to some interesting observations by those who have watched this "cover-the-legislature-at-all-costs" phenomenon. First, coverage of other state government activities, programs, and individuals often is neglected as a result. Why? "[I]t's a lot easier to cover the legislature.... Stories are easy to get. Legislators seek out reporters, doling out juicy quotes and swapping hot rumors." Plus, editors want their reporters to be there. "When reporters aren't there, editors want to know why not." [14]

Second, there have been changes in the nature of the capital press corps. There tend to be fewer gray beards than in the past and more younger reporters. The tradeoff seems to be youth, vigor, and inexperience versus age and experience; hence the coverage may not be as good as in the past even though there may be more media folk involved. For example, the capital press corps in one state capital once operated under the following set of rules for new reporters: "(1) Don't fall down; (2) Don't get sick; and (3) Don't *ever* look like you don't know what you are doing." [15] No one knows what the rules might be now.

Another major factor influencing how state governments and politics are covered by the media is the location and size of the state capital. In some states, the capital city is not the largest city; instead, it seems to be a "compromise" city between two large urban centers. Examples of this include Springfield, Illinois, located about two-thirds of the way from Chicago toward St. Louis, Missouri;

Jefferson City, Missouri, located midway between St. Louis and Kansas City; and Trenton, New Jersey, located closer to the Philadelphia metropolitan area than to the New York area.

Some other state capitals are near the geographic center of the state, such as Little Rock, Arkansas; Des Moines, Iowa; Oklahoma City, Oklahoma; and Columbia, South Carolina. However, several capitals are in what seems to be out-of-the-way locations, including Sacramento, California; Annapolis, Maryland; Albany, New York; and Carson City, Nevada. Still other states put their capital in the largest city, where most of the action takes place. Some examples of such capitals are Denver, Colorado; Atlanta, Georgia; Boston, Massachusetts; and Providence, Rhode Island.

When the state capital is in an out-of-the-way location, the media may find it more difficult to cover events since the government may be the only game in town. When there is not much action—or when the legislature adjourns—many in the press return to their home cities, leaving state government uncovered. When the state capital is located in the state's largest and most active city, there may be better coverage of state government, but that may be drowned out by the coverage of all the other activities in the city.

The National Media and the States

How does the national media treat what goes on in the states? One quick answer is that the national media doesn't cover the states unless a disaster occurs. Media specialist Doris Graber calls the national media's coverage of state issues "flashlight coverage." [16] She argues that there are basically two types of news in the eyes of the national media: high priority news and low priority news. The former is news that "has been judged in the past as intrinsically interesting to the audience by the usual news criteria. . . . [It is news that is] exciting, current, close to home, about familiar people, and audiences are likely to deem it relevant to their life." On the other side of the coin is low priority news, which "has been judged intrinsically uninteresting although it may be important." [17]

Graber argues that state news traditionally has been in the low priority news category, with only an occasional "entertainment or convenience item" receiving "a brief spotlight" in the news. However, when state news can be tied to high priority news, such as national elections, coverage increases. [18]

A recent study of the media coverage of the 1989 Virginia gubernatorial election is instructive of another aspect of what national coverage can mean during a state-level election. [19] This race was in an off-presidential year, which meant there wasn't too much political news. In addition, the Democratic candidate, L. Douglas Wilder, was vying to become the nation's first elected black governor. The study showed how two "local" papers covered the race (the *Richmond Times-Dispatch* and the "Metro" section of the *Washington Post*), and how the national media covered it (included were articles from the *Christian Science Monitor, Los Angeles Times, New York Times, Wall Street Journal, Newsweek, Time,* and *U.S. News and World Report*).

The results are revealing. The national coverage focused narrowly on the historical aspect of the race, and on the fact that Wilder was prochoice on the abortion issue while his opponent was prolife. The local papers focused more broadly on the substantive issues, and provided candidate and voting group profiles. The national media obviously concentrates on the aspects of a story that appeal to a broad audience; however, this treatment does not ensure coverage of the whole story—or even the correct story.

Working with the Press

There is another side to the media-government relationship: how those who serve in state government react to the role of the media. Most governors, some state agencies, and a growing number of legislatures have established press offices to work with—and even cater to—the media and its needs. This means each governor has a press secretary or communications director. Recently, state legislators have realized the need for a media liaison who works either for a party caucus or the party leadership. Many agencies in state government also are developing offices that work with the press.

For press offices, working with the media on a daily basis usually entails distributing press releases and answering queries. But press offices are also responsible for making sure that their bosses handle themselves properly with the media corps. At the 1982 New Governors Seminar sponsored by the National Governors' Association, newly elected governors were given the following advice on dealing with the media:[20]

● Good press relations cannot save a poor administration, but poor press relations can destroy a good one.

● Never screw up on a slow news day.

● If you don't correct an error immediately, in the future you'll be forced to live with it as fact.

● Never argue with a person who buys ink by the barrel.

● When you hold a press conference and are going to face the lions, have some red meat to throw them or they'll chew on you. It should be something of substance, as long as the governor isn't the Christian.

● Never make policy at press conferences.

Part IV provides some perspectives on the media in the states. Rob Gurwitt from Congressional Quarterly examines the changing nature of the press covering the state capitols. Ferrel Guillory of the (Raleigh) *News and Observer* analyzes the changing nature of newspaper readers, as perceived by the media. Kevin Finch of *Illinois Issues* raises the interesting question of journalists losing their citizenship rights due to their occupation as objective observers of politics and government. Finally, Jim Hoefler of Dickinson College identifies what may be the medium of the future in political campaigns—cable TV, with its ability to deliver messages to a highly segmented audience.

Notes

1. Thad L. Beyle and G. Patrick Lynch, "The Media and State Politics." Paper presented at the annual meeting of the Midwest Political Science Association, Chicago, April 1991.
2. William T. Gormley, Jr., "Coverage of State Government in the Mass Media," *State Government* 52:2 (Spring 1979): 46-47.
3. Ibid., 47.
4. V. O. Key, Jr., *Public Opinion and American Democracy* (New York: Alfred Knopf, 1961), 381.
5. Terry Sanford, *Storm Over the States* (New York: McGraw-Hill, 1967), 51.
6. Bureau of the Census, U.S. Department of Commerce, "Daily and Sunday Newspapers— Number and Circulation, By State: 1988," *Statistical Abstract of the United States, 1990* (Washington, D.C.: U.S. Government Printing Office, 1990), 556.
7. Table A-40, "Daily Newspaper Circulation per 100 Residents, 1987," *State Policy Data Book, 1989.*
8. Table A-41, "Number of Television Stations, January 1985," *State Policy Data Book, 1989.*
9. Table A-42, "Number of Radio Stations, January 1985," *State Policy Data Book, 1989.*
10. Sanford, 50.
11. Ibid.
12. Ibid., 51.
13. Quoted in Sanford, 52.
14. Jack Betts, "When the Legislature's in Session, Does Other News Take a Back Seat?" *North*

Carolina Insight 12:1 (December 1989): 63.

15. Jack Betts, "The Capital Press Corps: When Being There Isn't Enough," *North Carolina Insight* 9:2 (September 1986): 48.

16. Doris A. Graber, "Flashlight Coverage: State News on National Broadcasts," *American Politics Quarterly* 17:3 (July 1989): 278.

17. Ibid., 288.

18. Ibid., 288-289.

19. Mark J. Rozell, "Local v. National Press Assessments of the 1989 Virginia Gubernatorial Campaign," *Polity* 24:1 (1991), forthcoming.

20. Thad L. Beyle and Robert Huefner, "Quips and Quotes from Old Governors to New," *Public Administration Review* 43:3 (May/June 1983): 268.

In the Capitol Pressroom, the Old Boys Call It a Day

by Rob Gurwitt

If it weren't for Bill O'Connell, there probably would be no civic center sprawled across an entire block of downtown Peoria, Illinois.

O'Connell had been sitting through sessions of the Illinois legislature for nearly 20 years when he dreamed the project up and helped steer it to passage along with his close ally, Representative E. J. "Zeke" Giorgi. After all those years, O'Connell knew as much as anyone in Springfield about how to work the corridors to take care of his hometown. "I have never been shy," he says, "about looking out for the interests of downstate." Those words would sound natural coming from some weathered municipal lobbyist or old-time legislator reared on the politics of pork. It's another matter when they're spoken, as they are, by the Springfield correspondent of the Peoria *Journal Star*.

O'Connell has been covering the Illinois legislature since 1955. He has been there five years longer than the next most senior reporter and nine years longer than the longest-serving legislator. "I am one of the last of the activists," he says, and he is. There will be no more Bill O'Connells in Illinois after he's gone. In fact, there are fewer and fewer like him in the pressrooms of state capitols all across the country.

O'Connell got his start in the business at a time when reporters practiced their craft differently than they do now, with less formality and a more relaxed set of standards. It wasn't just that the whiskey bottle tended to come out of the drawer in the morning, or that anyone wandering into the pressroom could sit in on the inevitable gin rummy game off in one corner. It was also that the line between newsmen and the legislators they covered was hazier. Some reporters, like O'Connell, felt free to dip an oar into the legislative process every once in a while. Most spent their evenings drinking with politicians, arguing politics and strategy, and building friendships.

That conviviality had a chance to flourish because statehouse reporters, in Illinois and in most other states, stayed around long enough to cultivate it. "The press corps used to have a lot of guys who were almost lifers," says Lee Leonard, United Press International's statehouse veteran in Columbus, Ohio. "They were cynical, gray-headed, wrinkled guys with real mean exteriors."

They were also veterans who not only knew every member of the institution they

Rob Gurwitt is a staff writer for *Governing*. This article appeared in *Governing* 3:10 (July 1990): 27-30.

covered, but could tell you its history and explain its byways better than most legislators. They were men like Sam Thompson, of Ohio's *Columbus Dispatch,* who was so well versed in legislative proceedings that parliamentarians in the House and Senate would check in with him on particularly complex or arcane calls. Or Eugene "Jep" Cadou Sr., who covered every session of the Indiana General Assembly from 1925 to 1967 for the International News Service, a UPI predecessor. By the end of Cadou's career, lawmakers had developed the habit of allowing him to address a joint session as the year's business wound down; a few years before he retired, the state Senate made him an honorary member.

That was another era. Today, in Illinois, of the 40-odd reporters who fill the capitol pressroom, only five besides O'Connell were there when [former] Republican Governor James R. Thompson took office in 1977. It's unlikely that many of the current crop will be there a decade from now.

Moreover, in their shorter periods of statehouse work, reporters do not get to know the legislature as intimately as they once would have. The distance between the press and politicians has widened in the past generation, pushed by evolving ethical standards on both sides, a mutual wariness that has mounted over the years with each new scandal and a variety of simple changes in state capital life. When a Peoria-area legislator alludes jokingly to O'Connell as "the 60th senator," he means it as a compliment; O'Connell, who often uses the word "we" when talking about the legislature's actions, would probably take it as such. A younger reporter, weaned in a more adversarial age, would wince.

Bill O'Connell is 61, a slightly built man whose glasses and mildly crooked smile combine to give him the curious air of an earnest wise guy. Which, as it happens, he is. Asked why he never drives from Peoria to Springfield—he hitches rides with legislators—O'Connell explains it's because he has no depth perception. "It's not because the secretary of state has my license," he cracks, "though he could probably get me if there was a law against drunken walking."

Opinionated, creatively profane and deeply knowledgeable about Illinois politics from Chicago down to the Kentucky border, O'Connell has spent his adult life trying to keep ordinary people interested in complex legislative business. For 25 years, O'Connell saw to it that the Peoria *Journal Star* periodically published a primer on how the legislature works, a basic course in the governmental process for the citizens of the town. He sees himself as writing for "Grace and Elmer," blue-collar people who work at Peoria's huge Caterpillar plant. "At the end of the week," he says, "I want to be able to sit in my backyard and have my neighbors understand what I was doing all week, and what the legislature was doing."

Often, over the years, that has meant walking a fine line between good fellowship and reportorial duty. Republican Lee Daniels, then-minority leader of the Illinois House, tells a story about spending a convivial evening with O'Connell talking about the legislature. As they drank—"Meaning no disrespect," Daniels says, "he can put it away"—O'Connell slid farther and farther down in his chair, and Daniels felt more and more comfortable about passing his thoughts along. The next day, there it all was in the paper. "He'd remembered it all, and he got it right," Daniels says.

Bill O'Connell has been willing from time to time to print news that embarrassed his legislative buddies. All the same, he has never seen anything wrong with supplying them with practical advice, such as when the time might be ripe for a particular bill. Nor has he minded taking new legislators from Peoria under his wing and introducing them around the capitol. And at certain crucial moments, he has done far more than that.

It was O'Connell, along with Democrat Giorgi, who came up with the idea of taking a legislator's bill to fund a civic center for his own hometown and turning it into a display of legislative generosity to a whole set of downstate cities, including Peoria. Even more important, it was O'Connell who helped get the whole idea the crucial backing it needed from the Chicago delegation.

The plan was to fund all these downstate projects by tapping racetrack revenues, the same source that was backing the bonds that had built McCormick Place, Chicago's lakefront exposition center. The idea worried the House majority leader, a powerful Cook County Democrat whose father-in-law happened to be general manager of McCormick Place. The majority leader was concerned that money the Chicago project needed might be drained away. O'Connell gave him a copy of the legislation to look over. Then he took him out for a beer. By the time their meeting was over, he had made it clear that McCormick Place would get its racetrack money first; the funds left over would be available for Peoria and the other towns downstate. O'Connell left not only with the majority leader's support but with a pledge of 60 additional votes.

None of the legislators who remember this episode are in any doubt about who was responsible for the result. "Bill O'Connell," says Zeke Giorgi, "is the reason Peoria got their metro center."

Bill O'Connell's legislative activism is a little unusual by the journalistic standards of the 1990s. But by the standards that governed Illinois statehouse reporting in the 1950s, it does not seem unusual at all.

In the mid-'50s, the Springfield press corps was dominated by one man—George Tagge, the legendary political editor of the

Chicago Tribune. Tagge was, in essence, the Springfield representative for Colonel Robert R. McCormick, the *Tribune*'s wealthy, conservative and strong-willed publisher—"the most eccentric publisher God ever put on this earth," as Bill O'Connell describes him.

Republican legislators from Cook County and the Chicago suburbs not only read what Tagge wrote, they listened politely when he spoke to them. "When I first came to the legislature as a staffer in 1968," says GOP Senator Bob Kustra, "I remember Republican legislators talking about taking orders from George Tagge."

Tagge spent almost a decade twisting arms and steering floor fights to get the Illinois legislature to issue bonds to build an exposition center on Chicago's Lakefront and name it after Robert McCormick; for their part, legislators nicknamed the building "Tagge's Temple," in memory of the reporter's years of lobbying. Bill O'Connell watched all that as a greenhorn in the capitol pressroom. More than a decade later, in a far less heavy-handed fashion, he took a page from Tagge's book in order to look out for the interests of his own hometown.

The state capitol environment that tolerated Tagge and trained O'Connell was a great deal cozier than the one that exists today. In the Springfield that Bill O'Connell went to cover, there were only a handful of reporters, representing the Chicago dailies, the St. Louis press, a couple of downstate papers and the wire services. The legislature met for six months every two years, but during those months politicians and reporters lived and drank together at three hotels near the capitol: the St. Nicholas for the Democrats, the Abraham Lincoln for the Republicans and the Leland for fence sitters and reporters whose papers' editorial policies weren't clearly partisan.

Today, those hotels have either been

A Scandal Survival Guide

... First, try to avoid ethics problems. While easily said, it is no less important for being obvious. Avoiding problems means more than simply following the law. In the minds of journalists and voters, ethics problems are a much broader category than legal problems.

One way for lawmakers to avoid problems is to bring in someone from outside the staff with excellent political sense to review their personal and financial life as well as office and campaign procedures. That person's charge should be to develop the strongest possible political case against a politician by weaving together that information in the form of possible negative attacks. If done properly, this procedure should provide a politician with a good sense of where problems lie and how they can be avoided. In addition, before taking action, a lawmaker should ask, "What is the worst light in which this could be put and how would I respond to that kind of question or attack?"

Lawmakers also should check with their legislative ethics committees or counsels before doing anything that may be deemed as questionable. Get the committee's opinion in writing. If these preventive measures fail, follow these rules:

● **Think through a game plan.** Too often, people caught in the middle of an alleged scandal allow themselves to be buffeted about by the situation because they have not developed a plan from the beginning.

● **Have the facts straight.** .... If getting the facts straight requires taking an extra day or two, take the time.

● **Admit everything at the first press conference.** The only thing worse than one day of scandal headlines is more than one day of scandal headlines. An immediate objective should be to contain the story as quickly as possible. Get it all out at once without leaving more for the second day's story. ...

● **Be honest.** A politician should tell his or her side of the story but not shade the truth. Journalists often are like sharks—the smell of blood drives them crazy. Once a lawmaker is in trouble, they will hunt for everything they can find to make it worse. If a lawmaker lies, it will be discovered.

● **Be apologetic.** Denying a mistake when it is clear to everyone else that one was made makes a lawmaker look worse to the public. It also gives the press more incentive to keep up its attack.

● **Don't take refuge in the law.** When a person says, "I did nothing illegal" the voters' first reaction is to say, "Yeah, but then you probably did something wrong."

Ethics issues are not primarily about what is legal or illegal but about right and wrong.

● **Don't overreact.** Voters are less interested in capitol gossip than are reporters and politicians. ...

When all is said and done, the primary question becomes not how an individual can deal with ethics problems, but more importantly, how can we repair the bond of trust between those who govern and those who are governed.

Improving the trust between society and its political institutions is a critical goal as we move toward the next century. Solving the problem will require creativity and attention, in addition to integrity.

Source: Mark S. Mellman and Edward H. Lazarus, "A Scandal Survival Guide," *State Government News* 33:4 (April 1990): 10-11. © 1990 by the Council of State Governments.

razed or converted to apartments, victims of the switch to a full-time legislature. Legislators and reporters alike tend to have their own apartments in the capital now, and usually repair to them at the end of the day. A few watering holes still pull in the evening trade, but they're filled for only a few hours with legislators, lobbyists and staffers; reporters generally drop by for a beer only when they have to find someone for a quote. The fraternity-like atmosphere that dominated many state capitals has been broken up by the presence of women in key positions both as reporters and as legislators, and the encroachment of family life upon what was once a male singles' subculture.

Indeed, in state capitals around the country, *Sacramento Bee* columnist Dan Walters suggests, it may be that the most common friendships that develop these days are between reporters and legislative staffers, who often live in the same neighborhoods and send their children to the same schools. Even in statehouses themselves, life has grown more formal. Jim Beaumont, a former Des Moines newspaperman who is now a vice president of the Illinois Chamber of Commerce, remembers that when he first arrived in Springfield in the early 1970s, the press corps sat in a large room on the same floor of the statehouse as the two legislative chambers, separated from the building's cafeteria by a low wall. "It was a very open environment, with that big pressroom smelling like hot dogs and the food line next to it, and people would congregate," he says. "It was like one big party; everybody was there buttonholing everybody else." Now, legislators and reporters all have their own offices and mingle far less.

But there has also been a clear change in the way reporters approach the politicians they cover, and in how legislators view the press. The physical separation between the two that began in Illinois in the mid-1970s was matched by a psychological separation that was spurred, in particular, by Watergate.

Adversarial reporting, of course, was born long before Watergate. Illinois newspapers have a long history of going after those in power. In 1956, state Auditor Orville Hodge, who was running for governor, had his hopes derailed when the *Chicago Daily News* disclosed that he had skimmed the state till of almost $2 million.

Still there is no denying that over the last decade and a half, the unguarded camaraderie that once marked statehouse society has suffered a universal decline. "After Watergate," says Steve Fagan, who edits the *Springfield State Journal Register,* "government officials at all levels became far more suspicious of the media than ever before. Maybe with good reason, because we saw a load of people come into this business with the idea that it was glamorous and with a desire to get a scalp and hang it on their belt." Not every reporter shares that agenda, and most statehouse journalists develop a loose affability with legislators they cover, but there's no doubt that relations are tinged more frequently with wariness than they were. In Illinois, O'Connell is pretty much the last vestige of the sensibility that prevailed when he first arrived. Like him, the next most senior reporters—Ray Serati of the Copley News Service and Charles Wheeler of the Chicago *Sun-Times*—are students of the institution who have devoted their lives to covering it; unlike him, they keep their views to themselves and are careful to keep a social distance from legislators. On a recent evening, when Senate President Phil Rock was hosting a fund-raiser that most of the state Democratic hierarchy and top lobbyists were going to attend, Wheeler was headed home to go to a school event with one of his children. Serati dismissed the affair by saying, "I see those guys all day, I don't need to take up my evening with them."

There have been tangible benefits to the end of the buddy system that used to prevail in state capitals. "There is less of a tendency," as Ohio's Lee Leonard puts it, "to print one-sided stories that are slanted toward legislators." Bill O'Connell himself is happy to be past the days when George Tagge would use his column to praise an obscure downstate legislator for his "little-noticed" work, omitting the legislator's one truly relevant accomplishment: the procurement and delivery of several bottles of liquor to the pressroom late one night after the regular supply had run out.

At the same time, though, there has been another change whose effects are more ambiguous: Reporters are committing less of their careers to covering the statehouse. For any number of reasons, including better pay in other professions, editors who believe reporters shouldn't stay on any one beat too long, reporters who want to become editors or move to Washington, there are not many young statehouse journalists now writing who will do what Bill O'Connell has done—spend an entire working life covering a state capitol.

A glance at the history of one newspaper gives a graphic picture of how things have changed. For the 38 years between 1937 and 1975, the Idaho legislature was covered for the state's biggest paper, the *Idaho Statesman* in Boise, by the same man, John Corlett. Corlett's successor as political editor, Steve Ahrens, stayed seven years and then went to work for a paper company. The next man, Rod Gramer, put in seven years at the legislature and four as political editor, but now works for a Boise TV station. The man after that, Randy Stapilus, also moved over to a local TV station, after three years.

None of this is to say that statehouses are filled with neophyte reporters. At many papers, the statehouse bureau is still a prestige assignment, and reporters will stay at the post for at least a few years before moving on.

Moreover, the job is complicated enough that journalists generally have to prove themselves elsewhere before being assigned there. "The legislature is such an arcane world, with regulars that go back so far, that if you put a brand new reporter in there he'd just get eaten up," says John Reed, who covers the capitol for the *Arkansas Gazette.*

Still, there is a difference between John Reed's generation and the one that came before. Many young journalists these days who have the talent and ambition to land a state capitol beat eventually begin thinking of other jobs that would offer more—more money, or more prestige, or just more of a chance to test how good they really are. "Increased mobility is just a fact of life both in and out of the profession right now," says Keven Willey, who writes for the *Arizona Republic.* Willey covered the legislature full-time for nine years; now, promoted to columnist, she is off the day-to-day beat.

What makes all this mobility important is that state government is more complicated today than it was 30 years ago. Budgets are far larger, the number of state agencies and departments has mushroomed, the complexity of the issues that state governments now tackle has grown immeasurably. The question is, as reporters lose the intimate familiarity with legislatures that they once had, how well are they keeping up with the changes?

There are at least a few politicians in any state capitol who are quick to answer, "Badly." Not only are too many reporters hell-bent to break sensational stories, they argue, but because they change jobs so often, and don't socialize with legislators as they once did, they don't understand the people they're writing about. "Guys like George Tagge, they'd been around a long time and knew the good guys from the bad guys," says Senate Republican leader James "Pate" Phillip of Illinois. "To think that reporters today know what's going on, that's a joke and a half." One who agrees with that is Nick Wilson, now completing two decades as a Democratic member of the Arkansas Senate. He remembers, in his early days as a legislator, spending hours talking to reporters about various personalities and why they did the things they did. Today, Wilson says, the press corps doesn't spend the time it takes to gather those insights. "Journalists," he says, "now have to work at face value with things that are going on—and if you work with politicians, you know that doesn't necessarily have anything to do with what's actually going on."

Some veterans think those sentiments amount to misplaced nostalgia. "To be honest," says Illinois Senator Bob Kustra, "I can't point to many people here and say, 'Oh gee, if only he knew more about state government and would carouse with us, things would be better.' I think it's healthier for the press and government when there's an arm's length relationship, and not a lot of carousing after hours."

Most current statehouse reporters say the same thing—that the institutional memory that has been lost in the last two decades can be offset by the fresh perspective new reporters bring to their job. Ohio's Lee Leonard began his statehouse career covering the Pennsylvania legislature in the 1960s, and recalls that at one point a relatively new Philadelphia re-

porter embarrassed the rest of his colleagues by writing about the longstanding practice House members had of alternating time in Harrisburg during the week; while one set was out of town, the other set cast their votes for them. The habit had never been written about because the pressroom old-timers simply saw it as a fact of life.

"They were good reporters," Leonard says of the statehouse veterans who were at work when he was young, "but in some cases they were around too long; they made too many friends and knew the system too well. When you know the system too well, you're no longer shocked by things. You're anesthetized and numbed to things that go on, and so you overlook them sometimes." Bill O'Connell has never been anesthetized—even if, late at night, he has sometimes seemed to be. He has always had a clear idea of what his job is, and what a legislator's job is. His job, more than anything else, is to be an interpreter for his community.

But O'Connell believes he has a second job, and that is interpreting his community's needs to the legislature. "I've always felt," he insists, "that if there's going to be a big pie, you should get your piece." That is why he schemed to get the Peoria civic center built. That is the view that makes him, the dean of the Springfield press corps, an anachronism in a much less rooted journalistic world.

Customers or Citizens? The Redefining of Newspaper Readers

by Ferrel Guillory

How should the readers—and potential readers—of American newspapers be defined? Do they form an audience or an electorate? Are they customers, or are they citizens?

Newspapers are in transition, and the way that newspaper managers define their targeted readership will determine how that transition is played out. The outcome will, in turn, have an influence on the vibrancy of American democracy.

... Newspapers—most notably the major-city dailies facing the task of attracting readers in sprawling suburbs—are not immune to the calls within the industry for a reassessment and repositioning in light of new technologies and shifting demographics. ... A refocusing that diminishes reporting and commentary on public affairs would be felt particularly in state and local politics and government.

"The newspaper can measure governing where the requirements of TV will rarely allow it to touch that subject," says Bill Green, a former ombudsman at *The Washington Post* and the developer of the Visiting Journalists Program at Duke University. "If newspapers give up some of their public affairs reporting—their watchdog role—it is not irrational to argue that democracy as we know it may be jeopardized."

Green, who recently retired after serving three years as a special assistant to U.S. Sen. Terry Sanford (D-N.C.), spent some of his last days as a Senate aide traveling around North Carolina to confer with newspaper editors. Green found newspapers healthy financially, at least in the short-term, and he detected no despair among newspaper people. But, he said, a "shadow" hangs over them as they drift into being "market driven."

Newspapers feel pressure stemming from changing lifestyles, developments in technology for collecting and delivering information, and diverse competition for advertising dollars. Still, the notion, widespread several years ago, that newspapers might fade away has given way to a renewed sense of the durability of the printed word. But if survival of newspapers as a medium of mass communication seems less-in doubt, there is much uncertainty as to how they will evolve.

Ferrel Guillory is government affairs editor for *The News and Observer* of Raleigh. This article is reprinted with permission of the N.C. Center for Public Policy Research, an independent research and educational institution formed to study state government policies and practices. It originally appeared in *North Carolina Insight* 12:4 (September 1990): 30-33, the quarterly journal of the North Carolina Center for Public Policy Research.

Two major lectures in 1989, each by a renowned journalist, illustrate the contrasting visions of newspapering that now vie for ascendancy in newsrooms ... across the United States. One was delivered by Anthony Lewis, twice a Pulitzer Prize winner and a columnist for *The New York Times.* The other was delivered by James K. Batten, a former reporter and executive editor of *The Charlotte Observer* and now president and chief executive officer of Knight-Ridder Inc., a large newspaper chain. ...

[The] Lewis [lecture] examined three major historical developments that had left the United States with a free press to speak out on powerful people and public policy: the rise and fall of the Sedition Act,[1] the landmark *Times v. Sullivan* libel ruling,[2] and the Pentagon Papers lawsuit over government secrets.[3] He warned of what he called the "rise of the national security state" and of the growing power of the presidency.

There is, Lewis said, a reluctance on the part of the courts to stand against these trends. The press itself is hesitant to challenge presidential authority, he said. Still, said Lewis, "The burden of checking the president increasingly falls on the press," and he asked rhetorically, "Do we want less scrutiny from the press?" The United States, said Lewis, "gambled on an open society." And part of that gamble, he said, is to tolerate the "annoyance of the press."

The Batten lecture[,] ... far from celebrating the "annoyance of the press," ... gave full voice to the school of thought that newspapers need to serve their readers as customers.

"Our newspapers' audience—actual and potential—is changing in ways that put it at odds with our traditional assumptions," he said, "and with our preferred definition of our own mission. Most of the best journalists I know were drawn to their careers by an intense interest in public affairs. They saw newspapers as indispensable instruments of American self-government. And they tended—we tended, to be more precise—to assume that ordinary Americans (all good newspaper readers, of course) shared—or at least should share—our voracious appetite for news of government and politics. That was a little naive. But today, that high-minded assumption is hopelessly inaccurate."

Batten offered the kind of statistics that make newspaper managers anxious not so much about current profitability as about the future: In the 20 years from 1967 to 1987, the percentage of adults saying they read a newspaper every day dropped from 73 percent to 51 percent. Despite population and economic growth, daily newspaper circulation—63 million in 1989—is only a million or so above the level of 1970.

What especially worries newspaper managers is a term of the trade known as "penetration"—which is a measurement of circulation as a proportion of potential subscribers. Since 1970, daily circulation rose only 1 percent, while the number of American households grew by 42 percent. Circulation of Sunday newspapers, which contain all sorts of feature sections, grew by 22 percent.

"We need to develop a new and fierce commitment to publishing newspapers that strain to please and satisfy our customers every day," said Batten. "The days when we could do newspapering *our* way, and tell the world to go to hell if it didn't like the results, are gone forever. ... Let's be done with the all-too-common journalistic queasiness about entertaining readers. Too many editors and reporters think there's something demeaning and unworthy—'pandering' is the favorite epithet—about making newspapers entertaining and enjoyable."

If Lewis and Batten were to debate each other face to face, they undoubtedly would find much in each other's lectures with which to agree. Batten surely would subscribe to Lewis' point that newspapers have rights, responsibilities, and challenges under the First Amendment. And Lewis would have to acknowledge that a newspaper losing—or about to lose—readers crucial to the health of the enterprise would ultimately be sapped of its viability.

As anyone who has read Frank Luther Mott's tome, *American Journalism,* would know, change is a constant in the history of the press in the United States.[4] In recent decades, the definition of news has expanded rapidly, as newspapers dramatically extended their reach into science, business, health, and the arts. Newspapers have long been a mixture of information and entertainment, offering readers crossword puzzles, comic strips, horoscopes, and gossip columns. What's at stake now is the balance within the mix.

It is easy—almost too easy—to attribute certain changes in American daily newspapers to the magnetic pull of *USA Today,* the color-snazzy national newspaper of the Gannett chain. Even though it is much maligned by some journalists for its short, shallow articles, *USA Today* has indeed had an influence on the industry, in terms of color and graphics and in the vivid example it offers of how newspapers can be adapted to the television age. But it is important to note that Batten does not come out of the *USA Today* milieu. Rather, he is the chief executive of a major newspaper chain, Knight-Ridder, which publishes some of the most substantive dailies in the United States—newspapers known for their investigative, national, and international reporting. That Batten would seem to suggest more customer-centered, as distinct from citizen-centered, newspapers is especially noteworthy.

Not only at *USA Today,* but throughout the industry, newspaper publishers, managers, and editors have become eager consumers of readership surveys and focus group studies. And they have discovered what politicians,

churches, businessmen, and others dependent upon public approval have learned about late 20th century Americans. This has become a more visual society with a shorter attention span. More and more people look inward, put their own wants and desires above public involvement, live in two-worker families, and thirst for an array of leisure activities. Too many people are nonvoters and nonsubscribers.

Batten urges newspaper people to become "more reader-driven, customer-driven." And *Editor and Publisher* magazine, the newspaper trade journal, reinforces the message. "One of the most pressing problems facing the nation's newspapers is declining market penetration," says a December 1989 article. "Nationally, just one out of two households receives a daily newspaper."[5] Another article in the same magazine begins, "The world is changing, people are changing, the newspapers had better adapt because their survival depends on it."[6]

Accordingly, newspaper managers have begun heeding the message—and in some respects with beneficial results. Circulation departments strive mightily to deliver newspapers on time and dry, regardless of the weather. The drive to make newspapers more visually attractive has led to a renewed appreciation of maps and use of color. And much more emphasis now goes to the organization of the newspaper, so that the same kind of material appears more or less in the same place, day after day.

And yet, the more readers and potential readers are treated as customers, to be served, pleased, and satisfied, the less they may be treated as citizens, to be educated, informed, and even challenged to think about public affairs. At the outset of the 1990s, the gravitational pull toward treating newspapers as customers remains strong.

Small samples of evidence point to larger

trends: On the day after Vice President Dan Quayle visited Charlotte in April 1989, *The Charlotte Observer*'s first edition carried a picture of Quayle in a schoolroom over a story with the headline, "Vice President Calls Busing a Failure." [7] *The Observer's* final edition, however, had the school picture and the busing story on an inside page, and it had replaced them on the front page with a photo of Quayle jogging and a story with the headline, "Visit Leaves Little Time for Relaxation." [8] . . .

As part of its redesign in late 1989, *The News and Observer* of Raleigh [North Carolina] shifted the "Under the Dome" column, a daily dose of political chatter and insider news about state government, from the front page to the first page of a section called "Local/State," a symbolic move indicating that the *N & O* appears headed toward becoming a more local newspaper. "Who wants to read all this government stuff?" an editor grumbled one day during the 1989 session of the General Assembly when I had budgeted an especially long list of stories. And then just before the Christmas holidays, another editor gave me some wry words of encouragement to continue pressing for news of government and politics. "It's good to have some dinosaurs around," he said.

To be sure, neither Batten nor the newspaper people who subscribe to his analysis call for an abandonment of government and political coverage. Batten's thesis is that newspapers will attract readers to public policy and hard truths by becoming more "warm and caring and funny and insightful and human." And he suggests some changes in the way newspapers approach politics and public debate: joining in an alliance, for instance, with get-out-the-vote programs. Moreover, he proposes that newspapers create their own news events by sponsoring local debates between public figures and experts and then printing stories and texts.

For the foreseeable future, newspapers will almost surely contain a mix of both trends: public policy here, customer-driven features and briefs there. While TV has bypassed newspapers as headline deliverers, newspapers—if they have the will to do so—can retain a franchise as the deliverers of what Walter Lippmann called "explained news."

That means hiring educated journalists who not only write well but know a thing or two about subjects they are covering. It means less grind-it-out daily coverage of legislative committees, but more updates on unresolved issues, trend stories, personality profiles of public policymakers, and articles about how government works and how government decisions affect the lives of real people.

If newspapers aren't in a drum-roll retreat from public policy, they plainly are seeing their readers more as customers and less as citizens. And, in Bill Green's view, as newspapers tie themselves to the findings of readership surveys, "They are less independent than they used to be."

It is a thought-provoking observation. For centuries, American newspapers have fought to keep themselves free from government intrusion. Moreover, newspapers—or at least the best of them—have had pride in maintaining their independence from the pressure of big advertisers. Now a diminishing of independence and integrity may come from a too-tight binding to public whims and attitudes of the times.

A repositioning of American newspapers that results in a substantial erosion of their devotion to public affairs would have an impact at all levels of government and politics. But the federal government and presidential campaigns would feel the impact least. This is so because Washington remains a focal point when major events break out and because the newspapers with a national scope, as well as the TV networks, have a competitive stake in maintaining their attention to the government and politics that flow out of the nation's capital.

More likely to fall through the cracks are state and local campaigns, and the debates and decisions that take place in state capitols and in city halls and county courthouses. With some exceptions, state and local candidates tend not to be the sort of celebrities or public figures that attract the public's gaze. Clashes over such issues as taxes and abortion will still draw coverage. But state and local issues tend to be less ideological and more mundane, however important such matters as public schools, poverty, health care, and environmental protection may be.

Newspapers have long used the metaphor of the mirror. They have defined themselves as mirrors held up for their communities to see themselves, warts and all, even to the point of annoyance. Now, the mirror metaphor increasingly may take a different connotation.

Newspapers may be drifting toward becoming mere mirrors of a public detached from public affairs and absorbed in private pursuits.

Notes

1. Sedition Act of 1798, 1 Stat. 596.
2. The *New York Times Co. v. Sullivan*, 376 U.S. 254 (1964).
3. The Pentagon Papers case: *The New York Times Co. v. United States*, 403 U.S. 713 (1971).
4. Frank Luther Mott, *American Journalism, A History: 1690-1960*, Third Edition, The MacMillan Company, New York, Fifth Printing, 1966.
5. M. L. Stein, "Adapting to Change," *Editor & Publisher*, Dec. 2, 1989, p. 24.
6. James Clark, "Shop Talk at Thirty," *Editor & Publisher*, Dec. 2, 1989, inside back cover.
7. *The Charlotte Observer*, April 18, 1989, p. 1A.
8. *Ibid.* at p. 4A.

The Press and Illinois' Political Process: Does Objectivity Limit Journalists as Citizens?

by Kevin Finch

College is a great place for esoteric discussions on ethics and other weighty matters. But sometimes philosophy can collide with the "real world." That's what happened to me while in graduate school at Sangamon State University a few years ago. The real world—in the form of a political candidate—strode into our ivory tower, a class called Illinois Government and Politics. Independent gubernatorial candidate Jim Nowlan brought his self-described quixotic campaign to our class, ostensibly to lecture about life as an independent in a two-party world.

When class was over, I signed his petition to get on the ballot. I admired the man's courage of convictions and I liked what he was fighting for: political plurality. But a classmate didn't admire what I had done. He burst from the line of students filing out of the classroom and said, "Uh, you shouldn't do that. You're a journalist."

"That's not cool," he told me. "*They* can look up your signature on that petition and use it against you."

I replied that I was technically not a full-time journalist. Besides, I reasoned, what harm could come of it? Nowlan would be lucky to get on the ballot, and he certainly wouldn't become a factor in the race. It turned out I was right about Nowlan. But the larger question of a journalist's participation in the political process remained unresolved. During the March primary, that issue once again raised its confused head in newsrooms across the state.

Just where do working journalists draw the line? Voting in Illinois' partisan ballot primary? Signing petitions? Donating money to candidates or causes? Just like those heavy philosophical discussions you had in college, there may not be any right or wrong answers. Nonetheless, with a national survey showing journalists' credibility on the wane, their unwritten ethics should be re-examined. Those who don't live on the fourth estate, including politicians, should also take note. The news media's importance in the political process has eclipsed even that of the political party. Just ask any candidate in search of "face time." Also, that elusive average citizen out there depends on the news media to provide clear, unbiased information to help make some voting decisions.

Kevin Finch is news producer at WTHR-TV (NBC) in Indianapolis. This article is reprinted with permission from *Illinois Issues* 16:8/9 (August and September 1990): 40-41, published by Sangamon State University, Springfield, Illinois 62794-9243. © *Illinois Issues*.

But all is not well in this democratic food chain if those who write, edit and announce the government and politics stories aren't sure of their own role. Let's examine the evidence. A Gallup poll commissioned by *The Times Mirror* and published in the January/February 1990 *Washington Journalism Review* shows more Americans question the independence, fairness and accuracy of news organizations. In 1985, 53 percent had their doubts; [in the 1990 poll] 62 percent [did]. [In the more recent poll], 68 percent of Americans [said] news organizations "tend to favor one side" in covering issues, compared to 53 percent in 1985. If a newspaper or news program can't be believed, it can't do its job. And that's bad for everyone.

Those responding to the survey also expressed concern about journalists getting too close to their sources, which brings us back to the question of a journalist's involvement in the process. How much is OK? As is often the case, it may be easier to answer what isn't OK. Case in point: Back in 1964, word got out in the WCIA-TV newsroom in Champaign [Illinois] that a reporter/anchor was working for a gubernatorial candidate on the side. Current News Director Dave Shaul recalled that his bosses quickly put an end to the double duty. Shaul said the anchor was told, "You either work here or for him." The off-hours campaigning ended before the station suffered any fallout.

One downstate newspaper reporter draws the line at voting. Anything after that—signing petitions, putting signs in the yard and actively campaigning—is out of the question.

Those sentiments echo the feelings of the majority of Illinois journalists surveyed [in] spring [1990]. Of 232 newspaper, radio and television journalists from Chicago and downstate, 72 percent vote in primaries, even though they have to openly declare a party (see survey results in box). Almost half the respon-

Survey of Illinois Journalists

(Of 415 surveys mailed in April [1990], 232 journalists working for Illinois newspapers, radio and television stations and other outlets responded).

Do Illinois journalists usually vote in primaries?

Yes 72% Reasons why:
46% Important to have a say in the process
13% It's a journalist's right as a citizen

No 26% Reasons why:
14% Putting party declaration on record compromises objectivity
3% Voting record is nobody's business

Do Illinois journalists sign petitions for political candidates or causes?

Yes 30%
No 68%

Note: Percentages do not add up to 100 because some respondents did not answer all questions.
Source: Kevin Finch, "The Press and Illinois' Political Process: Does Objectivity Limit Journalists as Citizens?" *Illinois Issues* 16: 8/9 (August and September 1990): 40-41.

dents consider their primary vote an important element in their role in the democratic process. Of the 26 percent who don't vote in primaries, the main reason cited was fear that a party declaration could compromise their perceived objectivity. That same concern is what keeps most Illinois journalists' names off political petitions. Sixty-eight percent will not sign on the dotted line; 30 percent do. The survey took the form of an objective questionnaire but was not purely scientific. The universe included a stratified mix of news organizations and geographic locations but when possible, was sent to friends or contacts to ensure a higher return rate.

In the comment section of the questionnaire, several respondents said the political involvement question was discussed in their newsrooms but usually without resolution and certainly without arriving at any hard and fast rules. So where do journalists learn how to answer such tough questions?

If they attended the University of Illinois School of Journalism, they learned from Associate Professor Bob Reid. Reid teaches his students to first identify ethical issues, then discuss pros and cons and alternatives. Reid said it should be left to the individual to decide his or her level of involvement in the political process. He lived by that philosophy during his 12 years as an editor for *The Southern Illinoisan*. But even Reid drew a line: He did not allow his employees to run for office.

Another former southern Illinois journalist said he left his employees to their own consciences while being very open about his own party affiliation. That former muckraker crossed all the way over the line to eventually become Democratic U.S. Sen. Paul Simon of Makanda.

Still another ex-journalist thinks it's fairly clear cut. "It's everyone's right to vote. ... I see no infringement on a journalist's objectivity by participation in the democratic process," said Sangamon State University Professor Bill Miller. But signing a petition, he said, could "pinpoint a possible allegiance."

There are some variables that make it even tougher for reporters and their professional kin to decide where they fit into the democratic picture. The journalist reticent to declare a party in a primary may feel particularly frustrated in a one-party town, a dilemma faced by one respondent from Chicago: "If you don't vote in the Democratic primary ... often times you effectively have given up your say in who ultimately gets elected." Then there's the case of the former general assignment reporter-turned-feature editor. Need the same ethical standards apply?

Those who cover politics on a regular basis think avoiding any political involvement is a given; they are much more concerned about intimacy with those they cover, about shying away from becoming part of the story. A subgroup of the Illinois survey is the Statehouse Press Corps. Of 17 responding, only three vote in primaries and only two sign petitions. But a former member of that group cites a much greater challenge to a political reporter's objectivity. Tim Franklin of the *Chicago Tribune* now runs the paper's Homewood bureau, but for years he worked in Springfield. He remembered how difficult it was to keep his distance while one of the boys on a particular candidate's bus. He recalled "an uneasy feeling-out process—they're trying to assess where you stand politically." One candidate even asked Franklin what he thought about a particular issue. Franklin's response: "It's not up to me; I just write about it."

There are some answers to the journalists' dilemma. Associate Professor Reid pointed out that everyone in the newsroom has conflicts of interest. Can a reporter cover a story on religion if he or she goes to church? Should a managing editor belong to the local chamber of commerce if there are business stories printed in his or her paper? Reid said, "Yes, with disclosure." Editors' notes—or anchor "intros" and "tags," the broadcast equivalent—can signal news consumers that the reporter writing the story has a particular interest in it.

Another idea would not be popular with the current political establishment. A small but significant number of those responding to the Illinois poll had some objection to the primary process—the two parties' domination of it and the required partisan declaration in order to get a ballot. Many of those suggest sweeping changes. One respondent declared, "Illinois should move to an open primary, period." Another even outlined a specific plan: "I think primaries should give the option of taking both or all ballots [into the booth] and returning only one—to be kept secret. . . ." No one is suggesting that the state's electoral process be altered simply to give a tiny minority—journalists—a clear conscience. Other citizens have been grumbling for years that the primary provides for a less-than-secret ballot.

Another way to bridge the gap between opinionated citizen and objective journalist is obvious, if not always easy. "I think the only way to establish a track record for objectivity is to *be objective* in reporting," said political columnist Pete Ellertsen of the Springfield *State Journal-Register*. He added, "I don't think primary voting really matters, as long as you report the news without putting your own spin on it."

That TV news anchor in southern Illinois said confusion about news people's role in a democratic society has been discussed frequently at that station, and that more talk is necessary to reach some ethical standards. But Franklin of the *Chicago Tribune* said, "I don't think that it's an issue that can ever be resolved."

Maybe one word is standing in the way of journalists' having clearer ideas of their mission of both covering and living in a democracy: objectivity. In her book *And So It Goes*, Linda Ellerbee contends that objectivity is impossible, that the best a news person can strive for is honesty or fairness.

Ever since that argument in grad school a few years ago, I have avoided primaries like the proverbial plague. But years of disenfranchisement have taken their toll. I'll swallow hard and request a partisan ballot next primary. But I won't feel comfortable about it.

A Barrage of Campaign Ads for State and Local Office: Just Around the Corner—On Cable TV?

by James M. Hoefler

Over the past decade we have seen a startling increase in the cost of elections for national office. Much of this well-documented rise in campaign spending has been attributed to the increased use of televised political advertising. Political parties have been supplanted by the media as the most prominent link between the voter and the national election process. It is neither party identification nor the "get out the vote" apparatus, but slick, high tech, thirty-second spot advertisements that make or break campaigns and candidates. It might be appropriate to suggest that Boss Tweed has been replaced by Boss Tube.[1]

Most voters are familiar with the use of paid political advertising by presidential and congressional candidates. Use of television advertising is not nearly so prominent in subnational elections, however, and for good reason. Although some gubernatorial and "big city" mayoral candidates have found extensive media campaigns to be both effective and affordable, many state campaigners and those running for local office find that traditional broadcast television spots are prohibitively expensive. Moreover, broadcasting commercials can be extraordinarily inefficient when the broadcast pattern for the television signals does not match the geographic boundaries of the

election district in which the campaign is being waged.

Cable television has the potential for changing all of that by creating a cost effective, "targetable" alternative to broadcast advertising. Indeed, cable systems may provide the vehicle for revolutionizing the way that political campaigns for state and local office are conducted. For better or worse, subnational campaigns may soon begin mimicking, on a smaller scale, the same media tactics that have become popular with campaigns for national office.

The Geography of Political Advertising

Today, much of the broadcast exposure purchased by state and local campaigns can be wasted on viewers who have no stake in the race. New Jersey and New Hampshire are prime examples. Both states are served primarily by out-of-state broadcast stations.

James M. Hoefler is assistant professor of political science at Dickinson College, Carlisle, Pennsylvania. This article is adapted from "Cable Television Advertising and Subnational Elections," *Comparative State Politics* 11:2 (April 1990): 37-42; and "Cable Ads Improve Candidates' Ability to Target Demagoguery," *Governing* 3:10 (July 1990): 70.

To reach New Jersey voters, candidates must purchase advertising time on stations that are based either in New York City or Philadelphia. Of course, much of the air time that is purchased in these markets spills out of New Jersey and into the New York City and Philadelphia metropolitan areas, respectively.

Meanwhile, candidates who insist on running television ad campaigns in the state of New Hampshire are forced to go shopping in Boston, the only major broadcast market that covers the Granite State. It is probable that New Hampshire candidates will attain—and pay for—exposure in many more households in Massachusetts than they will in their home state. Ultimately, much of the money spent by candidates in New Jersey and New Hampshire is wasted plucking the heartstrings of nonresidents.

In stark contrast to the broadcast market, which casts its signals over an indiscriminate landmass, cable systems "narrowcast" their programming and advertisements into geographically discrete communities. This difference represents a potential boon for campaigners in states that share the problems faced by candidates in New Hampshire and New Jersey. Advertising time can be purchased, at greatly discounted rates, so that it only reaches communities within the state.

Moreover, geographic targeting makes it possible to run a campaign composed of community-specific themes, each theme addressing the issues that are salient for specific communities. In each case, the community's name can be invoked, local politicians can be referred to, and parochial issues can be raised since only viewers who subscribe to the local cable station would be likely to see the "narrowcasted" ad.

The cable systems have gone to great lengths to facilitate the kind of discriminate media purchasing suggested here. To streamline operations, local cable systems that operate in the same market typically join together to form a "cable interconnect": industry jargon for a collection of cable systems that agree to market their local advertising time through a common agency. For example, one agency—a cable interconnect called Cable Adnet—manages advertising time for a dozen independent cable operators in south-central Pennsylvania. Cable Adnet makes it possible for candidates to purchase time on one, several, or all twelve systems in the area by contacting one central vendor.

In North Carolina, another Adnet interconnect manages advertising time for all thirty cable systems in the state's three primary broadcast viewing areas. Iowa's Heritage Cablevision interconnect handles all cable ad purchases for the four systems in that state. And Boston Interconnect manages the sale of local advertising time for the dozen independent cable system operators that serve forty-one different New England communities. Boston Interconnect can sell candidates time in any subset of these forty-one contiguous communities.

In each case, the candidate has only to chose which communities to cover, and with what. While officials running for local office buy time on individual systems, candidates for the state legislature can combine cable system purchases to reach their geographic constituency, or soft spots therein. Candidates for state-wide office can easily cobble together a package of ads to cover the entire state, or they may chose to focus their attention only on communities in marginal sections of the state. The alternative strategies are as numerous and varied as the communities served by the cable systems.

The Demography of Political Advertising

Some programming on broadcast television is designed to appeal to demographically specific groups. Saturday morning cartoons are broadcast for children, of course, while sports events that are covered later in the day are intended to attract more of an adult male audience, though the female audience is growing. These and a few other exceptions aside, however, much of the programming on broadcast television is oriented to a general, relatively heterogeneous collection of viewers.

In contrast, cable systems carry channels that are entirely dedicated to special, often very discrete, demographic groups. And market research conducted by viewer rating services such as Nielsen and Arbitron reveal that cable channels are relatively successful in this pursuit.

For instance, sporting events carried on ESPN attract an overwhelmingly male audience with higher than average incomes, and programming on the Lifetime channel is geared to attract a predominantly female audience. The Financial News Network (FNN) and the Nashville Network (TNN) also have their own distinct viewer profiles. Black Entertainment Television (BET) and Galavision—a Spanish-language channel serving Los Angeles, San Antonio, and Miami— present two more opportunities for candidates interested in reaching homogeneous subsets of the general population.

In all, cable systems carry varying mixtures of over two dozen specialty channels, each with an audience that is more discrete than the general broadcast viewing audience. It does not take much imagination to predict how market-savvy media consultants might capitalize on such opportunities.

The Economics of Political Advertising

The cost of advertising time varies greatly, depending on the size of the broadcast market, a local station's market standing, the program's rating share, and time of the broadcast. Broadcast time is always expensive, however, compared to advertising time on cable. For example, a spot on a popular, pre-prime time game show such as "Jeopardy" would cost approximately $200 in Harrisburg or Des Moines, while fetching $400 in Charlotte, and as much as $3,500 in Boston.

Not surprisingly, ad slots on popular prime time shows are even more expensive. A thirty-second spot on "Dallas" or "60 Minutes" would sell for around $600 in Harrisburg, $900 in Des Moines, $2,500 in Charlotte, and $14,000 or more in Boston. Federal regulations require that television stations sell time to political candidates at the lowest market rate, so campaign ads might be purchased for somewhat less than these commercial rates. Still, the typical campaign budget for a state or local election would be consumed in short order if much advertising time were purchased even at discounted rates.

In contrast, cable advertisements can be bought for a fraction of what broadcast ads cost, and still a substantial percentage of the available households would be reached.[3] For example, most cable systems that serve smaller municipalities might charge only a couple of dollars per thirty-second ad on a popular channel such as Cable News Network (CNN). In larger markets, such as Harrisburg, Pa. (70 percent of 110,000 households subscribing to cable), a thirty-second spot on CNN would cost about $15. The same CNN ad would cost $30 in Des Moines (61 percent of 123,000 households subscribing), or $23 in Charlotte (64 percent of 200,000 households subscribing). On a smaller scale, a candidate could advertise in Nashua, N.H., where 85 percent of the 21,000 households subscribe to cable, for about $10 per advertising spot.[3]

For candidates interested in expanding from the central city to the greater metropolitan area, the cable interconnect can arrange package deals. Commercials running simultaneously on all twelve cable systems within the

Harrisburg broadcast area (covering approximately 70 percent of the area's 350,000 households) would cost about $70 each. The same $70 would buy thirty-second spots on the eleven cable systems in the Charlotte broadcast viewing area (a much bigger market, but only 28 percent of the 800,000 households subscribe to cable in that part of North Carolina). The entire state of New Hampshire could be covered (reaching about 55 percent of the state's 354,000 households) for about $200 per thirty-second ad.

Sales representatives from the broadcast television stations are quick to question what these bargain rates buy. They rightly point out that the percentage of households subscribing to the local cable system can vary substantially, as noted in the case of the greater Charlotte area, where only 28 percent of the households are hooked to cable. Even when a high percentage of an area's households subscribe, rating services indicate that the market share for any of the mainstream cable networks is minuscule.[4] Most cable networks manage to attract, on average, only about 2 percent of the viewers in the available audience. Broadcast networks, in comparison, attract between 15 and 20 percent of the available viewers on a typical night. One campaign consultant suggests that, as a result, it would take ten repetitions of a cable system ad to reach the same number viewers as a single spot ad on broadcast television. Given the ratings picture sketched here, that math seems about right.

At the same time, market research suggests that cable viewers are more affluent, more professional, better educated, and, ultimately, more politically active than the general public. Moreover, the "narrowcasting" of messages to geographically and demographically targeted cable audiences minimizes "waste circulation" and makes it possible to combine the power of media with the focused impact of direct mail. State and local campaigns often turn on the kind of narrowly focused issues that cable television's pinpoint marketing can accommodate. And this can be done at prices that even candidates should be able to afford.

The Ethics of Political Advertising

Many state and local races are run today the way they have been for years—with lawn signs, bumper stickers, and palm cards as the primary vehicles for communicating with the electorate. The cable option promises to change all of that in the coming years. Candidates running for offices at the state and local levels will be able to target, demographically and geographically, specific markets on cable for a small percentage of what advertising time costs in the broadcast market.

This development may be viewed positively as a way to increase voter education and mobilization in subnational elections. At the same time, this medium makes it possible for a candidate to run a coordinated campaign of contradictory messages and targeted demagoguery. This, of course, raises important issues of accountability.[5]

The broad, heterogeneous audience of the broadcast market enforces discipline on political advertisers. Divisive and derisive messages are watered down and handled subtly, if they are handled at all, because the body politic is exposed to these messages en masse. This market discipline is lost—or at least substantially mitigated—in cable advertising. Distorting, inflammatory messages designed with specific audiences in mind may never come to the attention of the whole body politic.

What, then, is there to keep tomorrow's cable ad campaigns honest in ways that do not invite serious First Amendment challenges? One solution might involve the formulation of voluntary guidelines for state and local political races by a respected, nonpartisan organization.[6] The resulting "code of conduct" might, for instance, require that candidates make copies of all ads available to the press, along with a schedule of time slots, cable systems, and program channels being used.[7] It would then be left to the press and broadcast media to identify candidates who ignore the published guidelines.

In addition, news outlets might cast reluctant candidates in an unfavorable light, implicitly or even explicitly suggesting that the candidates who do not adhere to the code have something unethical or misleading about their campaigns to hide. Ultimately, editors would be expected to take guideline adherence into account when making endorsements.[8]

The greatest potential for abuse may be in state and local elections, where the impact of targeting is high and where the attention of the media, the parties, and the public is relatively low. All state and local races bear watching, then, in the emerging post-broadcast age of the 1990s.

Ultimately, there is an almost unlimited potential for cable advertising as a positive and efficient vehicle for communicating information and mobilizing voters in state and local races. Without some method of accountability, however, the potential for abuse seems equally unlimited. And given the track record of media handlers in races for national office, all bets are that self control will not be especially effective. It will be left to the media and the voters to monitor critically the barrage of state and local campaign ads that is just around the corner on cable television.

Notes

1. Hedrick Smith, *The Power Game: How Washington Works* (New York: Random House, 1988), 36.

2. Nationwide, subscriptions to cable television have nearly tripled in the last ten years, from 19 percent of all households in 1980 to 56 percent in 1990. Now, in many areas of the country the traditional broadcast viewing area is entirely blanketed by a patchwork of independent cable television systems where, taken together, two-thirds or more of the area households subscribe.

3. All of these are average costs per thirty-second spot when purchased as part of an advertising package. A typical package might include twenty-one spots to be run over a one-week period, where an ad is run once in every eight-hour period.

4. The market rates and advertising costs quoted here for CNN are somewhat inflated due to coverage of the Persian Gulf war. It is presumed that they will decline.

5. Political scientists traditionally have minimized the impact of slick television advertising, arguing that political ads neither create nor alter preferences but merely reinforce existing beliefs. But political scientists and operatives closer to the world of political advertising are now rendering an alterative judgment: Sophisticated negative advertising can and does work.

6. Maybe the League of Women Voters would be willing to take up the cause.

7. Federal Communications Commission regulations already require that advertising contracts be made a matter of public record. The guidelines proposed here would simply facilitate the process.

8. Some major newspapers have already begun experimenting with "truth in political advertising" watches. For example, three major papers—the *San Francisco Chronicle*, the *Los Angeles Times*, and the *Sacramento Bee*—used "truth boxes" in their reporting of California's 1990 gubernatorial campaign. Highlighted boxes appeared on the front page of selected editions, with candidate claims extracted from commercials appearing beside researched presentations of the facts. While not foolproof, the proliferation and refinement of such efforts do seem to constitute steps in the right direction.

V. STATE LEGISLATURES

In theory, state legislatures fulfill the representative democracy function in state government. Each legislator represents a particular district with particular interests. Legislators then meet in the state capital to meld the interests of the districts they represent with the interests of the state as a whole. The results of this tugging and hauling are the state budget, state policies, and occasionally a constitutional amendment.

In practice, however, state governments operate somewhat less democratically. Subject-area specialists both within and outside the legislatures have an inordinate amount of power over legislators, especially those legislators who chair or are on money committees: finance or revenue, and appropriations. Because of their heavy workload, individual legislators increasingly must rely on these experts—their peers and lobbyists—for guidance on how to vote. Once the legislation has been signed into law, administrators of state agencies and programs are largely on their own to interpret and implement the laws.

One Person, One Vote

Until the 1960s, everyone in a state was not equally represented in the legislature. State legislatures determined how district lines were drawn and thus who would be represented in the legislature and to what extent. Legislatures used various devices such as the gerrymander (excessive manipulation of the shape of a legislative district to benefit a certain incumbent or party) or silent gerrymander (district lines were left intact despite major shifts in population).[1] Both types of legislative legerdemain resulted in underrepresentation of minorities and those living in the cities.

As a result of this misrepresentation, the U.S. Supreme Court ruled in the landmark decision *Baker v. Carr* (1962) that federal courts had the power to review legislative apportionment in the states. Two years later, in *Reynolds v. Sims,* the Court ruled that both houses of a state legislature must be apportioned on the basis of population—that is, "one man, one vote." And in the *Davis v. Bandemer* case (1986), the Court gave political parties standing in court suits over apportionment if a particular political party felt gerrymandered unfairly. And which party won't feel treated unfairly if it does not get the legislative apportionment plan that helps it the most? In *Colgrove v. Green* (1946), the Court indicated that it wanted to stay out of the "political thicket" of apportionment; forty years later it jumped squarely into that thicket.

We are now in the midst of coping with the results of the 1990 census. Most state legislatures are in the process of reallocating and redrawing congressional and state legislative districts. The party controlling the governorships and the houses of the state legislatures should be able to draw lines to its own benefit in the current 1991 legislative sessions—albeit under the the various court constraints already noted. Redistricting is one of the most politically charged items the states will find on their 1991 agenda since it directly affects the legislators themselves.

Currently, Democrats control twenty-seven of the fifty governor's chairs and seventy-one of the ninety-nine partisan legislative chambers (Nebraska has a one-house, nonpartisan legislature). Two governors are independents, although they previously were Republicans. Democrats control both houses in thirty states, and split control with the Republicans in ten states; and five are controlled by Republicans. Four states have an even partisan split in one house, while the other house is controlled by either Democrats (Alaska) or Republicans (Idaho, North Dakota, Vermont).

But party numbers do not always add up to party control since several state legislatures can be run by informal, bipartisan coalitions. These coalitions may be the result of deep divisions in the majority party over the choice of house speaker. Other coalitions can be due to divisions over ideology or specific issues. Still others occur when the minority party grows in strength and seeks to redress what it sees as an abridgment of its rights by joining in a coalition with dissidents from the majority party in seeking new leadership.[2]

A unique problem of party control occurred in the Indiana house, where a 50-50 member party tie led to a dual leadership system of "speakers *du jour*" or "stereo speakers," which resulted in a difficult 1989 legislative session. One solution adopted by the legislature was to increase the membership in the House from 100 to 101 to preclude the possibility of a tie in the future.[3] But the problem was resolved when, near the end of the 1989 session, one Democratic member switched his party affiliation to Republican.

How important are the redistricting stakes involved? Former U.S. representative Lynn Martin (R-Ill.), who is now the secretary of labor, argues: "We're talking about changing the face of America. That's how important this is."[4] But, unlike such struggles in previous decades, there is now a third actor in the redistricting game: the federal courts. The U.S. Supreme Court, in *Davis v. Bandemer,* for the first time agreed that such mapping of districts is subject to court challenge if discrimination against *identifiable political groups* can be proved. The definition of such groups, however, is not entirely clear from the Court's opinion.[5]

Legislative Reforms

These reapportionment decisions coincided with a general revival of state government during the mid- to late 1960s. The revival came at a time when the states sorely needed a new, more positive image. Television news programs pictured southern governors blocking school doorways to keep minority students out. Numerous publications described the apparent failures, unrepresentativeness, and corruption of state governments.[6] It took national legislation such as the Civil Rights Act of 1964 and the Voting Rights Act of 1965 and U.S. Supreme Court decisions to force state governments to fulfill their responsibilities to those they represented.

In the 1970s and 1980s, state after state passed laws that drastically reformed state legislatures and improved their public image. The following examples are representative of the kinds of laws passed:

● Tighter deadlines and improved scheduling procedures for considering legislation
● Automated bill status and statute retrieval systems
● Computerized systems for the state budget process
● Relaxation of constitutional restrictions on what issues legislators can consider
● More flexible and rewarding systems of legislative compensation
● Greater staff capability in bill drafting, legal services, budgeting, and postaudit and program evaluation
● Longer sessions, and the replacement of biennial sessions with annual ones
● Longer terms for legislators, and individual offices for each legislator
● Expanded personal staffs

Separation of Powers

Other parts of state government, not just the legislatures, were reformed in response to the "indictment" of the states in the 1960s. Gubernatorial powers were strengthened to make governors the chief executives of the states in fact, rather than just in theory. However, these reforms did little to reduce the natural conflict between the executive and legislative branches that is built into state constitutions.

The U.S. Constitution and state constitutions share a fundamental principle: separation of powers. Consider, for example, this article from the Colorado Constitution that clearly separates legislative, executive, and judicial authority:

> Article III. Distribution of Powers. The powers of the government of this state are divided into three distinct departments, the legislative, executive and judicial; and no person or collection of persons charged with the exercise of powers properly belonging to one of these departments shall exercise any power properly belonging to either of the others, except as in this constitution expressly directed or permitted.

The principle of separation of powers is expressly adopted in the constitutions of thirty-eight states. Twenty-nine of these states include some exceptions to a strict interpretation of the principle. (The last clause of Article III above is an example of such an exception.) Nine states require strict separation with no exceptions allowed. But twelve state constitutions do not include any separation of powers provisions.[7]

Executive Branch Appointments. Appointments are perhaps the area of greatest tension between the executive and legislative branches of state government. Legislatures often have a constitutionally mandated power to confirm gubernatorial appointments. They can cause the governor problems with this authority, as Republican governor George Deukmejian of California found out in 1988 when he tried to appoint Republican U.S. representative Dan Lungren as state treasurer. In the Democratically-controlled legislature, the House approved the appointment by a 43-32 vote, but the Senate voted against the appointment 19-21. This split vote raised an interest-

ing constitutional question: Deukmejian argued that a nomination is confirmed unless rejected by both houses, but the legislative counsel argued that either house could veto an appointee. The state's attorney general, John Van de Kamp, a Democrat, agreed with the legislative counsel. Part of the politics of this situation was Lungren's ambition to run for governor in 1990 and the Democrats' view that Lungren's appointment would strengthen his future candidacy.[8] Lungren did not run for the governorship but Van de Kamp did and lost in the Democratic primary.

In some states, legislatures have the statutory or constitutional authority to make appointments to boards and commissions; they even can appoint their own members to these positions. Only four states strictly ban legislators from serving on boards and commissions. Eleven states allow legislators to serve on advisory bodies only. However, twenty states permit legislators to sit on boards and commissions that exercise management responsibilities.[9] This "legislative intrusion" into the executive branch has been challenged successfully in Kentucky, Mississippi, and North Carolina.

Legislative Veto. A second area of tension lies in the increasing use of the legislative veto—a procedure permitting state legislatures (and the U.S. Congress) "to review proposed executive branch regulations or actions and to block or modify those with which they disagree."[10] In lieu of legislative veto legislation, some states have enacted laws regarding review of administrative rule-making procedures.

Over the past decade, there has been a rapid rise in the use of the legislative veto—up to forty-one states by mid-1982. However, the tide recently has turned against this legislative bid to gain increased control over the executive branch. Courts, both state and federal, have invalidated the legislative veto as an unconstitutional violation of the separation of powers principle.[11] And voters in several states have rejected their legislature's use of a legislative veto.[12]

Legislatures and Citizens

Between 1980 and 1985, voters in at least ten states made their legislatures the target of the initiative process. Nineteen separate initiatives aimed at state legislatures ranged from redistricting and reapportioning, to regulating the size of the legislature and the amount of legislative pay, to moving to a unicameral legislature, to barring the state legislature from repealing initiatives.[13] As discussed in the introduction to Part II, voters in several states during the 1988, 1989, and 1990 elections also addressed issues concerning the legislatures, both initiated by the legislature itself and by the voters through the initiative process.[14] But legislatures were the losers as pay raises were rejected in Arizona, Massachusetts (by a ratio of 4.8-1), Nevada, and Texas, where voters also rejected an increase in legislators' daily expense allowances. In addition, South Dakota voters decided that their legislature no longer may place initiatives on the ballot. And several states placed limits on the number of terms legislators could serve.[15]

Why are voters targeting their legislatures? One reason might be the continuing decline in public esteem of state elected officials. In a 1985 national poll, only 16 percent of the respondents rated the honesty and ethical standards of state political officeholders as high or very high—although this was better than in 1977 when only 11 percent did so. At least state officials were rated three times better than car salesmen, who were at the bottom of the list at 5 percent.[16] A recent study compiled the results of state polls that asked citizens their views on the overall performance of their state legislatures. The results indicating the legislature was doing a fair or poor job

outnumbered those saying it was doing a good or excellent job.[17] Comparing these results with a multistate study in the late 1960s, which asked a similar question, it is clear that citizens' views of legislative performance have declined over the past two decades.[18]

Legislative Activity

There is a rhythm to what happens in most state legislatures. Even-numbered-year sessions tend to be much quieter than those held in odd-numbered years. Why? It is tied to the electoral cycle. Most state legislators are elected in even, nonpresidential years such as 1990. Many others are elected in the even, presidential year elections, as in 1988. During election years, legislators and governors usually adopt a "play it safe" strategy and avoid taking positions on controversial issues that could cost them votes. Some states do not even convene their legislatures in election years; others have short sessions.

Policy initiatives in numerous areas—education, health care, economic development, and hazardous waste disposal, to name a few—are being undertaken by the states and their legislatures rather than by the federal government and Congress. This full agenda leads columnist Neal Peirce to argue that "it's not in Washington that the future of American politics is being written."[19] A major conservative spokesman agrees, lamenting that "the Great Society may be over in Washington, but it has just begun in the states."[20]

As the states enter the 1990s, one major issue has taken precedence over all others—state budgets and the need to either cut services or raise taxes. Legislators are facing decisions that are almost impossible to make even in nonelection years. While the size of state budget deficits seems small when measured against that of the national government, some of these deficits are so great that basic changes in what state governments do and how they pay for it are being made. For example, the California deficit is so great that even if they dismantled all educational programs beyond the high school level, the deficit would still be in the billions!

Part V explores different aspects of state legislatures. Rob Gurwitt of Congressional Quarterly examines how the new breed of legislative leaders is developing and extending its hold on power through the use of political dollars. Richard Paddock of *State Legislatures* discusses one state's effort to address some of the ethical problems legislators face. And John Hill of *State Legislatures* provides a case study of legislative politics in Louisiana, one of our most interesting states, politically.

Notes

1. The term "gerrymander" originated in 1812, the year the Massachusetts legislature carved a district out of Essex County that historian John Fiske said had a "dragonlike contour." When the painter Gilbert Stuart saw the misshapen district, he penciled in a head, wings, and claws and exclaimed: "That will do for a salamander!"—to which editor Benjamin Russell replied: "Better say a Gerrymander"—after Elbridge Gerry, the governor of Massachusetts. Congressional Quarterly's *Guide to U.S. Elections*, 2d ed. (Washington, D.C.: Congressional Quarterly, 1985), 691.

2. Malcolm E. Jewell, "The Durability of Leadership," *State Legislatures* 15:10 (November/December 1989): 11, 21.

3. James Grass, "Legislative Deadlock Makes for Full House," *USA Today*, April 19, 1989, 6A.

4. Quoted in Tom Watson, "Drawing the Line(s) in 1990: A High-Stakes Game to Control the Legislatures," *Governing* 1:8 (May 1988): 20.

5. Ibid., 20-21.

6. See, for example, Frank Trippet, *The States—United They Fell* (New York: World Publish-ing, 1967).

7. Jody George and Lacy Maddox, "Separation of Powers Provisions in State Constitutions," in *Boards, Commissions, and Councils in the Executive Branch of North Carolina State Government* (Raleigh, N.C.: North Carolina Center for Public Policy Research, 1984), 51.

8. "Politics: Split Vote Leaves Rep. Lungren Dangling," *Congressional Quarterly Weekly Report*, February 27, 1988, 549.

9. "Legislators Serving on Boards and Commissions," *State Legislative Report* (Denver: National Conference of State Legislatures, 1983), as reported in George and Maddox, "Separation of Powers Provisions," 52.

10. Walter J. Oleszek, *Congressional Procedures and the Policy Process*, 3d ed. (Washington, D.C.: CQ Press, 1988), 297.

11. The U.S. Supreme Court case was *Immigration and Naturalization Service v. Jagdish Rai Chadha* (1983).

12. New Jersey in 1985, Alaska and Michigan in 1986, Nevada in 1988.

13. David B. Magleby, "Legislatures and the Initiative: The Politics of Direct Democracy," *The Journal of State Government* 59:1 (Spring 1986): 35-36. Some of these initiatives failed, some passed, some are still in circulation seeking the requisite number of signatures to be placed on the ballot, and one was disallowed.

14. Sandra Singer, "Voters Dabble with Legislative Details," *State Legislatures* 15:1 (January 1989): 30.

15. Rae Tyson, "Environmentalists take a drubbing," *USA/Today* (November 8, 1990), 4A.

16. "An Erosion of Ethics?" *Public Opinion* 9:4 (November-December 1986): 21.

17. Patrick Cotter, "Legislatures and Public Opinion," *The Journal of State Government* 59:1 (Spring 1986): 47-50.

18. Merle Black, David M. Kovenock, and William C. Reynolds, *Political Attitudes in the Nation and the States* (Chapel Hill, N.C.: Institute for Research in Social Science, 1974), 186.

19. Neal R. Peirce, "Conservatives Agony: The States Turn Left," *State Government News* 30:11 (November 1987): 14.

20. Quoted in Peirce, 14.

How To Succeed
at Running a Legislature:
Pack a Mighty Wallet

by Rob Gurwitt

In June 1990, at the Aladdin Shrine Temple on the outskirts of Columbus, Ohio, House Speaker Vern Riffe [threw] a birthday party for himself. Like the previous ones, it [was] a sparkling affair, . . . a small combo playing jazz off in the corner as guests spread through the huge hall, stopping to fill up at the bar or graze the buffet tables of fried chicken legs, egg rolls, pasta, vegetables and broad trays of cheeses.

Where the event [was] truly impressive, though, [was] in the sheer number of Ohio movers and shakers there. As many as 2,000 politicians, lobbyists, union officials and corporate executives [paid] their respects to the Democratic speaker at a cost of $300 each.

The same month, in Illinois, House Speaker Michael Madigan host[ed] a similar event at the Island Bay Yacht Club on Lake Springfield, a few miles away from the statehouse. This one [was] not a birthday celebration but a salute to the Democratic majority, of which Madigan [was] leader.

To anybody who wandered in, these parties would look like elaborate versions of the individual candidate fund-raisers that have become a staple of American politics in the past generation. But the purpose was different. Riffe and Madigan were not raising money for

their own campaigns. Each was raising the money so he could give it away to colleagues—in hopes of locking his party into legislative control and maintaining his own personal grip on power.

This is the leadership fund-raiser, circa 1990. It is a physical symbol of the most important campaign finance development in state politics in the last decade: the political fund managed and controlled by legislative leaders. In part because it has become so popular, the whole enterprise is raising a slew of questions about what the proper role of a legislative leader should be.

The idea is not all that new. It was created in the mid-1960s, in California, by Jesse Unruh, the state's buoyantly inventive Assembly speaker. For years afterward, California represented the state of the art. This past decade, the Assembly's Democratic leadership, headed by Speaker Willie Brown, spent between $2 million and $4 million each election year to keep itself in the majority and maintain Brown in power. Voters have put something of a crimp in Brown's activities by approving two initiatives banning transfers

Rob Gurwitt is a staff writer for *Governing*. This article appeared in *Governing* 3:8 (May 1990): 26-31.

from one campaign committee to another—a move that reformers in a few other states are pushing as well—but Brown has made it clear that he intends to find ways around the measures.

Whatever happens in California, however, the system that was developed there is thriving all across the country. In 1987, New Jersey Senate President John Russo's "Senate Majority '87" had $2 million to spend on Democratic candidates; in Illinois, Madigan's "Friends of Michael J. Madigan Committee" collected $947,000 in the 1987-88 election cycle. In less brazenly partisan states, such as Maine, Minnesota, Oregon and Wisconsin, the amounts raised by speakers and party leaders have been smaller but often just as significant, given the lower overall election costs.

All this spending seems at first glance to be directed at a simple result—legislative leaders are helping their parties do better at the polls. "It's made us much more effective," says Minnesota House Speaker Robert Vanasek, a Democrat. Party leaders are targeting vulnerable incumbents on the opposing side and then sinking resources into defeating them, often with considerable success. At the same time, they're helping vulnerable members of their own party survive the opposition's onslaught.

There's no doubt, though, that the move by leadership into the vanguard of campaign finance is having a much broader impact on state legislative life. For one thing, it has given leaders one of the few new weapons they have come up with in recent years to combat the rules changes and party atrophy that have cut into their power over rank-and-file members. In several states, as legislative parties take the place of political parties, their leaders are gaining renewed influence not only over their own caucuses but over the entire state scene. To those who have bemoaned the decline of authority and leadership in legislative bodies

all over the country, this can only be seen as a good thing.

At the same time, the practice has added a new dimension to the entire debate over the ethics of campaign finance. That is because a House speaker or a Senate president can hold the entire thrust of a legislature's work in his hands, controlling what bills come up and when. The issues surrounding leadership fund raising are, therefore, much more important than those raised by an ordinary legislator's dependence on special-interest money.

"It's not so much that individual votes are being purchased; where PAC giving may create ethical problems is in controlling the agenda," says Paul Hillegonds, a Republican who is Michigan's House minority leader. "To the extent they weigh in with key committee chairs or with the leadership, I sense that they have a great deal of influence in what bills will be debated or what will make it out of committee. There are all sorts of implied connections between fund raising and giving and which bills are moving forward." Leaders who set out to feed the campaign machinery in their states quickly become part of it. They are hybrids: part leader of their party, part legislative leader and part special interest. In accepting money from donors and handing it out to other politicians, they are creating a relationship between the donor and the legislature itself that did not exist in very many places in the country a decade ago.

The whole phenomenon might not exist at all if legislative campaigns had not become so expensive over the past few years. A legislative seat may still be a bargain in Kansas, New Hampshire or Rhode Island, where the number of voters who have to be reached is generally fairly small. But in a growing number of states where legislative campaigns used to be measured in the low tens of thousands of dollars, the price tag has been rising well ahead of the inflation rate.

In 1989 in New Jersey, candidates in the 80 Assembly districts alone spent an estimated $7.7 million, up from $5.5 million in 1987, when both Assembly and Senate seats were up. Oregon had its first $100,000 House race in 1986, when three candidates topped that mark. In 1988, 26 of them did. "Each year's wretched excess becomes next year's norm," says Terry Nelson, director of the state's Common Cause affiliate.

In those circumstances, not every candidate can raise the amount of money he or she needs. Leaders come up with the money that keeps a vulnerable incumbent afloat or makes an ambitious challenger competitive.

That's especially true in states where the party apparatus is either traditionally weak, as in California and Oregon, or has withered over time. In Oregon, where there have never been strong parties, House Speaker Vera Katz has become central to the Democrats' strength in that body. The party's financial fortunes have come to rest so heavily on Katz's shoulders, in fact, that some Democrats are beginning to worry about what will happen to them politically whenever she steps down. "We don't have a real working group of caucus members," one of them says. "When Vera isn't there [any longer], it will become apparent that we don't have anyone raising money; we could lose the House."

In Ohio, Senate President Stanley Aronoff, a Republican, traces the fund-raising effort by his own party leadership to the decline of the state's GOP in the 1970s. "We were receiving very little help from the state party," he says. "It became difficult to recruit candidates, unless some support could be offered by way of media, campaign managers, money and so on." The Republican Senate Campaign Committee, which Aronoff helped direct even before ascending to the Senate presidency, was designed to fill that gap. In Minnesota, Wisconsin and several other states, committees like Aronoff's have become the new political parties at the legislative level, recruiting candidates, providing consultants and conducting polling and get-out-the-vote campaigns.

The arrival of legislative leaders as sources of campaign money has meant, among other things, that the money is used in a more efficient way. Traditionally, the corporations, labor unions and other interests that fund these campaigns have steered it to those who have needed it least—influential but politically secure incumbents. When they give the money to a leader or to his PAC, the leader can target it to the incumbents who need it. Incumbents running in relatively safe districts generally get less funding from their leadership.

Even more important, a leader's ability to hand out funds means that nonincumbents, who usually have a hard time raising money, are more likely to get a boost. "I don't believe we gave any money to incumbents last time," says Celia Mason, an aide to Katz in Oregon. "Once you're established in the legislature, it's much easier to raise money on your own." Be that as it may, legislative leaders do give money to incumbents; sometimes, they give lots of it. And that raises the question of how much leverage it gives them over those members who get the money.

As easy as it is to imagine a House speaker using the explicit threat of withheld campaign funds to keep rank-and-file legislators in line, it doesn't happen very often. In highly competitive states, where every seat counts, no leader is likely to force a member to cast a vote that will place re-election in jeopardy, just for the sake of discipline. "You can't play too many games with your members," says the Minnesota House's Vanasek. "Whether someone follows your lead on issues or not, you've still got to have them there when you organize."

More to the point, if leaders are inter-

When Legislative Leaders Control PACs, It's Good for the Political System

PACs managed by legislative leaders—the speaker, the majority leader, the minority leader or the leaders of the party caucuses—dilute the power of special-interest PAC dollars. These PACs attract a variety of special-interest contributors. The leader then distributes the money based not on who will support the goals of the contributor but on who among the candidates of the leader's party needs additional campaign resources. In this way, the leadership PAC insulates the individual candidate from the pressure of narrow interests.

For example, a leadership PAC will receive contributions from both doctors and chiropractors, or from the business lobby and the labor lobby. The leader thus has successfully raised necessary campaign funds but has also diluted the special-interest giving, because the candidate receiving the contribution doesn't even know where the funds originated. The leader himself is also insulated from the special-interest pressures because the money has come from competing groups.

You could, and likely will, end up with situations where dollars from the telephone industry end up going to a reform-minded, consumer-oriented legislator who is battling that same industry with various legislative proposals.

Leadership PACs also improve the political process by increasing the potential for competitive elections in a larger number of legislative districts.

Legislative leaders have few, if any, priorities higher than achieving majority status if their party doesn't have it or maintaining that status if it does. Therefore, they use their PACs mainly to defeat incumbents of the opposite party or to protect vulnerable incumbents of their own party. They seldom contribute to incumbents in safe seats, which is exactly where most of the direct PAC-to-candidate contributions go. Thus, leadership PACs make elections more competitive not only between the two political parties but also between incumbents and challengers.

Leadership PACs also improve the political debate in an election by giving challengers a source of campaign funds free of direct special-interest ties. As a result, the challenger has the resources needed to raise issues for the voters about an incumbent's record of defending one or more special-interest groups.

Finally, leadership PACs help a leader to lead the caucus once the election is over.

When a leadership or caucus PAC has played an effective role in electing or re-electing a legislator, it has created an obligation on the part of the legislator to leaders of the party in the legislature and loyalty to the leaders' efforts to define and enact the party's agenda. Legislators realize they have not only a voice in the decision-making process of the party caucus but also an obligation to implement the consensus decisions of the caucus.

Source: Robert Vanasek, "When Legislative Leaders Control PACs, It's Good for the Political System," *Governing* 3:6 (March 1990): 74. Robert Vanasek, a member of the Democratic-Farmer-Labor party, is speaker of the Minnesota House.

ested in boosting their party's legislative strength, they'll tend to give money to candidates in the marginal seats that are harder to win. That means that on policy matters, the legislators elected from those districts may need the freedom to part company with the leadership on key issues if they're going to survive. "It doesn't matter what these people do, they've got to be taken care of," says Alan Rosenthal, director of the Eagleton Institute of Politics at Rutgers University.

Still, campaign funding doesn't need to be held like a stick over a politician's head to be an important source of power for a legislative leader. It may be used as a carrot, an effective tool for building loyalty and a sense of obligation. In a situation where leaders are recruiting first-time candidates and then putting thousands of dollars into their campaigns, it doesn't take too long to build a group of legislators who owe their positions to the leadership. "Mike Madigan has people standing behind him in the House who are totally dedicated to his leadership," says Lester Brann, president of the Illinois Chamber of Commerce. "He's been the major force in getting them into the legislature."

When a powerful leader shows a willingness to drop $20,000 or $30,000 on the campaign of a favored ally who's in trouble, as Madigan has done in Illinois and Riffe in Ohio, an ambitious legislator needs no road map to figure out that going along with the speaker may pay off handsomely should he or she ever face a stiff challenge.

Still, there are legislators who wonder whether such largesse holds dangers. The biggest contribution Ron Gerberry has ever received as a Democrat in the Ohio House was $1,500. It came from Speaker Vern Riffe's political action committee. Gerberry took the money but still voted against Riffe on a bill the speaker wanted; he paid for it by losing a committee chairmanship. "Now, I don't sell my soul for $1,500," Gerberry says, but he wonders whether he or any member could afford to be equally courageous if the contribution were much greater. "If someone comes in and dumps $20,000 on me," he adds, "then I don't think it would be in one's best judgment to accept that." Some members who start out thinking they can do without Riffe's money learn from experience that they can do better with it. June Lucas, a liberal Democrat from Ohio's industrial Mahoning Valley, found herself opposing the speaker on her first vote in the state House. Riffe was backing a tort reform measure, and Lucas was against it. "To me, it was just another giveaway to the insurance companies," she says.

So when a reporter called her and told her that Riffe was going to cut her out of any money for her re-election bid, she responded angrily that she didn't need any help from him. As a result, even when she found herself in a tough re-election fight, she felt unable to approach Riffe for help. He did not offer any. Lucas ended up raising $53,000 on her own and survived. But she feels no particular smugness about it. "It was hard," she says now. . . .

Occasionally, the shadowy bonds of loyalty and obligation resolve themselves into a naked fight over power, and at that point, a leader's fund-raising ability plays a much more obvious role. In Rhode Island, Senate Majority Leader David Carlin, a sociology professor at the Community College of Rhode Island, won his post in 1989 with a slight majority of the Democratic caucus, which makes up 41 of the 50 seats in the Senate.

Carlin is a liberal who, despite his position as majority leader, is something of an outsider in state politics, which is dominated by ethnic clubhouse politicians from Providence and the smaller industrial cities. The ethnic faction within the Senate is led by John Bevilacqua, son of a former House speaker, who in 1989 wooed enough Republicans into a coalition to strip Carlin's majority leadership of most of its power.

. . . The split between the two camps hurt fund raising, because lobbyists are unwilling to commit heavily to either side. Even so, both sides will almost certainly be able to raise enough to wage full-scale war against each other. . . .

In doing so, they will be following the classic model established in California in 1980. There, Assembly Speaker Leo McCarthy found himself the target of a takeover attempt by Majority Leader Howard Berman. The two Democrats carried their intra-party warfare into that year's primaries, coldbloodedly raising money to target each other's allies. The result was that neither man became speaker. Willie Brown, a third Democrat who was able to combine some of McCarthy's support with votes from the Assembly's Republican minority, outflanked both of them. Nearly a decade later, Brown is still the Assembly speaker.

For a conscientious legislator, there are quite a few dilemmas posed by the rise of the leadership campaign fund and the pressures and temptations that can be generated by a powerful speaker such as Vern Riffe. But those issues may be minor compared to the ones raised by the relationship between the leader and the interest group that donates the money.

Leaders themselves argue that because they get their money from so many different sources, their fund-raising activity is, if anything, a way to reduce special interests' influence on the legislative process. "If a senator is totally reliant on winning on his or her own resources, he or she may have to accept too much from one source," says Ohio's Aronoff. "I almost think it's better that there be a Senate campaign committee that is so diverse that it can't be said to be captive of anyone." But it is not easy to sell that argument to those watching from the outside.

In Ohio, the Akron *Beacon Journal* has insisted repeatedly that because of leaders' power over legislation, the effects of special-interest contributions to them can be pernicious. In a series of articles over the last few years, the newspaper has drawn a link between heavy campaign contributions by several industries in the state to leadership funds and specific legislative enactments. The episodes illustrate what the newspaper refers to as the "pay to play" system—"a rarely acknowledged understanding," according to the *Beacon Journal,* "that those seeking favorable treatment in the Ohio Legislature can pay—in the form of political contributions—to get it." In one instance, the paper reported that $54,000 in campaign contributions from employees and lobbyists connected to Blue Cross of Ohio flowed to the legislature in the months before and after it considered legislation the company desperately wanted. Of that, half went to campaign committees under Speaker Riffe's control. The legislation passed. By the same token, the paper also found that some $79,000 in contributions from telephone industry employees and PACs went to the Senate Republican leadership campaign committee, mostly during 1987 and 1988, when the legislature was considering—and eventually passing—bills favorable to the industry.

Both leaders, Republican Aronoff in the Senate and Democrat Riffe in the House, insist that the paper's accusations are unfounded. "There is no correlation between fund-raising efforts going on in the statehouse and legislation that's pending in the House," says Riffe's spokesman, Kent Carson. "If you look as far back as you want to go, at any industry, you'll find issues they've won or lost. Political fund raising is a fact of life." What is undeniable, though, at least in some states, is that the corporations, lobbyists and interest groups that once were roundly accused of trying to buy influence with their campaign contributions are now beginning to fret about the pressure they feel to contribute. Even if there's nothing in the message from a Riffe or an Aronoff to suggest that their interests hang in the balance, that is the way some read it. "I think there is a general feeling that if you don't contribute, you don't get dealt a hand," says Alan Rosenthal of Rutgers.

"Sure there's pressure," says one Illinois lobbyist who asked not to be identified. When Speaker Madigan's aides get in touch, he says, "often they want people to bring checks in there payable to Joe Blow, to be handed to Joe Blow by the speaker." Another Illinois lobbyist, asked whether he'd ever been pressured by Madigan to make a contribution, all but answered the question by avoiding it. "You're not going to get anybody to tell you right before the session starts that the speaker or any other leader puts pressure on you," he said.

Still, in some states, lobbyists have begun to talk publicly about pressure. In January 1990, New Jersey's Karen Kotvas, who directs a lobbying group for trial lawyers called Lawyers Encouraging Government and Law, went public with allegations that she had been shaken down in 1989 for a contribution by four Democrats who were angling for the speakership. By the end of summer 1990, it had become fairly clear that Democrats were not only going to win New Jersey's governorship but would take over the Assembly as well. So when the four candidates for speaker rented space together across from the statehouse in Trenton and called in a number of special-interest representatives, Kotvas wasn't quite sure what to expect.

What she got, she says, was "a heavy-handed script." Kotvas says she was told that her group was being asked to donate $20,000 to a Democratic campaign fund the four were putting together. When she demurred, arguing that her organization's bylaws allowed her to donate only to individual candidates, "the

pressure built up. They said, 'You're looking at the next speaker; one of us is going to be the next speaker.'" And then one of them, Kotvas alleges, told her, "Your members are not going to be happy if your bills don't get posted."

All four Democrats who were there—Joseph Doria, who is now speaker, Deputy Speaker John Paul Doyle, Majority Leader Wayne Bryant and Speaker Pro Tem Willie Brown—deny Kotvas' allegations, contending that they met with her and other lobbyists to talk about campaign strategy and to ask for donations but not in specific amounts. The state attorney general's office and the FBI are investigating.

If it happened, the Kotvas episode is probably an aberration. Money has become so important to the system that, just as a presiding officer can get a measure of loyalty without putting direct pressure on a member, so a leader can get his point across without pressuring donors. Fear and the sense of competing for access with other donors will do that.

Paul Romain, a lawyer and lobbyist in Portland, Oregon, numbers among his clients the state's beer and wine distributors. "We've never been a big contributing group," he says of this group, "but this next biennium we're planning on somewhere close to a $100,000 PAC. I've told them that we can't get by with $100 contributions anymore; we're competing against someone who's given five grand. We're forced into a position where we have to play that game, and all we've done is raise the stakes so we can get back to an even playing field."

It may be true, as the leaders themselves insist, that in most places all a hefty contribution does is give an interest the right to sit down with a leader and hash out the issues. It may even be true, as Rosenthal asserts, that "everybody gets access; it's just that some are expected to pay for it and others get it free."

But it is nevertheless also true that some of the sources of the money are getting weary of it all. Oregon's campaign-finance reform initiative is being spearheaded in part by Romain, the beer and wine lobbyist. In Kansas, not long ago, a move by rank-and-file legislators to hold individual fund-raisers was nipped in the bud by the state's leading lobbyists, who told legislative leaders that they would stop contributing at all unless fund-raisers were limited to leadership groups in the House and Senate.

On the other hand, it might not be wise to read too much into those complaints and frustrations. It is one thing for lobbyists to complain about how much money they are being asked to give; it would be quite another for them to stop giving it. In Illinois in 1989, a number of interest groups also began talking openly of some sort of moratorium on campaign donations, at least while the legislature was in session. The move failed, and for a simple reason. "You couldn't carry out a moratorium unless you had complete support from all the lobbyists," says business lobbyist Lester Brann. "We'd be sitting it out, and everyone else would be participating, and we'd be held out as the guys that deep down didn't want to give money. I'd hate to have us get that reputation."

California's Tough New Ethics Law

by Richard C. Paddock

When the California Legislature convene[d] in December [1990] for the 92nd session, its members . . . face[d] tough new restrictions on the way they conduct their personal and legislative business. Gone [are] the lucrative honoraria of the past. No longer [are] legislators . . . able to accept expensive gifts or free foreign trips paid for by corporate sponsors. And for the first time, California lawmakers . . . face the possibility of a fine for voting on matters in which they have a conflict of interest.

The new standards of conduct are the result of Proposition 112, a ballot measure approved by the state's voters in June [1990]. "It's the toughest ethics law in the country," said Ruth Holton, a Common Cause lobbyist. "It's the toughest in that it is so comprehensive. It not only addresses honoraria, but all the ethics questions. It puts the pieces together."

Proposition 112 was placed on the ballot by the Legislature itself in an attempt to improve its tarnished image among the state's voters. In recent years, legislators have faced growing pressure to accept less money from special interest groups. "The voters had indicated they wanted changes in the way the Legislature conducts its business and we welcome the opportunity to bring that about," said Senate President Pro Tem David A. Roberti, the leading sponsor of the ballot measure. "It's a major step forward [for] ethics reform in the state Legislature and I think it's a model for all legislatures."

The results of the balloting on Proposition 112 make it clear that voters are willing to pay legislators a higher salary in exchange for limiting their outside income. In addition to setting new ethical standards, the ballot measure . . .pave[d] the way for a substantial pay raise for legislators by creating a commission to set the level of compensation for the state's elected officials. The . . . increase in lawmakers' pay [takes] effect without a vote of the Legislature. . . .

The new code of conduct for legislators is a wide-ranging law designed to limit the influence of groups that have a stake in legislative actions. Specifically, the law bans all honoraria and limits gifts to no more than $250 annually per donor. Free trips to foreign

Richard C. Paddock is a reporter in the Sacramento bureau of the *Los Angeles Times*. This article is reprinted with permission from *State Legislatures* 16:7 (August 1990): 9. © 1990 by the National Conference of State Legislatures.

countries are prohibited unless they are paid for by a government agency or a non-profit group. Furthermore, legislators who vote on matters affecting their own financial interests will be subject to a fine of up to $2,000. Legislators who leave office will be banned from lobbying their former colleagues for 12 months. All legislators, staff members and lobbyists will be required to attend courses on ethical conduct at least once every two years. In addition, the ballot measure wrote into the state constitution the requirement that the Legislature hold most of its meetings in public.

Calls for ethics reform had been mounting both inside and outside the Legislature during the last several years. Barred by the constitution from giving themselves a large salary hike, some legislators had made a practice of supplementing their income by accepting thousands of dollars in honoraria for speaking to groups that are pushing bills in the Legislature. Assembly Speaker Willie Brown was the champion speech-maker, receiving more than $130,000 in honoraria in 1988 and 1989.

Roberti acknowledged that the ballot measure also was prompted in part by an FBI sting investigation that resulted in the conviction of Senator Joseph B. Montoya on racketeering and extortion charges. Among the evidence presented at the trial was a videotape of Montoya accepting a $3,000 "honorarium" for having breakfast at a restaurant with two undercover operatives. Earlier . . . , a federal grand jury filed similar corruption charges against former Senator Paul Carpenter, now a member of the state tax board. Illustrating the crisis in confidence faced by the Legislature, the *Los Angeles Times* Poll found [in] December [1989] that most of the state's voters think it is commonplace for California legislators to take bribes.

Proposition 112 and bills passed by the Legislature to implement the ballot measure

were the result of more than 18 months of legislative hearings and behind-the-scenes negotiations. In the Assembly, Speaker Brown created a special committee that spent nearly a year drafting its proposal. In the Senate, Roberti and his staff produced a similar proposal. Ultimately, the two were merged by a conference committee that included the top

---

Virginia

. . . In Virginia disclosure [of lobbying expenditures] is . . . hampered by a law that requires lobbyists to report expenditures incurred from November through February only. This "wonderful loophole," says [Julie] Lapham [, executive director of Common Cause/Virginia], allowed one of Virginia's largest paper manufacturers to pick up the tab for a summer picnic for the staff and families of an elected official, but not report it because it fell outside the reporting period. The picnic was only discovered when a staffer sent an announcement to a newspaper.

The law lacks a clear definition of lobbying, says Lapham, and that gives lobbyists a lot of leeway in reporting. The Virginia League of Savings Institutions, for example, seems to pick and choose what to report. Its 1988 report listed a $42,000 reception the group hosted for lawmakers at Richmond's plush Jefferson-Sheraton Hotel—even though League lobbyist Mark Saurs says no lobbying occurred. Meanwhile a $5,000 contribution to Gov. Douglas Wilder's 1990 inaugural fund went unreported, because, says Saurs, "it was not considered a lobbying expense."

Source: Amy E. Young, "In the States," *Common Cause Magazine* 7:1 (January/February 1991): 43. Reprinted with permission. © 1991 *Common Cause Magazine*, Washington, D.C.

leadership of both parties among its members.

Some legislators criticized the proposal for not going far enough to curb abuses by legislators and for linking the new ethical standards to a salary increase. "They're saying to people: 'Pay me more money and I'll be honest,' " protested Assemblyman Richard L. Mountjoy, a leading opponent of Proposition 112.

But the measure won the support of such groups as Common Cause, the League of Women Voters and the California Chamber of Commerce, which argued that the new ethics code was needed and that legislators deserved a higher salary.

"It puts in the constitution and guarantees in the constitution a number of reforms that have been long overdue," Roberti said. "We felt that something should be done and we should be the ones doing it. Even though this will make stricter rules for the Legislature, I think there will be a sigh of relief. There will be clear guidelines of what should be done.

Louisiana Senate Unseats Governor-Backed Leader

by John Hill

Even for Louisiana's Mediterranean-style, anything-goes politics, the mid-term change in the Senate presidency on May 9 [1990] was stunning.

In a coup d'etat unprecedented in the state's often Byzantine political scene, the Senate voted 21 to 18 to oust Senate President Allen Bares, a conservative Democrat who was Governor Buddy Roemer's hand-picked leader.

Former Senate President Sammy Nunez—who himself was ousted by the Roemer forces when the governor and the new Legislature took office in 1988—staged the coup. In a surprise attack that the Roemer forces did not take seriously until it was too late, the Nunez crowd lined up a coalition that gave them a three-vote margin to regain power. Within two days, Nunez, a former president of the National Conference of State Legislatures, had punished senators who fought him up until the last minute by removing them from committee chairmanships and positions of leadership, replacing them with his backers and realigning committees.

The coup was partly a move toward legislative independence in a state with the nation's most powerful governorship, partly a negative reaction by senators who dislike and distrust Roemer and partly just another in a long line of battles between the two almost equal halves of Louisiana's strange body politic: the populist, more liberal heirs to the Long faction of the state (who just regained control), and the more conservative, pro-business successors to the anti-Long faction.

Unlike the English colonies back East, Louisiana was alternately a French and Spanish territory. The governors of Louisiana ruled with royal powers, usually naming relatives to important tax collecting posts, each getting his cut as the money went back toward the crown.

When the Americans arrived after the 1803 Louisiana Purchase, they built their homes away from the terrible influence of the French and Spanish, who then lived in what is now the French Quarter. But from their Garden District mansions, they recognized a good political system for the in-crowd and so Louisiana's Constitution was written to incorporate enormous gubernatorial power. Today's governor has control over the construction budget and every dime in the operating budget.

John Hill is the bureau chief of Gannett News Service in Baton Rouge, La. This article is reprinted with permission from *State Legislatures* 16:6 (July 1990): 17. © 1990 by the National Conference of State Legislatures.

So Louisiana's Legislature is weak. The House—truly representative of Louisiana's ethnic gumbo—has historically been unable to get enough factions together to elect its own speaker.

The Senate was somewhat different. Until the new Constitution was written in 1974 giving the Senate the power to elect its own officers, the lieutenant governor presided. After the new Constitution took full effect in 1976, the Senate elected as its president a man who was philosophically in line with populist Edwin Edwards, then governor.

When that president was convicted of federal fraud charges in a private business affair, the Senate in 1983 simply promoted Nunez, then the president pro tem.

But Roemer, a conservative businessman, swept the state in 1988, forcing Edwards to withdraw from a runoff campaign. Roemer wanted a new team, so rather than try to work with Nunez who had served as president for six years, the new governor fought him, corraling a slim majority to install the more philosophically agreeable Bares.

The wounds never really healed. Then a power vacuum occurred in 1989 when Roemer, whose massive tax revision proposals were turned down by voters, went into what he later admitted was a depression. He iso-

lated himself in the governor's mansion and for long months the state was in a free fall.

When the Legislature returned April 17 for the 1990 session, Roemer used his opening day address to apologize to legislators publicly for being too hard-headed, too neglectful. But for many senators, it was too little too late: some disgruntled by Roemer's cavalier treatment, broke ranks to join the Nunez faction.

At a quiet hotel meeting called to explore the possibility of a coup, 19 senators showed up. Two others had pledged support. The coup was launched on the spot.

Nunez has pledged cooperation with, but independence from, the governor, with whom he quickly held a meeting. "This is not an anti-Roemer move," says Nunez. "This is a move toward Senate independence."

"It is a get-Roemer move," says Senator Randy Ewing, a Roemer backer. "Whenever anybody said anything bad about Bares, they mentioned Roemer in the next breath."

"Bares was more of a floor leader for the governor than a leader of the Senate," says Senator Foster Campbell.

Nunez says his support is mixed. "I had support from the Democrats, Republicans, blacks, whites, conservatives, liberals and moderates. It was a coalition for the independence of the Legislature."

How a Bill Becomes State Law

This graphic shows the most typical way in which proposed legislation is enacted into law in the states. Bills must be passed by both houses of the state legislature in identical form before they can be sent to the governor to be signed or vetoed. Of course, the legislative process differs slightly from state to state.

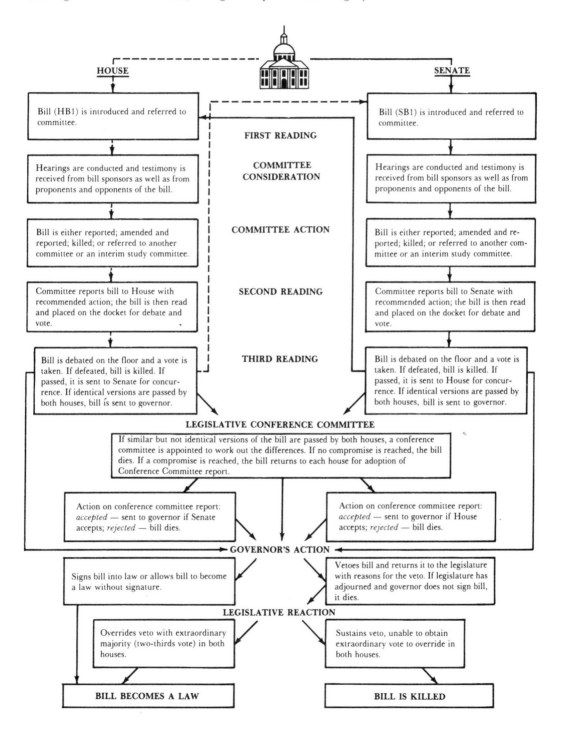

HOUSE

SENATE

Bill (HB1) is introduced and referred to committee.

Bill (SB1) is introduced and referred to committee.

FIRST READING

COMMITTEE CONSIDERATION

Hearings are conducted and testimony is received from bill sponsors as well as from proponents and opponents of the bill.

Hearings are conducted and testimony is received from bill sponsors as well as from proponents and opponents of the bill.

COMMITTEE ACTION

Bill is either reported; amended and reported; killed; or referred to another committee or an interim study committee.

Bill is either reported; amended and reported; killed; or referred to another committee or an interim study committee.

SECOND READING

Committee reports bill to House with recommended action; the bill is then read and placed on the docket for debate and vote.

Committee reports bill to Senate with recommended action; the bill is then read and placed on the docket for debate and vote.

THIRD READING

Bill is debated on the floor and a vote is taken. If defeated, bill is killed. If passed, it is sent to Senate for concurrence. If identical versions are passed by both houses, bill is sent to governor.

Bill is debated on the floor and a vote is taken. If defeated, bill is killed. If passed, it is sent to House for concurrence. If identical versions are passed by both houses, bill is sent to governor.

LEGISLATIVE CONFERENCE COMMITTEE

If similar but not identical versions of the bill are passed by both houses, a conference committee is appointed to work out the differences. If no compromise is reached, the bill dies. If a compromise is reached, the bill returns to each house for adoption of Conference Committee report.

Action on conference committee report: *accepted* — sent to governor if Senate accepts; *rejected* — bill dies.

Action on conference committee report: *accepted* — sent to governor if House accepts; *rejected* — bill dies.

GOVERNOR'S ACTION

Signs bill into law or allows bill to become a law without signature.

Vetoes bill and returns it to the legislature with reasons for the veto. If legislature has adjourned and governor does not sign bill, it dies.

LEGISLATIVE REACTION

Overrides veto with extraordinary majority (two-thirds vote) in both houses.

Sustains veto, unable to obtain extraordinary vote to override in both houses.

BILL BECOMES A LAW

BILL IS KILLED

VI. GOVERNORS AND THE EXECUTIVE BRANCH

Governors Cannot Halt National
Guard Missions Overseas, Court Rules

147

As the head of state politics and government and the elected representative of the people, governors must perform a wide variety of duties. They greet visitors, travel to other states and even other countries to lure new businesses to their states, rush to the scene of disasters to demonstrate concern, prepare annual and biennial agendas for government activity, and, on occasion, discuss important issues with the president. From state to state the record varies on how well these and other gubernatorial responsibilities are fulfilled. Some governors are reelected to another term, others are excluded from service, and still others are elected to higher office.

Since its weak beginnings after the overthrow of colonial rule, the American governorship has grown in power and influence. The extensive reforms of the past two decades are becoming evident throughout the executive branches of the fifty states. As Larry Sabato reports, "Within the last 20 years, there has been a virtual explosion of reform in state government. In most of the states, as a result, the governor is now truly the master of his own house, not just the father figure." [1] Many of the powers that were restricted have been expanded, and governors now have new powers at their command, such as the ability to reach the people directly through the media and to serve as the key state official in the intergovernmental system of grants and programs.

Moreover, the caliber of the individuals who serve as governors has changed in recent years. Most states have been able to say "goodbye to good-time Charlie" and hello to "a thoroughly trained, well regarded, and capable new breed of state chief executive." [2] This does not mean that all governors have spotless records. There have been several cases of governors and former governors who have run afoul of the law and spent time in prison. [3] One governor, Evan Mecham (R-Ariz., 1987-88), was impeached by the state House, convicted by the state Senate, and removed from office. In 1990, Mecham tried to come back by running for the Republican nomination for governor. He was able to do so because the Arizona legislature at the time of his impeachment failed by a slim margin to adopt the "Dracula clause"—an act by a state legislature that drains the lifeblood out of a politician by forbidding his or her return to electoral politics.

Governors Edwin Edwards (D-La., 1972-80, 1984-88) and Bill Sheffield (D-Alaska, 1983-87) had well-publicized escapes from legal and ethical problems in the mid-1980s, but were turned out of office when the voters did what the authorities could not do. In 1991, Edwards is seeking to return to the office despite his less than glorious departure at the hands of the voters four years previously. More recently, former governor Arch Moore (R-W.Va., 1969-77, 1985-89) agreed to plead guilty to charges of extortion, mail fraud, tax fraud, and obstruction of justice, crimes that he committed during his last two races for governor and during his last term in office. [4]

These governors' activities, other gubernatorial missteps, and what he decried as one of the weakest groups of newly elected governors in 1986 led one careful "governor-watcher" to wonder if the trend toward having better governors may be ebbing in the states. [5]

Governors and the State Ambition Ladder

An interesting aspect of the governorship is its place on the "ambition ladder" that eager politicians climb to attain higher and higher levels of success. Of the 196 governors who served between 1970 and 1990, 53 percent previously had served at some time as an elected state legislator, 28 percent as an elected state official, 27 percent as a law enforcement official, and 14 percent as an elected local official. Only 13 percent had served as a U.S. representative, and one in the U.S. Senate.

If the penultimate or last office held before winning the governor's chair is considered, fifty individuals (26 percent) moved up from a statewide elective office (usually attorney general, lieutenant governor, or even former governor). Forty-two (21 percent) moved from a legislative seat (usually a leadership position in the legislature). Ten jumped from a local elective position to the governorship (5 percent). Only twenty-four governors (12 percent) stepped directly into office from the U.S. House of Representatives, and only twelve (6 percent) never held any previous position in government.[6]

In the last full round of gubernatorial elections (1987-90), there were fifty-three contests.[7] Of the thirty-three incumbents who sought reelection, twenty-five (76 percent) won, and three of ten former governors seeking a comeback won. Thus, governors and former governors won twenty-eight of the fifty-three races. However, eight governors and ten former governors lost their bids, giving all governors a 61 percent success rate (twenty-eight of forty-six). Other winners who previously had held statewide office were secretaries of state (three), lieutenant governors (two), state treasurers (two), and a state auditor. No state attorneys general were elected although eleven tried.

With thirty-six of the fifty-three races (68 percent) being won by these current or former statewide officials, the importance of a major statewide office for winning a gubernatorial election is clear. Other successful launching positions for six of the twenty-eight new governors (21 percent) were Capitol Hill in Washington; three sitting members of the House and one sitting and two former U.S. senators won. Others came from the private sector, although some had previously served in the state legislature. Though four former mayors of large cities assumed governorships up to the 1990 elections, only one governor moved up from a mayor's office in 1990, former Cleveland mayor George Voinovich in Ohio.

What do these figures tell us about making a successful climb to the governor's office? Those who succeeded in becoming governor tended to use a "state-based" career ladder: the legislature and other state elective positions. Moving up from a local position, usually as mayor of a large city, has not been built into this ladder, although recent results suggest this might be changing in some state political systems. While moving from a federal position—representative, senator, or cabinet member—has not been part of this ladder in the past, using the U.S. House of Representatives as a launching pad to the governorship appears to be developing, as evidenced in the most recent elections in Louisiana, New Hampshire, New Jersey, and North and South Carolina.[8] Even members and former members of the U.S. Senate are looking at this track.[9] Still, capturing the governorship from a position outside state politics appears to be difficult.

But what is the next step after the governorship? Is it a higher elective office? Two of our most recent presidents were governors— Jimmy Carter (D-Ga., 1971-75) and Ronald Reagan (R-Calif., 1967-75)—and sixteen former governors are serving as U.S. senators.[10] Also, the 1988 Democratic candidate for president, Michael S. Dukakis (D-Mass., 1975-79, 1983-91), was a governor. But this is the exception rather than the rule. Most governors do not attain higher elective office. Of the governors who served between 1970 and 1981,

62.5 percent had not been elected to another position by 1982.[11] Looking at just those governors who have graduated from the governorship in the 1980s, only ten of sixty-nine have run for and won another office: six have won a U.S. Senate seat, one a House seat, and three have reclaimed the governor's chair. Nine others tried to extend their political careers, but six lost in attempting to move to the U.S. Senate and three in trying to become governor again.

Most former governors enter the private sector, usually to develop a lucrative law practice. These governors must give up what former governor Lamar Alexander (R-Tenn., 1979-87) called "the very best job in the U.S.A." [12] Ronald Reagan indicated that "being governor was the best training school for this job [of being president]." [13] Is there life after being governor? The National Governors' Association (NGA) asked some former governors what had happened to them since leaving office. Yes, there was life, but the quality of that new life can be determined only by the individual. By planning early for the transition, NGA suggests, the governors "can also help ease their own adjustment to the 'good life.' " [14]

Gubernatorial Campaign Costs

Being elected governor is not as easy as it once was. One reason is the new style of campaigning that has led candidates to create their own organizations instead of relying solely on their political party. Opinion polls, political consultants, advertisements tailored to specific audiences in the major media markets, direct mailings, telephone banks, and air travel are extremely expensive, and full-time fundraisers often are needed to help gubernatorial candidates wage winning campaigns. Without the party to alert the faithful and bring in the straight-ticket votes, candidates must create what Sabato calls their own "instant organization" or "party substitute." [15]

Second, there is a growing number of wealthy individuals who aspire to the governorship and have the means to succeed. Some come from "old money" and are the descendants of those who first amassed the family fortune: Nelson Rockefeller (R-N.Y., 1959-73); Winthrop Rockefeller (R-Ark., 1967-71); John D. "Jay" Rockefeller IV (D-W.Va., 1977-85); and Pierre S. "Pete" du Pont IV (R-Del., 1977-85). Others have "new money" and are spending it: Fob James (D-Ala., 1979-83), William P. Clements Jr. (R-Texas, 1979-83, 1987-91), Wallace G. Wilkinson (D-Ky., 1988-), and Gaston Caperton (D-W.Va., 1989-).

Third, gubernatorial races are more competitive. Awareness of the importance of state government and of the key role of the governor in state politics has increased the number of candidates for the office. In the fifty-three separate gubernatorial elections between 1987 and 1990, there were 376 candidates seeking their party's nomination for governor, for an average of 7.1 candidates per election. Of these candidates, 215 were strong enough to receive more than 10 percent of the party primary or convention vote. In 1990, nineteen candidates sought the governorship in California, fifteen in Nevada, fourteen in Texas, and twelve each in Hawaii and Minnesota. Clearly, there is no shortage of people who wish to become governor of their state.

The fourth and most obvious reason of all is inflation. Like everything else, the cost of politics rises when inflation erodes the dollar. If the 1987 dollar is used as the base point, the dollar was worth forty-three cents in 1972 and eighty-five cents in 1982.

Until the passage of state campaign spending laws in recent years, little information was available on gubernatorial campaign costs. California records go back to 1958, when the Fair Practices Commission was established, but in other states spending information was simply unobtainable, unless some scholar had studied a particular election. Even if officially reported monies raised and spent became public knowledge, unofficial funds spent on a candidate's behalf by organizations and individuals, or time and services contributed by supporters, were not recorded.

Today, more information is available. States are requiring candidates to report campaign finance information. The 163 gubernatorial contests between 1977 and 1989 cost more than $1.032 billion calculated in constant 1987 dollars.[16] This is an average of $6 million per race, although the cost of some states' races can skew this upward. (The 1986 Texas contest cost at least $35 million, the most expensive governor's race ever.) In 1986, the thirty-six races for governor cost about $260 million in 1987 dollars, the three 1987 races cost slightly more than $40 million, the twelve 1988 races cost $49 million, and the 1989 races in New Jersey ($26.2 million) and Virginia ($21.7 million) were the most expensive campaigns in those two states' political history.[17]

Looking at the gubernatorial elections in the fifty states between 1977 and 1989 using 1987 dollars, there are six states in which these races have averaged more than $14 million each: Texas ($26.8 million), Louisiana ($21.7 million), New York ($20.7 million), California ($20.5 million), Kentucky ($18.4 million), and Florida ($14.0 million). Note that in addition to the largest states included in this high-cost races list, there are three southern states, suggesting that as the Democratic party declines in importance there, money politics is replacing it. At the bottom of the list are the eight states in which the average cost is still below $2 million: Montana ($1.7 million), Wyoming ($1.6 million), Idaho ($1.5 million), South Dakota ($1.4 million), New Hampshire ($1.2 million), Vermont ($.8 million), Delaware ($.7 million), and North Dakota ($.6 million).

One Among Many

The governor is not the only official in the executive branch of state government who is elected statewide. The states elect more than 500 officials, including forty-three attorneys general, forty-two lieutenant governors, thirty-eight treasurers, and thirty-six secretaries of state. There are even five land commissioners, five secretaries of labor, and one commissioner of mines elected by the voters of some states. Ten states elect their boards of education, and eleven states elect their superintendents of public instruction. The legislatures appoint some state officials, mainly in the postaudit function, and the lieutenant governors in a few states have some appointive power. This means that governors have little or no power over some parts of state government, except their own power of persuasion or the power they can create through the budget.

Fragmentation of executive branch leadership complicates the politics between the actors involved. In the early 1980s, for example, the governors and the lieutenant governors of California, Missouri, Nebraska, and New Mexico were pitted against each other over the issue of who is in charge of state government when the governor is out of state. Can the lieutenant governor make appointments to office or the bench (patronage)? Call a special session of the legislature? Issue pardons? And who receives the governor's salary while he or she is absent? More recently, some governors have had difficulties with other elected officials: in Virginia, the governor and lieutenant governor fought over the budget surplus and taxes; in Idaho, the governor and the attorney general have been squabbling over regulating the amount of timber exported from the state; in Georgia, the fight was between the governor and the attorney general, with the two officials battling over the state's open meetings law and personnel matters; and in North Carolina, the governor and attorney general fought over the governor's right to contract leases and appoint certain officials.[18]

Executive branch fragmentation has other consequences. Perhaps most importantly, it restricts what governors can accomplish in high priority areas such as education. A gubernatorial candidate may pledge to improve primary and secondary education, but, once elected, have difficulty fulfilling this goal because other elected officials with responsibility in the education policy area may have different views on what should be done.

Recent federal court decisions have begun to restrict a chief executive's ability to remove or fire government employees, an action often needed to open up positions for appointing the executive's own team. In the 1976 *Elrod v. Burns* decision, the U.S. Supreme Court held that "patronage firings" violate the First Amendment's protection of an individual's freedom of political belief and political association.[19] In the 1980 *Branti v. Finkel* decision, the Court reaffirmed its position but did indicate "if the employee's private political beliefs would interfere with the discharge of his public duties, the First Amendment rights may be required to yield to the state's vital interest in maintaining governmental effectiveness and efficiency."[20] In its 1983 *Connick v. Myers* decision, the Court again affirmed its position but held that "the First Amendment does not protect from dismissal public employees who complain about their working conditions or their supervisor."[21] All three cases concerned local government situations but, by extension, affect governors as well.

In 1990, the Supreme Court decided narrowly in *Rutan et al v. Republican Party of Illinois* that state and local government violates an individual's "First Amendment rights when they refuse to hire, promote or transfer . . . [an employee] on the basis of their political affiliation or party activity."[22] This case, which focused on the patronage process of the Illinois governor's office, highlights a basic tension in these situations. There is a tension between the right of employees to be protected for their political beliefs and the need of an executive to put into place individuals who will seek to achieve the goals for which that executive was elected.

The most significant restriction on a governor's ability to be governor is the relationship that he or she has with state legislators. There are many types of advice and counsel that governors give each other on this relationship; consider these comments by incumbents to newly elected governors in 1982:

> Don't necessarily judge your success by your legislative score card. . . . Avoid threatening to veto a bill. You just relieve the legislature of responsibility for sound legislation. . . . A governor successful in managing the selection of legislative leadership gains a Pyrrhic victory. . . . It's too easy to dismiss one or two legislators because there are so many. You do so at your own peril. . . . Legislators will complain about your spending too much time with the staff, but what they really mean is you don't spend enough time with them. . . . If someone urges your support on a bill by saying it's a "merely" bill, sew your pockets shut; there are no "merely" bills. . . . Legislators will learn that press coverage comes from opposition to the governor.[23]

Part VI provides a close-up view of the governorship as we enter the 1990s. Alan Ehrenhalt of Congressional Quarterly discusses the differences between how issues are addressed during the campaign and what one must do when in the governor's office, a difference of pretending there are no hard choices and then having to face the hard choices. Charles Wheeler of *Illinois Issues* provides a political biography of the nation's senior governor in service, James Thompson (R-Ill., 1977-1991). Carolyn Lukensmeyer, who served as chief of staff to Ohio's governor

Richard Celeste, spells out some tough lessons that new governors must learn. Finally, the issue of gubernatorial control over the National Guard is discussed in an article from *Governors Weekly Bulletin*.

Notes

1. Larry Sabato, *Goodbye to Good-time Charlie: The American Governorship Transformed*, 2d ed. (Washington, D.C.: CQ Press, 1983), 57.
2. Ibid., xi.
3. Otto Kerner (D-Ill., 1961-68), Spiro Agnew (R-Md., 1967-69), Marvin Mandel (D-Md., 1969-77), David Hall (D-Okla., 1971-75), and Ray Blanton (D-Tenn., 1975-79).
4. "Former Governor of West Virginia to Plead Guilty," [Raleigh] *News and Observer*, April 13, 1990, 8A.
5. Query by Larry Sabato at the "State of the States" Symposium, Eagleton Institute, Rutgers University, New Brunswick, N.J., December 18, 1987.
6. Gubernatorial election data for 1970-89 may be found in Thad L. Beyle, "Governors" in *Politics in the American States: A Comparative Analysis*, 5th ed., ed. Virginia Gray, Herbert Jacob, and Robert B. Albritton (Glenview, Ill.: Scott Foresman, 1990), 203-208.
7. New Hampshire, Rhode Island, and Vermont had elections in 1988 and 1990 because their governors serve only two-year terms.
8. James G. Martin (R-N.C.) in 1984 and 1988; Carroll A. Campbell Jr. (R-S.C.) in 1986 and 1990; Buddy Roemer (D-, now R-, La.) in 1987; Judd Gregg (R-N.H.) in 1988 and 1990; and James J. Florio (D-N.J.) in 1989.
9. Henry Bellmon (R-Okla.) in 1986; Lawton Chiles (D-Fla.), Lowell Weicker (I-Conn.), and Pete Wilson (R-Calif.) in 1990.
10. The U.S. senators are: Dale Bumpers (D-Ark., 1971-75); David Pryor (D-Ark., 1975-79); Bob Graham (D-Fla., 1979-86); Wendell H. Ford (D-Ky., 1971-74); Christopher S. Bond (R-Mo., 1973-77, 1981-85); Jim Exon, D-Neb. (1971-79); Bob Kerrey (D-Neb., 1983-87); Richard H. Bryan (D-Nev., 1983-87); Terry Sanford (D-N.C., 1961-65); David L. Boren (D-Okla., 1975-79); Mark O. Hatfield (R-Ore., 1959-67); John H. Chafee (R-R.I., 1963-69); Strom Thurmond (R-S.C., 1947-51); Ernest F. Hollings (D-S.C., 1959-63); Charles S. Robb (D-Va., 1982-86); and John D. "Jay" Rockefeller IV (D-W.Va., 1977-85).
11. Thad L. Beyle, "Governors" in *Politics in the American States*, 4th ed., ed. Virginia Gray, Herbert Jacob, and Robert B. Albritton (Boston: Little, Brown, 1983), 217.
12. Lamar Alexander, *Steps Along the Way: A Governor's Scrapbook* (Nashville: Thomas Nelson, 1986), 9.
13. "Inquiry: Being Governor Is Best Training for Presidency," *USA Today*, September 11, 1987, 11A.
14. "Is There Life after Being Governor? Yes, A Good One," *Governors' Weekly Bulletin* 86:32 (August 8, 1986): 1-2.
15. Larry Sabato, "Gubernatorial Politics and the New Campaign Technology," *State Government* 53 (Summer 1980): 149.
16. "Total Cost of Gubernatorial Elections: 1977-1989," *The Book of the States, 1990-91* (Lexington, Ky.: The Council of State Governments, forthcoming).
17. Thad Beyle, "The 1989 Gubernatorial Races," *Comparative State Politics* 11:2 (April 1990): 29-32.
18. "People: Some Governors Get No Respect," *Governing* 1:2 (November 1987): 67.
19. Elder Witt, "Patronage Firings," *Congressional Quarterly Weekly Report*, July 3, 1976, 1726.
20. Elder Witt, "Supreme Court Deals Blow to Public Employee Firings for Solely Political Reasons," *Congressional Quarterly Weekly Report*, April 5, 1980, 899-900.
21. Elder Witt, "Employee Rights," *Congressional Quarterly Weekly Report*, April 6, 1983, 791-792.
22. Cheri Collis, "Cleaning Up the Spoils System," *State Government News* 33:9 (September 1990), 6.
23. Thad L. Beyle and Robert Huefner, "Quips and Quotes from Old Governors to New," *Public Administration Review* 43:3 (May-June 1983): 268-269.

The American Political Pretense: No Hard Choices

by Alan Ehrenhalt

In fall 1990, when William F. Weld was running for governor of Massachusetts, he used a simple analogy to explain how easy it would be to cut the state budget. It would be, he said, "like squeezing water from cheese." Nothing important would be lost. The product would be just as good.

In those same weeks, David Walters was telling the voters of Oklahoma what they might expect from him if he won the governorship. "We are going to change Oklahoma," he vowed. There would be substantial commitments to funding the 1990 education reform law, improving the correctional system, rehabilitating prisoners with new programs in literacy and vocational training. The money would be there: In a $6 billion state budget, a competent administrator should be able to find $100 million right away by stamping out inefficiency.

Just how many voters believed those assertions is impossible to say. Presumably millions of them did, because Republican Weld and Democrat Walters were both elected. In the crunch of a gubernatorial campaign, it still pays candidates to talk of funding an ambitious set of commitments painlessly, without new taxes or drastic service cuts, through the simple expedient of making gov-

ernment more efficient. Waste, fraud and abuse are the Loch Ness Monster of American politics. Candidates keep insisting they have seen it, and if given a chance, they will prove that it exists. The fact that they never produce much evidence of it after the election only seems to give the legend more credence with every passing election year.

People who have watched a few rounds of this won't be very surprised at what has happened in Massachusetts and Oklahoma in the few months since Governors Weld and Walters took office. Walters offered a budget that did manage to provide about $3 million in new money for prisoner rehabilitation, but not by any magic streamlining process. His budget took painful hits at the departments of Health, Mental Health and Veterans Affairs, and at the programs they operate. The "water" that Weld proposed to squeeze out of the Massachusetts governmental cheese turned out to include severe cutbacks in health programs and support for the elderly and a sharp reduction in aid to localities. During the campaign, Weld had insisted that local aid was "not where the hammer is going to fall."

Alan Ehrenhalt is a staff writer for *Governing*. This article appeared in *Governing* 4:8 (May 1991): 11-12.

I don't begrudge any new governor the right to make substantial spending cuts at a time of budget austerity, and I certainly don't doubt that health departments and local aid programs all over the country contain their share of trimmable fat. What I find so depressing is the whole political sequence: the continued willingness of politicians to pretend that there are no hard choices involved, the eagerness of the voters to believe them and the absence of any mass outcry when, just a few weeks after the election, the process generates exactly the kind of pain that the newly installed leaders insisted it wouldn't.

The difference between the limitless promises of fall and the austerity of late winter is, of course, the difference between campaigning and governing. Governing is choosing among competing goods, deciding to honor some of the items on one's wish list and putting others aside. It's possible for a new governor like David Walters to pour money into education reform or into prisoner rehabilitation, or to keep taxes from going up. It's just not possible to do all of those things at once, not in this year of budget shortfalls, and not in any year that is coming up soon.

Deciding which dreams to fulfill and which ones to delay or abandon isn't a simple matter of administrative competence, as candidates like Walters and Weld like to insist. It is a painful process in which many people get hurt and some people feel betrayed.

There are many things wrong with the American political system these days, but surely one of the most important of them is this: Too much of it takes place in situations like the gubernatorial campaigns of 1990, situations in which it is possible for the important players to pretend that no hard choices have to be made.

Governors, especially ones as intelligent as William Weld and David Walters, know perfectly well that it is pretense. Once they are inaugurated, they set about the sobering business of raising taxes and reducing services in precisely the painful ways that the legal necessities of a balanced budget require. Legislators understand it too, and in the end they cast the unpleasant votes that move the process along. But it is all made that much more painful and dishonest by the aura of fantasy that envelops the fall election campaign.

It raises a chicken-and-egg question. Do cynical politicians brainwash the innocent, well-meaning voter with empty promises? Or do voters generate the promises by rewarding those who make them and punishing candidates who dare to talk openly of trade-offs and sacrifices? Maybe a little of both. I think it is safe to predict that as soon as the voters start refusing to support candidates who try to sell them the Brooklyn Bridge, nobody will be out there selling it.

But pointing out villains is not really the important issue. What is important is a lesson that this particular flaw in our politics ought to teach us: We should be extremely suspicious of any governmental institutions that do not have trade-offs and hard choices wired right into them. Gubernatorial campaigns are not the only such institution.

There is, for example, the process of creating laws by the direct initiative of the voters. California made the initiative famous, but nearly half the states allow it in one form or another, and more are considering it. The governor of Kansas, Democrat Joan Finney, was elected in 1990 on a populist platform that stresses the right of the people to make their own laws, and she describes enactment of an initiative law as a major goal of her four-year term.

Defenders of the initiative process like to portray critics as arrogant elitists who do not believe the American people are competent to make sensible decisions about important public policy. But the most important argument against initiatives has nothing to do with intelligence or elitism. It has to do with the absence of hard choices. Voters who cast initiative ballots are allowed to mark in favor of massive environmental cleanup campaigns or guaranteed levels of educational spending without having to think about how to pay for them. They are allowed to support drastic reductions in state taxes without considering which of their services they would like to see taken away in consequence.

Given an extensive enough education campaign, of course, a pressure group that opposes a particular tax cut or spending initiative can make its consequences seem so horrendous as to kill it off altogether. This happened in Massachusetts in fall 1990, when opponents of Question 3, the $2 billion spending reduction initiative, managed to convince 60 percent of the voters that its passage would decimate the state's social service delivery system. In that situation, some astute campaigning and fund raising turned an initiative into a genuine hard choice.

Most of the time, that does not happen. The voters are essentially being asked whether they would like to give themselves a Christmas present, and they say yes. It is the job of the state legislature, months and years afterward, to pay for it, as Massachusetts is paying now, with an enormous deficit, for the 1980 initiative that placed a ceiling on local property taxes and forced large increases in state aid to localities. And as California is paying for Proposition 98, the law that requires a level of state education funding that the state's current revenues cannot reasonably support.

Most judges no doubt believe that they inhabit a world of hard choices, and in their way, they do. The judge who commands a state to spend more money on its prisons or mental institutions, or declares a school financing system inadequate, or orders the doubling of a local property tax, as happened in Kansas City, Missouri, may genuinely agonize over the decision. He may see it as a last resort to protect the constitutional rights of prisoners, or mental patients, or schoolchildren.

But it is a one-dimensional decision, nonetheless. Judges don't have to choose between more money for prisons and more money for schools; they are perfectly free, if the right cases happen to come before them, to insist on both. There is no built-in limit on the number of evils they can try to remedy at once.

The concept of limits makes its appearance only when the legislature or the city council tries to cope with the cumulative impact of all its judicial mandates and obligations and finds it impossible to do so, given the reluctance of the voters to accept any sizable tax increases. Only then are we talking about a hard choice—a choice between worthy causes, in which somebody who deserves better has to lose.

The fiscal troubles that are causing hardship all over the country in 1991 have been made worse by years' worth of decisions and commitments on the part of political actors who chose not to frame them as the hard choices they really were. Governors who campaigned simultaneously for more programs, lower taxes and no painful reductions in spending; citizens who voted themselves tax cuts without renouncing any of the services the taxes were providing; judges who pronounced huge school systems inadequate, and then left it to legislatures to tidy up the details.

Most of us learned a long time ago in our private lives that we cannot have everything we want, at least not all at once. There is a reason why "no free lunch" has become a cliche; the reason is that we all know it is true. It makes so much sense, in fact, that the sooner we start applying it to our public life, the better off we will all be.

Gov. James R. Thompson, 1977-1991:
The Complete Campaigner,
the Pragmatic Centrist

by Charles N. Wheeler III

On January 14 [1991], a remarkable era in Illinois politics and government [drew] to a close. Hand on Bible, Jim Edgar [took] the oath of office as the state's 38th governor, and after 5,117 days in office, James Robert Thompson Jr. [was] no longer ... the state's chief executive. The mark that Illinois' longest-serving governor [left] upon the state may well be indelible, from the glass walls of Starship Illinois in the Chicago Loop to the rustic outposts of Dixon Springs prison boot camp in deep southern Illinois. During his eventful years, Illinois' economy survived the nation's worst times since the Depression and continued its post-World War II evolution from a manufacturing and agricultural base to one in which high tech, service industries and tourism are key components.

At the helm throughout was Thompson, eager to shape government in order to nurture the change and to prepare Illinois for its role in the global economy of the 21st century. Along the way the governor, too, evolved:

● From a crime-busting federal prosecutor who put away some of the biggest names in the Cook County Democratic machine to a canny wheeler-dealer ready to reward friends and contributors with prestigious appointments and lucrative no-bid contracts.

● From a neophyte first-termer chided for a do-little agenda to the author of Build Illinois, the state's most massive public works program enacted in modern times.

● From a party outsider berated by Republican chieftains for giving jobs to Democrats to the architect of a GOP patronage operation so blatant it forced the U.S. Supreme Court to take notice.

After 14 years, the Thompson record include[d] a host of impressive accomplishments, tempered by some notable failures and even a few downright embarrassments. More than anything, it's a record of sometimes surprising contrasts, dominated by the personal charm of a man it's almost impossible not to like.

What will future historians make of Thompson, who arrived on the state scene in 1977 bringing "Camelot to the cornfields," in one reporter's words, and who [left] a self-described "Boss Tweed of modern-day patronage" ... ? On one point, at least, there is likely

Charles N. Wheeler III is a reporter in the *Chicago Sun-Times* Statehouse Bureau. This article is reprinted with permission from *Illinois Issues* 16:12 (December 1990): 12-16, published by Sangamon State University, Springfield, Illinois 62794-9243. © *Illinois Issue.*

to be scant disagreement: Big Jim was among the most gifted campaigners the state has ever seen, able to reach out beyond a Republican base and appeal to Democrats, independents, Illinoisians of any and all political persuasions.

He may have started slowly—long-time associates recall that he seemed almost shy, diffident, when he first took to the campaign trail and the county fair circuit back in the summer of 1975—but his quick wit, affability and boyish charm made him a natural. One of his pollsters confided early on that Thompson was among the very few candidates he'd ever handled who actually inspired people to want to vote for him.

Perhaps his self-effacing manner touched the egalitarian spirit so deeply rooted in our culture. Leave the button-down, suit-and-tie look to other candidates; Thompson preferred blue jeans, T-shirts and a good time along the way, and he could be equally at home knocking back early-morning shots of Lebanese "white lighting" with Cat workers at an East Peoria bar or clapping along with worshipers at a west side Chicago church. . . .

Thompson's relaxed manner sometimes irritated his Democratic opponents, particularly Adlai E. Stevenson III, whose own patrician air was little help in his two losses to Thompson. When an earlier foe, Michael J. Bakalis, groused that Thompson's casual manner and pet dogs won him vacuous and uncritical TV exposure, the governor responded, "That's his hang-up, not mine. I can't help it if he doesn't like dogs." . . .

Thompson's penchant for rapprochement with the legislature was born of personal preference and political necessity. The new governor set the tone from the start: "There will be no tactics of confrontation, no politics of division," he said in his brief inaugural address in 1977. It was a marked—and most welcome—change from the man he replaced, Democrat Dan Walker, who four years earlier told lawmakers: "The free ride is over." Walker's deliberate confrontational style produced four years of debilitating warfare between the executive and legislative branches, even though his fellow Democrats controlled both chambers his final two years.

Thompson, in contrast, never had the luxury of a Republican General Assembly. In only one two-year span, 1981 to 1983, did his party control a single chamber, and even then the GOP grasp was tenuous because of the hold House Minority Leader Michael J. Madigan had on some city Republicans. Thus Thompson [was] a conciliator, a compromiser, a consensus seeker who . . . enjoyed enormous rapport with a legislature in which his party [was] a consistent minority.

Only once was the spirit of cooperation truly violated, but the exception to the rule produced no long-lasting ill will. In perhaps the boldest political move of his career, the governor in 1981 tried to snatch Senate leadership from a badly splintered Democratic majority. As called for by the Constitution, the governor was presiding over the Senate at its first meeting to choose its own presiding officer. While the 30 fractious Democrats squabbled, with dissident holdouts refusing to support the reelection of Senate President Philip J. Rock (D-8, Oak Park), Thompson declared elected Sen. David C. Shapiro, an Amboy dentist who was the unanimous choice of the Senate's 29 Republicans. Ultimately, the Illinois Supreme Court sorted out the mess declaring that the votes of a clear majority of the 59 senators, or 30 votes, were needed to elect a Senate president, not just a plurality of the votes cast. Rock, an intensely decent man, harbored no grudges and, in fact, stood by Thompson more steadfastly in later budget battles than did Republican legislative leaders.

A more chronic irritation was the amendatory veto power. Lawmakers complained throughout Thompson's tenure that too often he remained above the legislative scrap as issues were hammered out, then stepped in after the fact to rewrite the bill with an amendatory veto. House Speaker Madigan was perhaps the loudest critic. The speaker ultimately resolved the issue by in effect consigning the revisions he didn't like to parliamentary limbo.

Thompson's role as a compromiser was easier because of the relationship he envisioned with the legislature, that of a partnership. A recurring theme in each of his State of the State messages was the accomplishments *we've* made, the challenges *we* face, always in tandem, working cooperatively for the people. "You have to understand that making government work for people is a shared partnership," he once reflected. "You just don't go in and command the General Assembly to do something; you work with the General Assembly." . . .

While the national Republican party turned hard right, Thompson remained a centrist; while a conservative White House collided with a liberal Congress, pragmatist Thompson colluded with a horse-trading legislature. The governor never acted as though his administration held a monopoly on good ideas; some of his most significant achievements were products of compromise, emerging from the legislative process in much different form than the governor's original proposals. . . .

The Thompson administration was virtually free of scandal, no small feat in a state with Illinois' checkered history, though Thompson himself came under fire for ethical blind spots. Perhaps the most embarrassing revelations occurred in 1982, when newspaper accounts detailed how Thompson accepted costly gifts, such as South African gold coins, art work and cash, from people with state government interests.

More troublesome for many as the administration grew older was the creeping

---

Veto Powers

Wisconsin voters in April [1990] passed a constitutional amendment with a 62% favorable vote to bar the "pick-a-letter" veto. The issue arises out of the item veto power of the Wisconsin governor, which most governors have. The extreme case was one in which the governor changed 48 hours in a child detention bill to ten days by selectively vetoing text to get the letters spelling ten days. The amendment was narrowly drawn, so it leaves at issue the selective vetoing of numbers to create new numbers. Actual example: using the veto to change a 1% cut to a 6% cut. . . .

Source: "Veto Powers," *State Policy Reports* 8:8 (April 1990): 24.

---

growth of pinstripe patronage, a catchy phrase for the no-bid consulting contracts, legal work, bond business, office leasers and low-interest loans channeled with distressing regularity to insiders with ties to the governor. Defending the practice in an interview, the governor said: "I don't think any press account of pinstripe patronage has ever pointed to an abuse of the process or has ever documented a case where the state got less than first-class service from its lawyers or its bond houses."

On the other hand, a 5-4 majority of the U.S. Supreme Court held Thompson's handling of what might be called "blue-collar" patronage—the conventional doling out of state jobs to party faithful—violated the U.S. Constitution. The court ruling affirmed what critics said all along: The hiring freezes Thompson imposed, more or less continuously, throughout his tenure were merely patronage tools used to ensure that worthy Republicans got available state jobs.

Early on, party leaders complained that Thompson was not grateful enough to those who labored in the GOP vineyards. "There is no patronage," chaffed one Republican during Thompson's first term. "He's got all those former assistant U.S. attorneys he brought with him who think patronage is a dirty word, illegal and immoral." Recalling such sentiments, Thompson mused: "It came as some irony that at the end of my administration, after all this, the Supreme Court of the United States certifies what these Republican chairmen refused to believe all along—that I had the best patronage machine in the nation, that it was a Republican machine."

As the curtain [was falling] on the state's longest-running administration and Big Jim Thompson [was striding] out of the spotlight— at least for the moment—how [did] his public rate his performance? Forty-eight percent of Illinois residents approve[d] of his handling of the job, while 43 percent [said] he [would] go down in history as above average or outstanding, according to a *Chicago Sun-Times* poll taken [in] September [1990].

Perhaps it's fitting that the final word on Thompson come from his No. 1 nemesis for much of his record-setting tenure. "In politics, the ultimate test is whether or not you won the last election," observed House Speaker Madigan when the governor announced his decision to forego a try for a fifth term "and so he leaves the office a complete winner."

Six Not-So-Easy Lessons for New Governors (and Others)

by Carolyn J. Lukensmeyer

As my days in the most exciting and challenging job I have yet held [drew] to a close and I [began] the transition back to the private sector, I [found] myself contemplating what I [had] learned over the [preceding] four years. I approach these thoughts from a dual perspective: first, as a buck-stops-here, hands-on manager of a large bureaucracy and political system, and second, as a practitioner and consultant with 20 years experience in organization design and development.

The leadership and management of government rests on a unique system. Every two, four or eight years, a startup organization is placed on top of a mature, entrenched bureaucracy. That creates both challenges and potential barriers for political leaders who are trying to effect change. They must find a way to link the newborn organization at the top to the established organization below if they are to get anything done.

That is just one of the ways in which running a government can be a more difficult task than running a business. In a democratic system, government must also value process as well as outcome. That means a collegial, broadly inclusive process. People must really be heard.

Most business enterprises focus primarily on outcome as a measure of success. I would argue that in today's world, the success of American business may rest on its leaders heeding the imperative of collegiality—in other words, running business more like a government.

For those in the public sector, I have identified six key lessons. I address them directly to governors, although they apply more broadly.

● Develop your vision and articulate it clearly to everyone, not just those closest to you. In the course of daily events, crises will command your attention. To keep your focus on the mandate that elected you, translate your vision into a strategic plan, complete with implementation strategies and timetables. Then stick to it.

● Establish relationships with your cabinet members quickly, and actively promote interagency cooperation. Recognize that many of the most important issues that face you—moving the children of dysfunctional families into the mainstream of American life; balancing the need to preserve the environ-

Carolyn J. Lukensmeyer was chief of staff to former-governor Richard F. Celeste (D-Ohio). This article is reprinted from *Governing* 4:2 (November 1990): 82.

1991 Occupants of Statehouses

Listed below are the governors of the 50 states and the year in which the next election for each office will be held. The names of governors elected in 1990 are in boldface.

Alabama — Guy Hunt (R) 1994 [1]

Alaska — Walter J. Hickel (I) 1994

Arizona — Fife Symington (R) 1994

Arkansas — Bill Clinton (D) 1994

California — Pete Wilson (R) 1994

Colorado — Roy Romer (D) 1994

Connecticut — Lowell P. Weicker Jr. (I) 1994

Delaware — Michael N. Castle (R) 1992 [1]

Florida — Lawton Chiles (D) 1994

Georgia — Zell Miller (D) 1994

Hawaii — John Waihee III (D) 1994 [1]

Idaho — Cecil D. Andrus (D) 1994

Illinois — Jim Edgar (R) 1994

Indiana — Evan Bayh (D) 1992

Iowa — Terry E. Branstad (R) 1994

Kansas — Joan Finney (D) 1994

Kentucky — Wallace G. Wilkinson (D) 1991 [1]

Louisiana — Buddy Roemer (R) 1991 [2]

Maine — John R. McKernan Jr. (R) 1994 [1]

Maryland — William Donald Schaefer (D) 1994 [1]

Massachusetts — William F. Weld (R) 1994

Michigan — John Engler (R) 1994

Minnesota — Arne Carlson (R) 1994

Mississippi — Ray Mabus (D) 1991

Missouri — John Ashcroft (R) 1992 [1]

Montana — Stan Stephens (R) 1992

Nebraska — Ben Nelson (D) 1994

Nevada — Bob Miller (D) 1994

New Hampshire — Judd Gregg (R) 1992

New Jersey — James J. Florio (D) 1993

New Mexico — Bruce King (D) 1994

New York — Mario M. Cuomo (D) 1994

North Carolina — James G. Martin (R) 1992 [1]

North Dakota — George Sinner (D) 1992

Ohio — George V. Voinovich (R) 1994

Oklahoma — David Walters (D) 1994

Oregon — Barbara Roberts (D) 1994

Pennsylvania — Robert P. Casey (D) 1994 [1]

Rhode Island — Bruce Sundlun (D) 1992

South Carolina — Carroll A. Campbell Jr. (R) 1994 [1]

South Dakota — George S. Mickelson (R) 1994 [1]

Tennessee — Ned McWherter (D) 1994 [1]

Texas — Ann W. Richards (D) 1994

Utah — Norman H. Bangerter (R) 1992

Vermont — Richard A. Snelling (R) 1992

Virginia — L. Douglas Wilder (D) 1993 [1]

Washington — Booth Gardner (D) 1992

West Virginia — Gaston Caperton (D) 1992

Wisconsin — Tommy G. Thompson (R) 1994

Wyoming — Mike Sullivan (D) 1994

1. Barred by state law from seeking re-election.
2. Buddy Roemer, elected as a Democrat, switched his party affiliation to Republican in 1991.

Source: Congressional Quarterly Weekly Report, November 10, 1990, 3840. This information was updated in May 1991 to include the results of the February 1991 runoff election in Arizona.—Ed.

ment with the need for economic development—extend beyond the jurisdictions of single agencies. Use your personal leadership to create an environment that supports and requires your cabinet members, and those who report to them, to work at working together. That is what it will take to create solutions instead of stalemates.

● Involve the bureaucracy. One of your first and primary tasks is to inspire its members to buy into your initiatives. Identify those places in your bureaucracy where there is real life and energy. Understand that these people are your major asset. Regardless of their political affiliations, and whether they had any previous links to you, they are your primary resource for changing the status quo. They are critical to the essential task of linking government to the wider community, which must be the foundation for any meaningful change.

● Be inclusive. As you first develop policy, invite into the dialogue all groups with a stake in the policy. Do not make the strategic decisions first and then allow other stakeholders to react. Pay closest attention to this in the areas you hope will become the legacy of your administration.

● Remember that a governor's board of directors is the legislature. Its members have the power to reject or enact your programs. Your ability to transform the mandate of the people into the political will of the legislature will determine your success or failure as governor. It is not a task to be slighted.

● Accept that in the four years you have as governor, the fundamental problems facing your state (and this country) will not be resolved permanently. But if you have succeeded in communicating your principles and goals to the citizens of your state, and in building coalitions of your supporters, then the new direction you have set for the state will become the basis of the dialogue between the public and your successor.

Good luck and have fun.

Governors Cannot Halt National Guard Missions Overseas, Court Rules

Governors do not have the constitutional right to block National Guard training assignments in foreign countries, the U.S. Supreme Court ruled unanimously [in June 1990]. Upholding a ruling by a federal appeals court, the Supreme Court said a 1986 law known as the Montgomery amendment is constitutional.

The Montgomery amendment overturned previous law that gave the governors authority to veto federal orders to place National Guard units on active duty in the absence of a national emergency. It provides that a governor's consent may not be withheld "because of any objection to the location, purpose, type, or schedule" of the active duty assignment.

Congress passed the 1986 law after several governors had refused to send their states' National Guard units on training assignments in Central America.

[Then-] Massachusetts Gov. Michael S. Dukakis and [then-] Minnesota Gov. Rudy Perpich had both challenged the law as unconstitutional.

The states had claimed that the Constitution left militia training at the state level. They argued that the ... amendment violated the Constitution's militia clauses, which give states "the authority of training the militia." The court decided that the responsibility for training the militia was a congressional determination, as in the Montgomery amendment.

In [the] ruling in *Perpich v. Department of Defense*, the court said that the Montgomery amendment does not infringe on a state's constitutional rights, but "merely recognizes the supremacy of federal power in the area of military affairs."

When the Minnesota appeal was filed, Gov. Perpich said that a lower court ruling upholding the Montgomery amendment was a "clear example of the federal government encroaching on state powers that have worked effectively in the past."

This article is reprinted with permission from *Governors' Weekly Bulletin* 24:23 (June 15, 1990): 2. National Governors' Association, 444 North Capitol Street, Washington, D.C. 20001-1572.

VII. STATE BUREAUCRACIES AND ADMINISTRATION

Just What Your State Wanted:
Great New Gifts from Congress

169

Departments and agencies within each state carry out the laws passed by the legislature and approved by the governor. These departments vary in size and in responsiveness to executive control. Transportation, human services, corrections, education, and health usually are large departments with sizable budgets and staffs. These "big ticket" agencies perform services quite visible to the public, and governors and legislators alike pay close attention to them. Governors appoint the heads of these agencies with great care, and the legislatures often must confirm the appointments.

Many parts of the state bureaucracy, however, appear to be remarkably immune to the vagaries of legislative and gubernatorial politics. The key to successful bureaucratic politics is to keep a low profile. Governors come and go, legislators come and go, but some agencies keep on doing what they have always done with minimum intrusion from outside. State government encompasses so many agencies and activities that it is virtually impossible for the governor and the legislature to keep track of them all.

Between a Rock and a Hard Place?

State bureaucrats—this is not a derogatory term—often are torn by competing values: economy and efficiency on the one hand and political expediency on the other. In the results-oriented world of politics, points often are scored for achieving an electorally advantageous goal rather than for saving money or doing a job efficiently.

Another problem is accountability. To whom are state employees accountable? To the governor, the legislature or particular legislators, the interest served by the agency, the public at large, themselves? The numerous lines of accountability give those in the state bureaucracy the opportunity to play one group against another and thereby do what they want.

In recent years important changes have been made that have improved the caliber of the states' work forces. The standards for hiring, promotion, and retention have been raised. Educational requirements are more exacting. In-service training has been upgraded. State employees who report wrongdoing in state government—"whistleblowers"— are better protected against retaliation. And more employees are covered by civil service and merit systems, which has reduced the number of patronage positions. Moreover, now minorities have better opportunities for employment and advancement within state government.

Another related development has been the growing political influence of state employee organizations. State employee groups and state employee labor unions have become stronger in almost all of the states. Like other interests, they lobby their own concerns and proposals before the governor and the state legislature— and with increasing effectiveness. What do they want for their efforts? Higher wages, better health and retirement benefits, and more recognition of their professional status. When it comes to preparing the budget, the most influential parties often are those who carry out the intent of the budget—namely, state employees.

Finally, we must note the dynamic growth of state governments over the last several decades. Since 1950 the number of state government employees has increased by 300 percent; only the increases in primary and secondary education employment were greater. While there was a consistent 'core' of about forty administrative agencies in most of the states in the late 1950s, this had grown to over seventy-five by the mid-1980s.[1] So both the number of people working for state government and the number of agencies in which they work have increased greatly.

Organizational Problems

How are state agencies organized? Some would argue they aren't. Governors trying to "run" state government or citizens trying to find out where to get help often are baffled by the apparent organizational chaos of the many departments and agencies. Periodically, the states reorganize their executive branch departments. This usually is done either to improve economy and efficiency, to clear up the lines of accountability so that the governor is the chief executive in fact rather than in theory, or to gain control over some agencies that are perceived as out of control—usually the control of the governor or of the legislature.

Not surprisingly, reorganization often is resisted by the agencies themselves and by groups with vested interests in the way things are. Those who know how the system works prefer the status quo and are extremely reluctant to learn new ways. And when the goal is to give the governor more power and influence, the agencies fight hard: they are far from willing to lose or share their power. Organizational battles are so difficult to mount and win that many governors and legislatures avoid them, believing victory is not worth the political costs.

Republican governors have been particularly attracted to setting up economy and efficiency commissions to survey state government programs, organizations, and policies in an effort to find ways to save the taxpayers money. These commissions, which usually are made up of members of the business community and supported by an out-of-state consulting firm specializing in such studies, review a state's budget, governmental organization, and programs. The commission issues a well-publicized final report pointing out waste in state

government and indicates 300-400 suggested changes as to how the state could save millions of dollars.

Some of the suggested changes make sense; others do not. They usually include some reorganization and consolidation of agencies, turning over some of what the agencies do to the private sector (privatization), eliminating some programs, charging or increasing user fees for some services, or transferring a program to another level of government.[2] One observer concludes that such studies have "been largely discredited" and may be more "a political than an administrative tool."[3] Even reorganizations have been criticized as doing more to spawn confusion "about program goals and work responsibilities" and sparking "political brushfires" that keep "managers from getting back to those basic issues of responsibility and accountability."[4]

Major executive branch reorganization efforts have occurred in twenty-two states since the 1960s. The goals usually articulated in these efforts were "modernization and streamlining of the executive branch machinery, efficiency, economy, responsiveness, and gubernatorial control."[5] Reorganizations are not apolitical events; they involve a battle for power among the branches of government. Aside from the built-in resistance that state bureaucrats have to such changes, legislators often oppose them as well because reorganizations usually increase the power of the governor over the executive branch at the expense of the legislature. For example, the number of independent boards, commissions, and agencies usually declines precipitously, such as in Georgia, where the number of such units dropped from 300 to 22, or in Louisiana, where the drop was from 300 to 19.[6] Furthermore, the few bodies that survive the reorganizations are often headed by a single gubernatorial appointee rather than by a multiperson board, which means more control for the governor and less access for the legislature. The most recent example of success in this occurred in 1989, when West Virginia Governor Gaston Caperton gained legislative approval for consolidating 150 executive boards and agencies into seven departments.[7]

Rather than seek major reorganization of the bureaucratic structure, state leaders may attempt partial reform when there is a pressing need to consolidate overlapping and confusing jurisdictions, or when they wish to tackle a particular problem facing the state by eliminating organizational barriers. This has been especially important in economic development, in the environmental area, and in the actual administration of state government.

Since the mid-1970s, thirty-six states have followed Colorado's lead and adopted some form of sunset legislation—legislation that calls for the automatic termination of an agency, board, or commission unless the legislature reauthorizes or reestablishes it. Licensing and regulatory agencies are the agencies most often governed by sunset laws. However, six states have since repealed their sunset laws, and six other states have allowed their laws to lapse into inactivity.[8] Many states also have passed "open government" laws to give the media and interested citizens better access to the activities and records of state government.

Management and Personnel Changes

Where the states have made the most headway is in adopting new management techniques. Budgets no longer are worked out in the back rooms of statehouses by employees wearing green eye shades; they are part of a larger policy-management process headed by the governor. In many states, policy, planning, and budgeting are treated as a whole process, not to be separated by competing political fiefdoms. However, according to two surveys, more than half of the states still have poor central management of state government.[9]

Changes in state government administration and personnel have been made but not without considerable furor. Controversies over affirmative action (Should minorities have a leg up in hiring and promotions?) and comparable worth (Should men and women be paid equally for dissimilar jobs of similar skill levels?) are bedeviling state legislators and administrators. A March 1987 U.S. Supreme Court decision, *Johnson v. Transportation Agency, Santa Clara County, Calif.*, supporting the promotion of a woman over a slightly more qualified man in a local government personnel situation, indicates judicial branch support for affirmative action principles. Another Supreme Court decision, *City of Richmond v. Croson* (1989), declared unconstitutional another state and local government affirmative action effort called set-asides, in which a fixed portion of public works funds are reserved for minority-owned companies. Using the legal concept of strict scrutiny, the Court argued any such program must meet a compelling state interest to be used. The concept of strict scrutiny historically has been difficult to specify legally, especially in the area of racial discrimination.[10]

Politically, it makes sense to open up jobs for women and other minorities; they are becoming more active in politics and their support often is needed to win elections. Hence, it is no surprise that the number of women in state-level cabinet positions increased by 114 percent between 1981 and 1989. In a 1989 survey of the forty states with a cabinet structure of government, women held 150 of the 703 cabinet-level positions, or 21 percent. The number of women in these cabinet positions varies from zero in Missouri to eight in Illinois and ten in Vermont.[11] The director of administration in Louisiana said she still sees evidence of male chauvinism in state government but felt "the good ol' boy network is aging and it is likely I will live to see their replacements." [12]

After the 1990 elections, women held 58 of the 331 available positions in state executive branches (17.5 percent). This compares to twenty-nine women holding such jobs in 1977.[13] Women also held 1,356 of the 7,461 state legislative seats (18.2 percent) after the last elections. This represents a quadrupling of the number of woman who served in 1969.[14] According to one observer of the state government scene: "We're going to have to move beyond the good ol' boy network to include in the profoundest way the good ol' girls and the good ol' minorities." [15]

There have been considerable changes in the type of personnel working at the administrative level in state governments. According to Deil Wright, who has studied state administrators since 1964, the 1988 cadre of administrators differed from their 1964 counterparts in the following ways: there were fewer males (83 percent in 1988 vs. 98 percent in 1964); fewer whites (91 percent vs. 98 percent); they were younger (median age of 43 vs. 53); and better educated (only 2 percent had a high school education or less vs. 15 percent, and those with graduate or professional degrees rose from 40 percent to 57 percent over the period).[16]

Ethics

How government officials, elected or appointed, behave while in office is increasingly a topic of concern at the state level. We generally recognize a corrupt act—or do we? Handing cash to a public official to influence a decision would seem to be a corrupt act. But what about a public utility political action committee that contributes funds to incumbent legislators' campaigns so that legislators might look more favorably on revising the utility rate structure? Is that a corrupt act? Or is that politics?

Like beauty, corruption and ethical mis-

behavior often are in the eye of the beholder. Some states are trying to clarify this issue by establishing ethics codes, standards, and commissions. Recently, several states have established inspectors general offices to probe into allegations of wrongdoing in state government. In some instances, the inspectors general have the authority to "identify programs or departments that *might be vulnerable* to corruption. . . ." [17] Some observers suggest that these steps, along with measures to open up electoral and governmental processes and to develop accountability measures, "have . . . been at least as significant as the other reforms" occurring in the states over the past few decades.[18]

While there are several state governments with a history of ethical and corruption problems, few can match the recent situation in West Virginia. Consider the following events, which occurred in about one year's time: the popular, recently reelected state treasurer A. James Manchin was impeached and resigned in July 1989 after auditors found losses of nearly $300 million in the state's Consolidated Investment Fund; state attorney general Charlie Brown resigned one month later after being accused of perjury during a custody hearing involving his ex-wife and daughter, and a grand jury that was investigating the perjury charges also subpoenaed Brown's campaign finance records from 1984 through 1988; three state senators were forced to resign, two over charges of taking money in return for votes, the other over a felony income tax charge; up to fifty other state and local officials were under investigation for alleged wrongdoing; and in April 1990, former governor Arch Moore (R, 1969-77, 1985-89) pleaded guilty to federal charges of extortion, mail fraud, tax fraud, and obstruction of justice.[19]

Part VII explores some of these and other controversies concerning state bureaucracies. Cheri Collis, in an article from *State Government News*, explores the impact of the recent

Supreme Court decision ruling against the time-honored practice of patronage. Karen Diegmueller, also of *State Government News*, discusses the effectiveness of sunrise and sunset legislation in controlling the number of boards and agencies in the states. Keon Chi of *The Journal of State Government* explores an increasingly common approach to multistate problems—multistate regionalism. Finally, David Rapp of Congressional Quarterly analyzes what many feel is at the heart of state fiscal problems: mandates from the federal government, most often from the U.S. Congress.

Notes

1. Deil S. Wright, Jae-Won Yoo, and Jennifer Cohen, "The Evolving Profile of State Administrators," *The Journal of State Government* 64:1 (January-March 1991), 30-31.
2. Tim Funk, "Efficiency Study Commissions: Is an Old Idea a Bad Idea?" *North Carolina Insight* 11:4 (August 1989): 42-43, 46-50.
3. James K. Conant, "Reorganization and the Bottom Line," *Public Administration Review* 46:1 (January/February 1986): 48.
4. Les Garner, "Managing Change Through Organization Structure," *The Journal of State Government* 60:4 (July/August 1987): 194.
5. James K. Conant, "In the Shadow of Wilson and Brownlow: Executive Branch Reorganization in the States, 1965 to 1987," *Public Administration Review* 48:5 (September/October 1988): 895.
6. Ibid., 902.
7. Elder Witt, "A Governor Seeks Less Government," *Governing* 2:9 (June 1989): 66.
8. Richard C. Kearney, "Sunset: A Survey and Analysis of the State Experience," *Public Administration Review* 50:1 (January/February 1990): 66.
9. Coalition to Improve Management in State and Local Government, *The Governor's Management Improvement Program: How to Do It* (Washington, D.C.: National Academy of Public Administration, 1985); and Office of State Services, *Reorganization and Management Improvement Initiatives: An Essay on State Experience* (Washington, D.C.: National Governors' Association, 1986).
10. Linda Greenhouse, "Ruling Ends Part of Affirmative Action Debate," *New York Times News Service*, reprinted in [Raleigh] *News and Observer*, January 25, 1989, 2A.
11. National Women's Political Caucus, "More Women Hold Top State Positions," *USA Today*, February 27, 1989, 6A.
12. Mireille Grangenois Gates, "More Women Join State Cabinets," *USA Today*, October 24, 1986, 3A.
13. Center for the American Woman and Politics, "Fact Sheet: Women in Elective Office 1991," Eagleton Institute of Politics, Rutgers University, March 1991.
14. Center for the American Woman and Politics, "Fact Sheet: Women in State Legislatures 1991," Eagleton Institute of Politics, Rutgers University, March 1991.
15. Comment by Jesse L. White, Jr., former executive director of the Southern Growth Policies Board and a public policy consultant in "On the Record," *Governing* 4:8 (May 1991), 18.
16. Deil Wright et al., 32.
17. Cheri Collis, "State Inspectors General: The Watchdog over State Agencies," *State Government News* 33:4 (April 1990): 13.
18. Fran Burke and George C. S. Benson, "Written Rules: State Ethics Codes, Commissions, and Conflicts," *The Journal of State Government* 62:5 (September/October 1989): 198.
19. No one has put together the whole story yet, but some of the pieces can be found in: "In Briefs: West Virginia," *Comparative State Politics Newsletter* 10:2 (April 1989); "West Virginia Woes," *State Policy Reports* 7:17 (September 1989): 30; "West Virginia Problems," *State Policy Reports* 7:24 (December 1989): 9; LaDonna Sloan, "In Briefs: West Virginia," *Comparative State Politics* 10:6 (December 1989): 37; and "West Virginia Problems," *State Policy Reports* 8:8 (April 1990): 24.

Cleaning Up the Spoils System

by Cheri Collis

Chicago Mayor Richard Daley's well-oiled machine established a tradition of political patronage in Illinois. The remnants of that may come to a grinding halt, however, with a narrow U.S. Supreme Court ruling in June [1990].

The justices said federal, state and local governments violated First Amendment rights when they refused to hire, promote or transfer employees on the basis of their political affiliations or party activities.

The court's decision of *Rutan et al* vs. *Republican Party of Illinois* promises to have a tremendous effect on state and local employment practices across the nation. In Illinois, the ruling could affect some 60,000 government positions.

But not everyone supports the decision. Those who favor patronage say it offers broad political benefits to a two-party system. They argue governors should have discretion to choose top-level managers who will be faithful. "Generally, Illinois believes that a limited patronage system is important to the preservation of a two-party system in this country," said Bill Ghesquiere, counsel to the governor.

Patronage supporters also say the ruling could prevent states from hiring qualified em-ployees because of the perceived threat of a lawsuit.

But patronage opponents say the state got what it deserved. They contend people should be hired on merit—not according to their campaign contributions.

One political scientist maintains that the number of patronage positions has significantly decreased in virtually every state, which eliminates the need for such a stringent ruling.

The ruling came in a challenge to [then-] Illinois Gov. James R. Thompson's hiring practices. Permission for hiring new employees was granted only after the governor's personnel office examined whether a job candidate voted in Republican primaries, made campaign contributions or worked for the party, according to the court opinion.

The five people who filed suit against the governor said they were discriminated against because they were not Republican Party supporters. They included a rehabilitation officer who said she was repeatedly denied promotions to supervisory positions; a road equip-

Cheri Collis is a staff writer for *State Government News*. This article is reprinted with permission from *State Government News* 33:9 (September 1990): 6-8. © 1990 The Council of State Governments.

Patronage Ruling: Threat to Political Parties, Promise to Individual Rights

An immediate effect [of the Supreme Court decision in *Rutan et al v Republican Party of Illinois*] was the issuance by [then-] Gov. Thompson on July 17 of Executive Order No. 1 (1990), strictly implementing the principles embodied in *Rutan*. About the past it says, "It has been the policy and practice of this administration to fill positions in the state only with individuals who are qualified for their positions." Indeed, recommendations to the governor's office have been made from lists of those qualified under civil service regulations, but apparently the attitude has been, "All other things being equal, hire the Republican." Now the record of past party affiliation, activity and voting is not to be considered. The order does not prohibit recommendations for those seeking employment by party officials, but these must deal strictly with the candidate's qualifications for the job and not with party loyalty.

Anyone who lives in Springfield will have to wonder whether job dispensers will be able to ignore the known party affiliation of the recommenders—but at least the Republicans have stopped attaching application forms for party membership to job application forms.

Source: F. Mark Siebert, "Patronage Ruling: Threat to Political Parties, Promise to Individual Rights," *Illinois Issues* 16:9 August/September 1990): 14-15. Reprinted with permission from *Illinois Issues*, Sangamon State University, Springfield, Illinois 62794-9243. © 1990 *Illinois Issues*.

ment operator who said he was denied a promotion; and a man who said he was unable to get a job as a prison guard.

Two other plaintiffs in the case said they were not recalled after being laid off because they lacked Republican credentials.

Terrence Brunner, executive director of the Better Government Association in Chicago, called the governor's hiring practices "a transparent attempt to ensure the building of a Republican patronage army."

Brunner said patronage demoralizes public employees. "Patronage is despicable because it takes our tax dollars and, instead of using them to hire the best people, uses them to hire political hacks," he said

Bill Ghesquiere, however, said the governor was surprised at the ruling. "It's a departure from 200 years of practice in this country of taking into consideration political factors in hiring people," he said.

"I don't believe that the patronage system in Illinois was that bad," he said.

Ghesquiere said a far bigger deal is being made out of patronage than the numbers support. He questions the accuracy of how many state employees are affected by patronage. He said many of those 60,000 are civil service employees and are therefore protected.

"I think this case throws the baby out with the bath water," said Ghesquiere.

Many party leaders feel the ruling provides a breeding ground for lawsuits nationwide. "Under this opinion, if employees allege they weren't a Republican, it puts the burden on the government to respond," Ghesquiere said.

Bob Gable, chairman of the Kentucky Republican Party, said the system becomes more bureaucratic under the ruling.

"Patronage is good," said Gable, adding that without it politicians would have difficulty hiring people who share their beliefs. He also fears employees will cry patronage whenever they don't get rehired or promoted.

Gable said worthy people will shy away from accepting important government positions for fear of lawsuits over hiring practices.

"It seems very hazardous—the job of being a public official with hiring responsibilities. You worry all the time if someone is going to sue you," said Gable.

Ohio Democratic Party Chairman Jim Ruvolo said employees will start blaming politics if they get fired.

"The courts have taken a dim view of patronage for quite a while but frankly I don't agree with it," said Ruvolo, who has been the state's Democratic Party chairman since 1982. "There's a place for patronage because the public gets better service."

Justice Antonin Scalia apparently shared this reasoning. Scalia wrote in his dissent that patronage "may sometimes be a reasonable choice, and should therefore be left to the judgment of the people's elected representatives."

States weren't the only ones with a vested interest in the case. Puerto Rico made it clear it sided with Illinois and filed a friend of the court brief.

The effects of the Supreme Court's ruling on patronage are unclear because many experts consider the ruling's language too vague. "The decision is ambiguous on some points. It's a little uncertain how far the decision goes," said Ghesquiere.

It also may be interpreted differently by government officials, said Larry J. Sabato, professor of government at the University of Virginia and author of several books on political parties and state government.

" Inevitably, the court will have to define more precisely what is a policy-making position," he said.

Sabato, whose work was cited by Justice William J. Brennan Jr. in the majority opinion limiting patronage, also said public officials should be allowed to use more discretion in choosing who will work for them.

He thinks the issue eventually will return to the court. Sabato said the four justices who voted for patronage are the younger, up-and-coming members of the court. "But with a 5-4 decision and with other younger leaders on the opposing side, it's not going to take but one personnel change and an appropriate case," said Sabato. "I'm not convinced it's over." . . .

Unions Applaud Decision

But Sandra Adams-Choate, an assistant general counsel for the American Federation of Government Employees, said the ruling will stick. More specific language may be necessary regarding the definition of policy-makers in the executive branch, but career employees needn't worry, she said.

Government employee unions applaud the court's decision. "Public service should be based on merit in a competitive system. The ruling affirms this," said Adams-Choate.

The American Federation of State, County and Municipal Employees, a union representing nearly 50,000 state employees nationally, also endorses the court decision.

But David Hoffman, the federation's public affairs field coordinator, described its effectiveness as "marginal at best" because many states already ban such arrangements.

Hoffman said the decision's impact will differ across the country. He notes many state and local governments already prohibit checking an employee's political background before promoting or hiring.

The Northeastern and Midwestern states generally have had long political patronage systems exemplified by big city political machines. Northern states were antipatronage and the South was a mixed bag, according to Sabato.

"There will be substantial changes in Illinois and Indiana. In most Western states, (people) won't even notice a decision was made," said Sabato.

Patronage In Decline

The Indiana Republican Party's 20-year machine ended when Gov. Evan Bayh, a Democrat, was elected in 1988, according to David Dawson, the governor's press officer.

At one time, Indiana had a formal political clearance card system in some executive departments, most notably the highway department, according to Dawson. "To apply for a position, you had to have a card filled out with the signatures of all the Republican Party officials," he said.

Some Indiana Republicans dispute the charge that patronage ended with Bayh's election. Rep. John Thomas, Republican from Brazil, Ind. who has held his House seat for 24 years, said, "if it was a machine under the Republican administration, it's an even more highly powered machine under the Democrats."

Bayh's administration is not free of the spoils system, opponents claim. Since Bayh took office, five former state employees have filed suit claiming they were victims of party politics.

Administration officials admit to a certain bias. Prior to the *Rutan* ruling, if two job candidates had similar qualifications, the Democratic supporter won out, Dawson said.

In Missouri, officials predict the ruling will not affect their state's employment practices.

"This court ruling will have very little impact on Missouri because our system is so different from the Illinois case presented before the Supreme Court," said Missouri Gov. John Ashcroft, a Republican.

Ohio officials say there is no ingrained patronage system in their state.

"There won't be any radical change based on this issue," said Elliot T. Fishman, senior staff counsel for Ohio's Division of Personnel. Ohio has a state version of the Hatch Act, a law that limits the political activities of state government employees.

Herbert B. Asher, a political scientist at Ohio State University, agrees. "Jobs are already protected and patronage is at the higher (work) levels where exemptions are allowed."

Ohio Democrat Party Chairman Jim Ruvolo, who also is vice chair of the National Democratic Committee, credited the demise of political patronage at the state level to civil service jobs and unionization.

In Illinois, however, the issue has yet to be settled. While the Supreme Court has ruled that patronage is wrong, a lower court in Illinois still must determine whether patronage existed in the state. Plaintiffs in the case face an uphill battle to win the lower court ruling.

The U.S. Supreme Court decision may have given patronage opponents another victory. But supporters of the spoils system say patronage has been the backbone of U.S. politics and the war isn't over yet.

One party leader likened the ruling to the overzealous punishment of a naughty child by an angry parent. "We're trying to perfect freedom and instead of letting people have their own way, we are trying to protect ourselves of any little perceived impropriety."

Sunrise, Sunset Cut Costs

by Karen Diegmueller

At the end of the tumultuous legislative session in August [1990], Louisiana's governor and Legislature were at loggerheads. All summer long they had clashed on such volatile issues as abortion, flag desecration and the censorship of music lyrics. The Legislature would pass a bill only to have Gov. Charles "Buddy" Roemer veto it. They were so mired in impassioned matters that the business of the state seemed to be at a standstill.

But inside the state Capitol in Baton Rouge, a task that had seemed insurmountable only a few years earlier had been accomplished. "We know how many boards we have," [said] Randall W. Womack, the special assistant for boards and commissions.

By some standards, this achievement may seem inconsequential. But following Roemer's election in 1987, his staff discovered that all the records pertaining to boards and commissions had been destroyed. Starting from scratch, they set out to identify what boards were in existence, what they did and whether they were worthwhile. However, when the governor attempted to abolish ones he believed were unnecessary, the Legislature rebuffed his efforts. In 1988, the Legislature refused to eliminate a single board. In 1989, lawmakers were persuaded to scrap 66. "We didn't abol-

ish any [in 1990], but we didn't create any," says Womack. "We're keeping a handle on what's getting created."

Nearly every state at one time or another has operated on the maxim, "Have a problem? Create a commission." Whenever a problem needed solving or a profession sought statutory officialdom, a new board or commission was born. If lawmakers have not entirely abandoned the practice, at least the halcyon days for these bodies appear to be over. Some states have introduced measures to control the proliferation of boards. Results are widely varied, but at the very least these strategies have focused attention on what has been a growth industry.

It's difficult to gauge exactly how many of these bodies exist throughout the United States because states don't keep up-to-date listings. But it's safe to say there are tens of thousands of state-sanctioned boards, commissions, authorities and other entities bearing a variety of names. Some are advisory in nature, others decide policy and make or enforce rules

Karen Diegmueller is a staff writer for *Education Week*. This article is reprinted with permission from *State Government News* 33:10 (October 1990): 7-9. © 1990 The Council of State Governments.

with the potential to affect sizable portions of society.

Although many are taxpayer-financed, their budgets represent only a fraction of overall state spending. Advisory boards in Califo nia, for example, account for about $16 million of the state's $56 billion budget. Even when all the state's boards and commissions are counted, including those funded by licensing and promotional fees, the sum is relatively small. In 1988-89 their budgets totaled $1.9 billion, according to a study by the Commission on California State Government and Economy.

Watchdog organizations and state officials nonetheless have called for oversight mechanisms to ensure accountability or, at a more elementary level, to provide a rationale for a board's existence.

Roemer's staff in Louisiana is engaged in such an endeavor. His office was able to hold the line against adding more boards ... by conducting a needs analysis of every bill that would produce an official body.

While Louisiana's method of controlling boards is information, other states have enacted legislation institutionalizing the procedure. Sunrise, as the practice is known, compels individuals or occupational groups who want to establish a new board or commission to prove it is prudent for the state to do so. Some 14 states have established a sunrise review.

Nebraska has been using sunrise since 1985. Recreational therapists were among those who asked the state to license them. In addition to bestowing the occupation with a certain official and prestigious status, regulation would have meant establishing a board to oversee its activities. As grounds for the application, therapists focused on the strides they had made as a profession rather than on the need to protect the public, says David A. Montgomery, administrator of the Nebraska

health department's credential review program. "It was seen as some kind of rite of passage for their profession."

The request was denied.

Since Nebraska adopted sunrise legislation, only five of 16 new health-related occupational groups seeking official recognition have been recommended for accreditation. The Senate (Nebraska is unicameral) has agreed with the credential panel in all but one instance.

Before sunrise, says Montgomery, it often came down to "who had the best lobbyists ... and who could get 30 votes." Now, he says, decisions are made "purely from a public health perspective."

The costs of the program have been supported by the professions. Operating expenses, which were $85,000 in 1985, [were] $80,000 in [1990].

Sunset Expires

Sunrise emerged from the shadows of sunset, the highly touted practice that began in Colorado in 1976. In its heyday, 36 states had adopted some form of sunset. Statutes varied but the core element was an automatic termination of a board, commission or agency unless the legislature acted to reauthorize the body.

In a survey of sunset laws published in *Public Administration Review* ..., Richard C. Kearney, a professor at the University of Connecticut, found that states have been defecting from sunset legislation. At last count, an even dozen have scuttled sunset or allowed it to expire.

Sunset legislation was inappropriate for such states as Illinois because they already had strong oversight mechanisms, says Kearney. Conversely, sunset was impotent in states with part-time legislatures and small staffs. "They don't handle the oversight responsibility very well anyway," he says.

As successful as sunrise has been for

Nebraska, sunset proved to be a disappointment and was repealed in 1982 after five years. The sunset review consisted of sending questionnaires to boards and commissions asking if they were working in the public interest. Says Montgomery, "They didn't ask the right questions and they didn't ask the right questions of the right people."

While sunset legislation was enacted for a noble purpose, Montgomery believes states went into it with false expectations. "A lot of people got into sunset thinking they were going to get rid of a lot of boards. We know that was naive."

Sunset's failure can be traced chiefly to politics. The boards and commissions frequently become bastions of special interests and appointments to them often are made to repay political favors. "It's extremely difficult to do away with one once it's in existence," says California Sen. Robert Presley, chairman of the Appropriations Committee.

Kearney agrees. "Few major entities have fallen. Most victims have been peripheral boards or commissions that had lost their usefulness or relevance, such as the Cascara Bark Peeling Board in Washington and the Stonewall Jackson Memorial Board in Texas," he says.

Without a mechanism to monitor their usefulness, boards can get embroiled in lengthy disputes. Before the interstate Commerce Commission assumed the responsibility, the Kentucky Railroad Commission set freight rates. "It used to be that the railroad commission had some authority in the state of Kentucky. We just don't have any anymore," says J. E. Combs, who was elected to the commission [in 1987] on a platform to abolish it. "It is just a ripoff of the taxpayers," he says, "They may have something on the agenda three times a year."

Unable to quash the commission without a constitutional amendment, Combs convinced the Legislature to phase out funding by July 1992. The other two commissioners have filed a lawsuit to prevent the loss of funding, which amount[ed] to $84,000 [in 1990].

From Sunrise to Sunset

Colorado, the birthplace of sunset legislation, continues to use the procedure. "In some states, [sunset] has been worthwhile. In some states, it's been a disaster," says Brad Mallon, director of the Office of Policy and Research in the Colorado Department of Regulatory Agencies.

If sunset by itself has been a disappointment to some states, it may see a new dawn as an adjunct to sunrise. Colorado now uses both. "Sunrise is the logical concomitant to sunset. If you're guarding the back door but you're not guarding the front door, it doesn't make sense," says Mallon.

In 1982, Colorado abolished the mortuary science board, Mallon says, because it was inactive, never disciplining any of the practitioners. Funeral directors and morticians [recently] tried to get their profession licensed anew but were thwarted as a result of the sunrise review.

California also is moving towards a dual system. Without any formal mechanism, the state in the past few years has warded off attempts by woodcutters and chimney sweeps to get licensed. Several pieces of ... legislation [were introduced that] would formalize the process.

To sort out the hundreds of state boards and commissions, Presley ... introduced a bill that would terminate all of them by a select date. Under the proposal, the Legislature could take action to preserve them individually.

"There are all kinds of them that are set up out there as advisory committees, and we have more advice now than we can absorb," says Presley. "We don't have to pay for any more advice."

Another bill, offered by Assemblywoman Delaine Eastin, would require proof up front that a new board or commission was necessary. Its conception would be evaluated on such criteria as the purpose of the body, the anticipated workload, the funding source and the anticipated results, says Michael V. Abbot, senior consultant to the Assembly Committee on Governmental Efficiency and Consumer Protection.

In the midst of efforts to curtail the formation of boards or trigger their demise, some government experts caution against proceeding for the sake of political expediency. While lawmakers pondered the budget crisis in California, several legislators sponsored bills calling for the elimination of certain boards as a moneysaving gesture.

"It had no rhyme or reason. It is just political posturing and it points up the vulnerability of these things," says Jack Hailey, consultant to the Senate Office of Research.

In some instances, "what you're doing is eliminating a board or commission and making a department of that. You're still going to have 300 employees and spend whatever," he says. Hailey contends that well-run boards are good government. They're "the cheapest, most effective way to get citizen review and advice."

Interstate Cooperation:
Resurgence of Multistate Regionalism

by Keon S. Chi

Multistate regionalism, a persistent phenomenon of the American political tradition, is reemerging as a viable strategy to deal with a multitude of state problems, ranging from economic development and social services to environment and education. The resurgence of regionalism is due in part to the gradual devolution of federal responsibilities, states' mutual interest in better planning and communication, and the desire to improve state management and programs.

Trends in Regionalism

The history of multistate regionalism is as old as the nation itself. Regionalism has been used over the years as a geographic, economic, planning, administrative and political concept. Since the creation of the Tennessee Valley Authority in 1933, the federal government has continuously used regional mechanisms to provide selected public services. And during the 1960s regionalism gained prominence with the creation of multistate commissions such as the Appalachian Regional Commission. In the past few years, state policy-makers have taken the lead in creating mechanisms for regional cooperation.

The resurgence of regionalism posits several significant trends. First, despite federal pre-emption of state programs and uniform state laws, "nationalization of American politics has not proceeded so far as to obliterate the regions," as political scientist Ira Sharkansky says. Regional differences persist and are sharper than ever in some respects. Also, state interests in regional activities remain strong. Record attendance at recent regional conferences of The Council of State Governments, for example, may be attributed to state policy-makers' interest in regional approaches to problems.

Second, unlike multistate regional mechanisms initiated and administered by the federal government during the 1960s and 1970s, states are developing regional strategies to tackle common problems without federal mandate or involvement. Moreover, some regional programs have been initiated by states without creating additional layers of bureaucracy.

Third, although the number of interstate compacts created has declined to less than 10 in the 1980s compared to 50 in the 1960s and 20

Keon S. Chi is a senior policy analyst at the Council of State Governments. This article is reprinted with permission from *The Journal of State Government* 63:3 (July-September 1990): 59-63. © 1990 The Council of State Governments.

in the 1970s, recent compacts tend to be more regional in scope. This is evidenced in the Great Lakes Interstate Sales Compact, Middle Atlantic Governors' Compact on Alcohol and Drug Abuse, Northeast Interstate Low-level Radioactive Waste Compact and proposed compacts such as the Northwest Compact for the Pacific Marine Resources Commission and the Midwestern Higher Education Compact.

Fourth, states are initiating regional innovations in policy and management areas without using the traditional form of interstate compact. These interstate regional innovations do not require congressional approval and can be implemented more easily. Over the years, individual states have been management and policy innovators within the American federalism system. Today states are contemplating regional innovations as well.

And, fifth, developments in multistate regionalism extend beyond national borders. States and provinces in the U.S.-Canadian and U.S.-Mexican border areas have initiated regional approaches. One example of such "borderless" cooperation is the Pacific Northwest Legislative Leadership Forum, established to explore greater regional unity for economic development. The forum consists of representatives from Alaska, Idaho, Montana, Oregon, Washington, Alberta and British Columbia. CSG's Eastern and Midwestern regional conferences also have begun cooperative programs with several Canadian provinces.

Regional Innovations

States are using non-traditional regional innovations and interstate compacts for efforts in economic development, social services, environment, education, management and regional trends analysis.

The South and the West are taking the lead in regional economic development efforts. The Southern Growth Policies Board, uniting 13 states, has been an effective vehicle for regional planning and cooperation as well as public-private partnership building. The group has been in the forefront in alerting state officials to economic development issues. Its publications have included "Foresight: Model Programs for Economic Development" and "SGPB: Analysis of Emerging Issues." At its 1989 annual meeting, the Board adopted a strategic plan for technology-based economic development in the South. The plan was prepared by the Southern Technology Council, which studies the interrelationship of science and technology and economic development. The regional plan, "Turning to Technology—A Strategic Plan for the Nineties," set goals, objectives and specific strategies for implementation.

The Southern region also is implementing a 10-year economic development plan completed in 1990 by the Lower Mississippi Delta Development Commission. The plan takes a comprehensive approach to economic challenges facing the South.

A strong case for regional cooperation for international trade was made by the Western Governors' Association in 1988 when the group adopted a regional plan, "Going Global: A Strategy for Regional Cooperation." The rationale for regional cooperation on international trade, investment and tourism is to create jobs in a more effective and less costly manner than states can do independently. The plan pointed out that "programs that are rational when viewed state-by-state can be seen as redundant or ineffective from a regional viewpoint." According to the plan, benefits of regional cooperation in export trade include: "cost reductions and economies from consolidation of efforts, increased impact from a more massive presence of the states when operating in combination, increasingly knowledgeable state officers as a result of pooling of experience; greater and more rational global coverage at little extra cost; and an effective presence for Western interests in Washington and overseas."

The Pacific Northwest Legislative Leadership Forum, another Western regional innovation, is a fresh approach for border states to compete more effectively in the world market, especially in the Pacific Rim and the European Community. The forum was sponsored by the Washington Legislature and the Northwest Policy Center at the University of Washington Graduate School of Public Affairs to explore regional economic unity. In 1990, delegates to the forum agreed that unified regional actions are necessary because each state or province is too small to compete effectively in the changing market. They also agreed to appoint two delegates each to a 14-member group to coordinate activities.

The creation of the Center for the New West in 1989 also is indicative of the desire for closer regional economic cooperation. A nonprofit private organization, the center provides information on economic development for 19 Western states.

States are cooperating to improve social services. The Southern Governors' Association and the Southern Legislative Conference conducted the much publicized Southern Regional Project on Infant Mortality in an effort to improve infant health. By sharing information on state innovations, the groups seek to reduce the South's high infant mortality rate.

To improve child support collection, 10 Southern states are tracking delinquent parents through an interstate computerized information system. Because the system shares information from state employment offices, corrections systems and drivers' license agencies, it can track absent parents by name or a previous employer as well as Social Security number. The Electronic Parent Locator has found absent parents in three of every four attempts.

Regional efforts also have been launched to fight drug abuse. In 1988, the Southern Governors' Association created the Southern Regional Drug Prevention Network, the first of its kind, to better address state and regional drug problems. A steering committee of the Mid-Atlantic Governors' Drug and Alcohol Abuse conference drafted a compact to establish a regional approach to substance abuse. The primary goal of the committee is sharing information on new laws and education and training programs. In 1989, the Midwestern Governors' Conference followed suit by adopting the Midwestern Compact on Drug Abuse.

In addition, the environment is the focus of several regional efforts. The Council of State Governments' Eastern Regional Conference created the Northeast Recycling Council in 1988 to share information on ideas and provide for policy implementation. Composed of the state recycling directors from 10 Northeastern states, the council focuses on the development and stimulation of markets for recycled products. The council recently sponsored forums with the region's newspaper publishers and state purchasing officials to promote purchase of recycled papers for newsprint. . . .

An interstate agreement for hazardous waste management became effective in 1990 in the Southern region. Alabama, Kentucky, South Carolina and Tennessee agreed to use regional facilities to treat and dispose wastes generated by industry within their borders. Other Southern states, including Florida, Georgia, Mississippi and North Carolina, are expected to join the regional agreement. Eastern states are considering an interstate compact on radioactive waste. . . .

The Chesapeake Bay is being restored through a cooperative effort involving the District of Columbia, Maryland, Pennsylvania, Virginia and the U.S. Environmental Protection Agency. Following the success of the 1983 agreement, a more detailed agreement was signed in December 1987. The agreement has led to the return of rockfish and an upsurge in osprey and eagles, as well as cleaner Bay waters. The regional program is used as a model for protecting other bays and estuaries.

Regional cooperation in higher education has proved advantageous in the Southern, New England and Western regions. The Western Interstate Commission for Higher Education, the agency created by the Western Regional Education Compact, is regarded as a model for regional cooperation in strengthening higher education. The Council of State Governments' Midwestern Legislative Conference is exploring regional cooperation in higher education through a similar compact. . . .

Recently, administrators in several states have initiated multistate management programs to conduct state business more efficiently. One area that has attracted attention is purchasing. In 1989, an interstate agreement was reached among Colorado, Minnesota and Wisconsin to jointly purchase pharmaceutical products. The DELMARVA cooperative was formed in June 1989 by Delaware, Maryland and Virginia to purchase items such as pursuit vehicles, road salt, light fixtures and insecticide. States also have discussed purchase of heavy equipment on a multistate basis. The cooperative has approached other states, including North Carolina, South Carolina, Pennsylvania and West Virginia. Western states also have considered a similar multistate cooperative to purchase recycled paper. In 1990, the National Association of State Telecommunications Directors formed a Joint Procurement Committee to evaluate purchases of telecommunications equipment.

State treasurers in four Southern states have acted to improve financial management. In October 1990, treasurers of Arkansas, Louisiana, Mississippi and Tennessee held their first Quad State Treasurers' Conference to discuss improving cash and debt management

and investment policies in an attempt to establish regional cooperative efforts.

The South and West are known for regional arts efforts. The Southern Arts Federation, which consists of nine state art agencies, recently adopted "The Southern Arts Agenda" with specific goals for states. The arts organization focuses on the relationship between culture and economic development.

The Rural Public Transit Consortium provides technical support services to transit systems in nine Southern states. Since 1984, the consortium has coordinated services among social service transportation agencies and local public transit operators. No other region has such a multistate rural consortium in public transit.

Individual states are taking a look at how regional, national and global events affect them. The Washington Legislature in 1989 launched an initiative to inject long-range thinking into the legislative process. The Washington 2000 project calls for long-range goals and objectives before legislation is drafted.

The southern Growth Policies Board and The Council of State Governments' Western Legislative Conference are known for their regional trends analysis projects. The SGPB has conducted regional futures projects by creating futures commissions with the help of members of the committees on Southern Trends. Participants in the futures projects have included governors, legislators, private sector representatives and academics. The widely publicized strategic plan for economic development, "Halfway Home and a Long Way to Go," was adopted by the Commission on the Future of the South in November 1986. The document is seen as a blueprint for action for the Southern states.

In 1989, the Western Legislative Conference released its Westrends group's first report, "The Dynamic West: A Region in Transition." It identified 10 trends shaping the West as the 1980s drew to a close. Those trends defined ways in which the West is distinguishable from the rest of the nation. In particular, it showed that rapid change in demography, the economy and politics was a distinguishing regional characteristic. The Westrends study and report are worthy efforts that assist state policy-makers in recognizing major forces in the Western region and the ways in which these forces influence each other.

As a result of the Westrends project, the Idaho Legislature recently considered establishing a task force to study regional trends affecting the state.

Regional Mechanisms and Prospects

Multistate regional cooperation can be initiated and implemented by federal agencies and individual states through interstate compacts or agreements. State policy-makers can use existing mechanisms as well as new vehicles for regional cooperation. . . .

States gain several advantages when taking a regional approach as compared to working alone. First, a regional approach allows state officials to pool their expertise and experience. Second, a regional approach raises policy issues more effectively and, as a result, has a greater impact. Third, such an approach helps states better deal with crisis situations by sharing resources and facilities. Fourth, a regional approach can exert more influence and enhance state visibility in Washington and overseas. And, fifth, it is cost effective.

The cost argument, however, is most appealing. While it is difficult to document cost savings from regional programs, a few examples are available. In the case of interstate child support collection, the 10 Southern states found the computerized system saved more than it cost to operate. Purchasing officials participating in the multistate cooperatives have reported savings for their states.

The greatest savings may come from reduction or elimination of duplicate programs in individual states. An example is the Western Regional Education Compact. The Western Interstate Commission for Higher Education's professional student exchange program has saved states from spending large sums on duplicate educational programs, especially those in health related areas. Because of the interstate compact, the Western region needs only three schools of veterinary medicine, one of which trains veterinarians for 10 states. The 15-state region has only 16 medical schools and eight dental schools.

Regionalism is not a panacea, however. Multi-state regional mechanisms initiated by the federal government have raised legal, administrative and fiscal questions. Some questions relate to the authority, jurisdiction and accountability of regional mechanisms. Whether regional approaches should be based on a permanent or ad hoc basis also is an issue. Moreover, sources of interstate conflict must be dealt with to launch an effective regional approach. Interstate conflicts stem from policy differences, poor communication, competition for jobs and investment, and in-state politics. The success of regional approaches depends on policy and program initiatives by state policymakers who are determined to look beyond short-term interests of individual states in favor of cooperative solutions to area problems on a long-term basis. . . .

Just What Your State Wanted: Great New Gifts from Congress

by David Rapp

Year-end 1990 taught America's governors a double lesson in hardball fiscal politics. First, they had to confront the anti-tax resentment of the voters, and six of them lost their jobs—the largest number in 20 years. Then they learned that while they were focused on campaigning, Congress had quietly presented them with a new set of expensive responsibilities it was not about to help them pay for. Precluded by the federal deficit from launching any meaningful programs of their own, House and Senate committees found it easier in the closing days of last year's session to promote their legislative agenda by passing the buck to the states.

The most important congressional buck-passing dealt with Medicaid. A year-long campaign by 48 of the 50 governors had sought a halt, for at least two years, to requiring states to expand health care coverage for the poor. Such mandates previously imposed by Congress were expected to cost states $6 billion more in fiscal 1991 than in 1990, and $33 billion in extra expenses over five years, mainly to add pregnant women, infants and the elderly to Medicaid's rolls. State costs for Medicaid in 1991 may exceed $35.5 billion.

But rather than declare a moratorium on program mandates, congressional health care advocates saw an opportunity to tack on a few more costly requirements. Working in the dead of night, House and Senate negotiators on the massive deficit-reduction bill wrote in language broadening the current requirements for states to use Medicaid to provide health care coverage for the poor and elderly.

The key players in this midnight gambit—Democrats Henry A. Waxman of California in the House and Lloyd Bentsen of Texas in the Senate—had been sympathetic to states' complaints about mandates. Still, neither wanted to give up a pet program merely to ease the qualms of governors. Waxman had originally crafted his plan for the elderly in a way that would make the federal government foot the bill. But Bentsen, chairman of the tax-writing Finance Committee, balked. The two started talking compromise.

At that point, every major interest and faction involved in the issue began working double time to argue its case. Yet when members of Congress looked around the room to see who would scream the loudest about new

David Rapp is a staff writer for *Governing*. This article appeared in *Governing* 4:4 (January 1991): 53.

changes in the Medicaid law, the states weren't there to complain.

Indeed, it turns out that state lobbyists had all but ignored this fight, having focused their time and energies down the hall on another life-and-death issue for governors: deductibility of state and local taxes in calculating personal income. The idea of limiting the deduction for state taxes had been mentioned as a relatively "painless" revenue-raising option to help President Bush and Congress break their tax-increase impasse. Governors saw it as the horror story of the year-end reconciliation showdown.

Their efforts kept the tax deduction intact. But in the meantime, Bentsen and Waxman cut a separate deal on Medicaid. Along with expanded benefits for low-income elderly, women and children, and the mentally retarded, it will also require states, one year at a time, to provide Medicaid coverage to children up to age 19 in families with incomes below the poverty line. Currently, only children up to age 7 must be covered. This will cost $1 billion-plus over the next five years.

It was an expensive lesson for the governors as well as their Washington lobbyists. Budgetary constraints may make new large-scale social programs impossible for Congress to enact, but that does not mean members are about to give up their personal agendas, especially if there is a handy escape valve—the states—to absorb the fiscal burden.

What kinds of burdens will Congress be looking to impose in the coming years of austerity? Big ones, like the expanded Medicaid benefits. But smaller ones, too. Often these little impositions aren't described or even intended as burdens; they may be meant to help solve genuine problems. But they end up costing the states lots of money nevertheless.

In the last few days of the 1990 session, while the Senate and House were tinkering with Medicaid, they were also dealing with water pollution. They approved a new law ordering coastal states to test beach water regularly. Congress was willing to put some money into this; it authorized $3 million in grants to cover the cost. The only problem is the size of the grant. Representative Porter J. Goss of Florida complained that it would take more than $2 million a year to test the 8,500-mile Florida shoreline alone. That leaves less than $1 million for more than 20 other coastal states.

Congress isn't about to appropriate the money that the program will actually cost, but it isn't going to drop the testing requirement either. In the committee rooms of Capitol Hill, that is known as federalism.

VIII. STATE COURTS

The third branch of state government, the judiciary, probably is the one part of state government with which most citizens would prefer not to have any dealings. State courts handle the crimes reported in the news—drunk driving, child abuse, robbery, murder, and rape. Personal disputes, divorce cases, and other civil matters also are tried in state courts.

Despite the importance of the judiciary in state politics, it is perhaps the least visible branch. One reason is because citizens want it that way; they want the courts to be above the hurly-burly of politics. The legislature may conduct its business in a circuslike atmosphere and the governor may crisscross the state to keep an impossible schedule of appointments, but the courts must be a model of decorum, a place where the rational presentation of facts and arguments leads to truth and justice.

The Court System

The several levels of state courts each have different responsibilities. At the lowest level are trial courts, where cases are argued and juries may be called to weigh the facts presented. Intermediate appellate courts, the next level in the state judicial system, are where the decisions of the trial courts and other lower courts can be appealed. (Thirty-five states have intermediate courts.) Finally, each state has a court of last resort, usually called the Supreme Court, but in Maine it is called the Supreme Judicial Court; in West Virginia, the Supreme Court of Last Resort; and in New York, the Court of Appeals. Here, the final appeals to lower court decisions are made unless a federal question is involved, which then means that appeal to the federal appellate courts is possible.

State court judges rule on a variety of concerns. Part of their workload is administrative (for example, the probating of wills).

Another part involves conflict resolution (for example, deciding which party is correct in contested divorce settlements and property disputes). And still another area of responsibility includes the criminal prosecution and appeals process.

In a broader sense, state court judges are policy makers. It is often in court decisions, rather than in legislation or constitutional amendments, that state policies are modified or set aside. Courts are reactive institutions of government, and their decisions are limited by the nature and timing of the cases brought before them. Judges establish new norms of acceptable behavior and revise existing norms to match changing circumstances. Their interpretations of the law may or may not have the backing of the public or of the governor or state legislature. Nonetheless, what they say goes—that is, of course, unless it is overturned by another court decision or by another decision-making body. In some instances, court decisions simply are ignored because the judiciary has no bureaucracy of its own to enforce decisions.

The norm of separating partisan politics from the judiciary is part of our national and state political cultures. But judges must be selected in some manner; and inevitably, politics become a factor.

Judicial Selection

The methods used to select judges vary from state to state. Sometimes judges are appointed by the governor and confirmed by the state senate. In Connecticut, the legislature appoints judges from nominations submitted by the governor. In Texas, judges are elected as Democrats or Republicans. Other states—Montana, for example—elect judges on a non-partisan basis.

Some states have adopted a variation of

the "Missouri Plan" to remove politics from the selection process as much as possible. In this process, a nonpartisan group such as the state or district bar association screens the many candidates and recommends the top contenders to the governor, who then makes the final decision. The argument is that merit will be the foremost criterion in the screening and nomination process.

The Missouri Plan also provides that when their terms expire, judges can "run again" on their record. The voters are asked: Should Judge X be retained in office? If the voters say yes, the judge serves another term. If the voters say no, the selection process starts anew. In this way, the judiciary is accountable to the citizens of the state.

The world of partisan elective judicial politics also is in considerable ferment. Political observers were startled in 1986 when three states—California, North Carolina, and Ohio—all had well-publicized, negative, and very expensive partisan races for their state's chief justiceship. California voters rejected liberal Democratic chief justice Rose Bird, appointed to that post by former Democratic governor Jerry Brown. The divisive campaign was centered around Bird's consistent objection to capital punishment. In North Carolina, the longstanding tradition whereby the governor appoints the longest-serving Supreme Court justice to the post of chief justice when that office is vacated was violated by Republican governor Jim Martin. Martin refused to appoint ranking Democratic supreme court justice Jim Exum and instead elevated his own newly-appointed Republican supreme court justice Rhoda Billings. This led to a series of political maneuvers, resulting in Exum's resignation and a subsequent successful challenge of Billings in the 1986 general election. In Ohio, Chief Justice Frank Celebrezze was defeated in a heated campaign after serving in a manner that provided for "rancor-

ous controversy and political infighting of a sort rare for state high courts." [1]

In early 1987, a U.S. district court judge in Jackson, Mississippi, ruled that Section 2 of the Voting Rights Act of 1965 applies to judges elected at the state level. At issue was the question of whether electing judges from at-large, multimember districts dilutes minority voting strength. The impact of the decision probably will mean that state judges will be elected from single-member districts, thereby offering the possibility of greater minority representation in the state judiciaries. [2]

In December 1989, a three-judge federal appeals court upheld the concept that the Voting Rights Act applies to judicial election districts. [3] So, in those states covered by the provisions of the Voting Rights Act, any changes in judicial district lines or the addition of judges must be precleared with the U.S. Department of Justice before being implemented. [4] In April 1990, the Department of Justice threw out Georgia's system of electing judges because it was discriminatory against blacks. The problem with the system was the election of judges in broad judicial circuits by a majority vote, rather than by a plurality vote. This has the same effect as at-large elections often do: diluting the strength of minority groups. [5]

In 1988, political fights swirled around the Texas Supreme Court as nine justices came up for election. This was the first time since Reconstruction that a majority of the court faced the voters at one time. The political contest had several elements: [6]

● In 1987, two justices were criticized separately by the Texas Commission on Judicial Conduct for improper ties to lawyers;

● The state supreme court was criticized by Texaco and the national press for refusing to hear the appeal of the $10.53 billion judgment by a state court trial judge against Texaco in favor of Pennzoil;

• Some of the leading contributors of political funds to the members of the current court turned out to be Pennzoil lawyers, although Texaco lawyers also gave money to some candidates (though they were outbid $315,000 to $72,700);[7]

• The resignation of Chief Justice John Hill in January 1988 to campaign for an appointed system of judgeships was quickly followed by the resignation of senior justice Robert Campbell to campaign for continuing the electoral system for selecting judges;

• Republican governor William P. Clements, Jr., appointed Texas's first Republican supreme court chief justice of the twentieth century and two well-known Democrats, all of whom ran for election to the court as Republicans.

The 1988 Texas Supreme Court campaigns, which cost an estimated $10 million, had "the nastiest, most negative campaigning I have ever seen," one Texas legislator told North Carolina's Judicial Selection Study Commission. "If you are before a judge in Texas now, you've got to be worried if you are a Democrat and he is a Republican."[8]

Is justice for sale as some critics suggest? Giving money to political campaigns, even judicial campaigns, is legal and "that's the problem," according to a Texaco spokeswoman.[9] One Houston lawyer suggested that "it looks just as bad for a lawyer to give a lot of money to a judge as for a judge to take a lot of money from a lawyer."[10] This is all cannon fodder for those wanting to remove the judicial selection process from electoral politics.

Tides of Judicial Policy Making

A current issue in the states concerns who should take the lead in the judicial system— the federal judiciary interpreting the U.S. Constitution, or the state judiciaries interpreting the individual state constitutions. For decades, the loud cry of "states' rights" masked inaction by state courts on segregation, malapportionment, and other unconstitutional practices.

During the 1950s and 1960s, under a broad interpretation of the Constitution (especially the Fifth and Fourteenth Amendments), the U.S. Supreme Court moved to upset the states' intransigence and, in some cases, illegal activities. Led by Chief Justice Earl Warren (the governor of California from 1943 to 1953), the U.S. Supreme Court overturned state laws upholding segregation, forced state legislatures to apportion themselves on a one-man, one-vote basis following each census, expanded voting rights, legalized abortion, and broadened the rights of the accused in the state criminal justice system. The Warren Court set minimal standards for the states to follow in these areas and often reversed state court decisions that narrowly construed the rights of individuals.

In recent years, the U.S. Supreme Court has become more conservative in its decisions. It has even backed away from some of the minimal standards it set earlier. Several state courts have decided not only to uphold these minimal standards but, in a new form of judicial activism at the state level, to exceed them. U.S. Supreme Court justice William J. Brennan, Jr., describes this trend as "probably the most important development in constitutional jurisprudence today."[11] Ronald Collins, an expert on state constitutional law, estimated that between 1970 and the mid-1980s state high courts issued approximately 400 decisions based on the higher standards of the state constitutions as opposed to the minimum standards established by the U.S. Supreme Court in interpreting the U.S. Constitution.[12] As New Jersey Supreme Court justice Stewart G. Pollock suggests, "Horizontal federalism, in which states look to each other for guidance, may be the hallmark of the rest of the century."[13]

175

California Supreme Court justice Stanley Mosk argues that liberals and conservatives alike can support this trend—liberals because it is a continuing expansion of individual rights begun under the Warren Court, and conservatives because such decisions are being made in the state capitals rather than in Washington, D.C.[14] North Carolina Supreme Court justice Harry Martin feels that this trend also gives "the people of the individual states greater protection of their individual rights because of the way people live in the different states." He argues that the state constitutions were designed to respond to the needs of each state, while the U.S. Constitution must respond to the needs of all fifty states. He cites as examples Florida's protection of citizens from unreasonable searches and seizures on boats, Alaska's similar protection of passengers on airplanes, and the right of North Carolina's citizens to a system of inexpensive higher education—all critical parts of each state's economy.[15]

Not all legal scholars and participants agree that this activism will have positive results. Former Oregon attorney general David Frohnmayer argues that "superimposing new and different state doctrinal rules on top of federal law is an open invitation to confusion and error on the enforcement front." He says the movement also means a greater responsibility will now be placed on the state legislators who draft state constitutional provisions and pass the statutes that can be questioned under the constitutional provisions.[16]

Why does such activism develop in a state's supreme court? One study of six state supreme courts from 1930 to 1980 found that dramatic shifts by state high courts from a relatively passive role to an active role take place in a relatively short period of time and are due mainly to a change in the composition of the court. The appointment of a "maverick" judge to a state's supreme court begins a process in which that judge dissents from the previous consensual and passive court decisions, soon swaying some supporters to the minority position. With additional appointments of more activist-oriented jurists, the court changes direction. Of import is the fact that once a transition to activism occurred, none of these courts moved back in the direction of nonactivism, at least not during the period studied.[17]

However, there still may be a question as to whether federal or state court decisions will affect states more. In recent years the U.S. Supreme Court has been making significant decisions affecting state politics. In *Davis v. Bandemer* (1986), the Court changed the ground rules of reapportionment by allowing a losing political party in a redistricting plan standing in a court suit to challenge the plan. In *Tashjian v. Republican Party of Connecticut* (1986), the Court threw out a state law mandating a closed party primary, thereby allowing independents to participate in the party nomination process. In *Johnson v. Transportation Agency, Santa Clara County, Calif.* (1987), the Court upheld local government affirmative action plans and decisions that discriminate in favor of women and minorities. In *Rutan et al. v. Republican Party of Illinois* (1990), the Court narrowly ruled against the time-honored patronage system of hiring political supporters to work in a gubernatorial administration.

Open Courts

Courtroom dramas such as "Perry Mason," "L.A. Law," and "The People's Court" portray how Hollywood feels justice is carried out. But these shows are misleading since most "real" justice proceeds at a very slow pace and is based on the rule of law and facts rather than on emotion. In fact, one lawyer argues that "trials are as exciting as watching paint dry." After the 1981 U.S. Supreme Court decision *Chandler v. Florida* rejected the argument that a defendant's right to a fair trial was violated by allowing cameras and microphones in a state courtroom, states have moved rapidly to allow such coverage by the media.[18] As of mid-October 1987, forty-four states allowed either still-picture cameras, microphones, or television cameras into their courts.[19] Interestingly, federal courts still ban these electronic devices.[20]

What is the impact of having cameras in the courtroom during trials? Some feared they would lead to behavior changes by participants in trials, such as grandstanding by lawyers. Not so, according to one Kentucky judge who feels the cameras cause lawyers and witnesses "to be a little bit more respectful because they know the tape will show the appellate court their tone of voice and body language, not just sterile written words." Other observers worried the cameras might be intimidating to lawyers or witnesses. There have been no such complaints in the Kentucky courts.[21]

Can videotapes replace the written record? In one Kentucky case, the tape playback refuted an appeal to a guilty plea entered when the defendant was supposedly insane. The tape showed the defendant to be "cogent and responsible." But there are some problems: it is often more difficult to find particular points or references on a tape than in a written transcript for a jury or appellate court seeking clarification.[22] Importantly, though, cameras in the courtroom increase the public's understanding of our states' judicial systems. According to the Kentucky judge, it "brings a whole new dimension to the idea of a public trial." [23]

Part VIII explores different aspects of the state judicial branch. Amy Young of *Common Cause Magazine* explores judicial politics in the states. Elder Witt and Rob Gurwitt of Congressional Quarterly document two of the most pressing issues that must be confronted

by the state judiciary in the 1990s: a staggering caseload and the gender bias that still pervades the courts. An article from *State Policy Reports* discusses the issues involved in a series of school finance cases that are being litigated across the states, and Jean Dykstra of the *New Jersey Reporter* shows how the courts in three states—Kentucky, New Jersey, and Texas—are coping with this litigation over school financing. Finally, Mark Siebert of *Illinois Issues* discusses one of the most difficult of all judicial decisions—whether to impose the sentence of capital punishment.

Notes

1. Katherine A. Hinckley, "Four Years of Strife Conclude with Ohio Chief Justice's Defeat," *Comparative State Politics Newsletter* 8:2 (April 1987): 13. Reprinted in Thad L. Beyle, ed., *State Government: CQ's Guide to Current Issues and Activities, 1988-89* (Washington, D.C.: Congressional Quarterly, 1988), 174-181.
2. "Mississippi Ruling Could Aid N.C. Suit on Judgeship Elections," [Raleigh] *News and Observer*, April 5, 1987, 32A.
3. The Voting Rights Act of 1965, extended in 1970 and 1975, banned redistricting plans that diluted the voting strength of black and other minority communities. The law suspended literacy tests and provided for the appointment of federal supervisors of voter registration in all states and counties where literacy tests (or similar qualifying devices) were in effect as of November 1, 1964, and where less than 50 percent of the voting age residents had registered to vote or voted in the 1964 presidential election. State or county governments brought under the coverage of the law due to low voter registration or participation were required to obtain federal approval of any new voting laws, standards, practices, or procedures before implementing them. The act placed federal registration machinery in six Southern states (Alabama, Georgia, Louisiana, Mississippi, South Carolina, and Virginia), Alaska, twenty-eight counties in North Carolina, three counties in

Arizona, and one in Idaho.

4. "Federal Court Applies VRA to State Judicial Districts," *Intergovernmental Perspective* 16:1 (Winter 1990): 20.

5. Peter Applebome, "U.S. Declares Georgia Judge Selection Illegal," New York Times News Service, in [Raleigh] *News and Observer*, April 27, 1990, 3A.

6. Peter Applebome, "Texan Fight over Judges Illustrates Politics' Growing Role in Judiciary," New York Times News Service, in [Raleigh] *News and Observer*, January 24, 1988, 14A.

7. Sheila Kaplan, "Justice for Sale," *Common Cause Magazine* (May/June 1987): 29-32.

8. Jane Ruffin, "Texan Warns N.C. Commission to End System of Electing Judges," [Raleigh] *News and Observer*, November 12, 1988, 3C.

9. Quoted in Kaplan, "Justice for Sale," 29.

10. Applebome, "Texan Fight over Judges," 14A.

11. Quoted in Robert Pear, "State Courts Move Beyond U.S. Bench in Rights Rulings," *New York Times*, May 4, 1986, 1.

12. Cited in Lanny Proffer, "State Courts and Civil Liberties," *State Legislatures* 13:9 (September 1987): 29.

13. Quoted in Pear, "State Courts," 16.

14. Stanley Mosk, "State Constitutionalism: Both Liberal and Conservative," *Texas Law Journal* 63:6/7 (March-April 1985): 1081.

15. Quoted in Katherine White, "North Carolina's Constitution Comes of Age," *North Carolina Insight* 10:2/3 (March 1988): 118-119.

16. Quoted in Proffer, "State Courts and Civil Liberties," 28.

17. John Patrick Hagan, "Patterns of Activism on State Supreme Courts," *Publius* 18:1 (Winter 1988): 97-115.

18. *Chandler v. Florida*, 449 U.S. 560, 101 S. Ct. 1802 (1981). John Bacon, "Across State Lines: Mich. Joins Pack, Allows Cameras in Courtrooms," *USA Today*, October 15, 1987, 8A.

19. Radio-Television News Directors Association, cited in Bacon, 8A.

20. Ibid.

21. Eileen Shanahan, "The Cameras Are Rolling in Kentucky Courts," *Governing* 2:1 (October 1988): 32-35.

22. Ibid.

23. Quoted in Shanahan.

Judicial Politics in the States

by Amy E. Young

Common Cause/Pennsylvania has been fighting for 12 years to reform the state judiciary, which one lawyer has described as "rife with decay, intellectual dishonesty and corruption." In June [1990] it scored a major victory with the unanimous passage of a reform bill that strengthens the judicial conduct review process. It will also make investigations public for the first time.

CC/Pennsylvania Executive Director Barry Kaufman says that next step in the two-pronged reform effort is to replace the state's partisan election system with a merit selection process. The state's current system, says CC/Pennsylvania State Chair Morris Slater, "is not selection by an informed electorate." According to a Pennsylvania Bar Association poll, when entering a voting booth to elect judges, more than 90 percent of the voters aren't familiar with the candidates' names or qualifications, and don't understand the different types of judges.

Nearly 80 percent of the nation's 24,000 state-level judges obtain or retain their position through an election. While proponents say the election process makes judges more accountable, critics charge that its political nature compromises the judiciary's independence.

Most states have no limits on campaign contributions, and special interests—some with cases pending before a court—are major donors. Two candidates for Ohio Supreme Court chief justice spent $2.7 million in their 1986 race. In 1988 candidates for the same position in Texas spent more than $3 million.

Pennsylvania Supreme Court candidate Ralph Cappy collected $1.4 million for his successful bid in 1989. More than $750,000 came from attorneys and related sources, according to a CC/Pennsylvania study. The study also showed that Supreme Court Justice Rolf Larsen raised more than $400,000 for his 1987 retention election, which took the form of an unopposed yes or no ballot question. More than 70 percent of Larsen's campaign contributions came from the legal profession.

"Judicial elections in Pennsylvania are dangerously dominated by special interests," says Kaufman, "especially the trial lawyers and PACs whose interests may later appear before the court." In addition, the political nature of the electoral system, says Marilyn Brill, president of the League of Women

Amy E. Young is an editorial assistant for *Common Cause Magazine*. This article is reprinted with permission from *Common Cause Magazine* 16:4 (July/August 1990): 41. © 1990 by *Common Cause Magazine*, Washington, D.C.

STATE COURTS

Washington Primary: . . .

With no statewide partisan or ballot propositions requiring voter decisions, the 1990 Washington primary drew the usual very small turnout of about 20 percent. But the outcomes of two nonpartisan state Supreme Court races resulted in surprises. State law provides that in Supreme Court, state court of appeals and superior court races any candidate receiving more than 50 percent of the primary vote will have his or her name appear alone on the general election ballot. The rationale for the law is that this relieves most incumbents from having to campaign during October when the Supreme Court convenes and other courts are crowded after summer recesses. In most cases the existing law has meant that a better-known incumbent will defeat a lesser-known challenger and then quit campaigning after the primary.

The legal establishment and press were shocked when Chief Justice Keith Callow, who had 20 years experience on the bench, was defeated by a little-known 39-year-old attorney, Charles Johnson, who polled over 52 percent. Johnson had no experience as a judge except for brief pro term sittings. He did not show up for evaluation by the bar, spent money only for filing, did virtually no campaigning and had not expected to win. Callow, first elected to the court in 1984, also did little campaigning but received bar and press endorsements and, from the beginning, was expected to be the easy victor.

Neither Callow nor Johnson could explain the outcome. A combination of factors undoubtedly helped Johnson. There is no statewide voters pamphlet in the primary. Such a pamphlet would have shown Callow's extensive record and Johnson's inexperience. The race was very low profile and Johnson is a much more familiar name than Callow. After the campaign Callow quipped that Johnson was a "very comfortable" name and that "everyone knows a Chuck Johnson some place or another." There was also some evidence of an anti-establishment vote in the general primary. Although practically every incumbent state legislator was renominated, a considerable number of challengers did better than usual. [In] June [1990], Callow participated in a unanimous decision upholding a city ordinance which placed restrictions on pit bulls and other breeds deemed dangerous. Kennel clubs in their newsletters and otherwise conducted a quiet campaign to defeat Callow and claimed, after the election, that they were a major factor in

Voters of Pennsylvania, "May be discouraging some of the most capable members of the bar from serving on the bench."

A CC/Pennsylvania-led coalition supports the creation of a Judicial Selection Commission made up of lay, legal and judicial members who would interview and recommend judicial candidates for gubernatorial appointment. Each appointment would be subject to Senate confirmation. Thirty-two states plus the District of Columbia have enacted some form of the merit plan to select some or

all of their judges.

The successful CC/Pennsylvania-backed judicial discipline bill meanwhile separates the investigative and adjudicatory powers of the state's Judicial Inquiry and Review Board (JIRB), which monitors the conduct of the state's judges and recommends action to the Supreme Court. The bill also makes an investigation public once charges have been filed; previously, JIRB proceedings were confidential. When board Chairman Edmund Spaeth Jr. resigned in March [1990], he cited the

180

... Judicial Politics

his ouster. Callow said he was unaware of the dog owners' opposition. Officials in the organization are hoping to work with their members in other states to mobilize into an effective single-issue force.

An interesting irony is that the legislature has for some time sought to place all contested judicial contests on the general election ballot. Supreme Court justices successfully lobbied against the proposals in the 1980s. It is reported that current justices are now having second thoughts. Some legislators are also calling for a review of how justices are selected and for election in November irrespective of the primary vote.

In the other race John Spellman, who served as governor from 1981-85, sought to win the supreme court position from Richard Guy who was appointed by Governor [Booth] Gardner to the court in 1989. Guy as a short term incumbent was essentially unknown and many believed that recognition of the Spellmans name would likely elect the former governor. This position attracted attention of the press from the Callow-Johnson contest and drew 30,000 more voters. Spellman maintained that his 18 years as a local and state executive gave him a greater breadth of knowledge and experience than Guy whose public life had been in the courts. Guy's billboards featured "a judge—not a politician" and claimed he better understood the law and judicial system.

Bar associations rated Spellman as "adequate" and gave a "well-qualified" endorsement to Guy. Editorially the press was bothered by the unprecedented fact of a former chief executive seeking a high judicial position with no experience on the bench. Some partisanship also marked its way into the campaign because Spellman was a Republican and Guy was appointed by the popular Democratic governor. Voters opted for Guy by a vote of 283,000 to 230,000. . . .

Source: Hugh Bone, "Washington Primary: Judicial Politics," *Comparative State Politics* 11:6 (December 1990): 45-47. Reprinted with permission. Hugh Bone is professor emeritus of political science at the University of Washington at Seattle.

board's lack of independence from the Supreme Court, the secrecy of its proceedings and the unfairness of the combined investigative-adjudicative function.

The reform push got a boost from a series of events that have rocked the state judiciary and public confidence in the judicial system. In 1983, after investigating allegations that Supreme Court Justice Rolf Larsen had engaged in political activities and racial slurs, the nine-member JIRB found Larsen not guilty of wrongdoing and voted to seal the record.

Then-JIRB member Robert Surrick tried to have the record made public but the Supreme Court—with Larsen voting—refused. (Larsen said he voted without knowing the case involved him.) Larsen then brought disciplinary proceedings against Surrick for allegedly violating the JIRB's confidentiality provisions; the charges weren't dismissed until 1989. Larsen also filed a libel and invasion of privacy suit against Surrick, the *Philadelphia Inquirer* and the *Pittsburgh Post-Gazette*. . . .

In May [1989] the *Philadelphia Daily*

News reported that a **JIRB** document indicated the board would recommend that the state Supreme Court suspend Larsen for two months for alleged improper contact with a lower-court judge concerning an estate case. Shortly after the newspaper report, Larsen sought and was granted by the Supreme Court a stay of any action against him pending a court ruling on his claim that four **JIRB** members contributed to the decision in violation of the state constitution. . . .

In 1987 it was discovered that nine Philadelphia judges had accepted cash from members of the Roofers Union. Although gifts to judges are not illegal in Pennsylvania, the **JIRB** recommended the judges' dismissal, saying the "conduct has nullified one of the most basic qualifications for the job. . . ." In 1988 three of the judges were convicted of extortion, racketeering or conspiracy.

Problems in State Courts

The following pieces, "State Courts Stagger Under Load" by Elder Witt and "Anti-Women Bias Found in Courts" by Rob Gurwitt, first appeared in different issues of *Governing* magazine. They highlight two of the most pressing issues confronting state courts in the 1990s.

State Courts Stagger Under Load

The truth is out. After years of talk about the mushrooming workload of the courts, it's now quite clear that state, not federal, courts are bearing the brunt of that load.

In 1988, 98 million new cases were filed in state trial and appellate courts, reports the National Center for State Courts. The comparable numbers for federal courts? A mere 327,000. And the number of state cases is growing faster: 4.3 percent in 1989, compared with 2.5 percent at the federal level.

"State courts are under unprecedented pressure, both trial and appellate courts," says David Rottman, director of the Court Statistics Project that produced the report.

There's no relief in sight. The current campaigns against drugs and drunk driving generate a significant portion of the 68 million new cases that involved infractions of traffic or other local ordinances, 12 million new criminal cases and 1.4 million new juvenile cases (16.9 million new civil cases were also filed in 1988). Indeed, at the current rate of increase, there will be twice as many criminal cases flooding into state courts by the year 2000.

What's to be done? More judges, yes, but that's just a small part of the answer, says Rottman. "We need to use judges more efficiently," he says. Change in the way courts handle cases is already well under way, including use of alternative dispute resolution, channeling particular categories of cases, like environmental ones, to special dockets and even an "emergency room system" of expediting more pressing cases.

"Caseload management is our number one priority," says Mary McQueen, Washington state court administrator. "At some point you can't cram more cases into the same number of hours a day. Eventually you have to change from a biplane to a jet engine."

Elder Witt and Rob Gurwitt are staff writers for *Governing*. Elder Witt, "State Courts Stagger Under Load," *Governing* 3:12 (September 1990): 14-15; Rob Gurwitt, "Anti-Woman Bias Found in Courts" *Governing* 3:10 (July 1990): 10.

McQueen advocates giving judges additional staff and the power to use them efficiently. "How many countywide elected officials have no secretary?" she asks. "We have some courts with 40 judges sharing five secretaries!"

Anti-Women Bias Found in Courts

California has become the latest state to study discrimination against women in the judicial system and uncover major problems. The ills it found range from demeaning treatment of female lawyers and witnesses to inadequate judicial response to the special problems of women whose cases come through the system.

The California study was done by the Judicial Council's Advisory Committee on Gender Bias in the Courts, whose members were appointed by former Chief Justice Rose Bird and by current Chief Justice Malcolm Lucas.

It found "pervasive" gender bias in the courtroom, including hostile behavior by judges toward female lawyers and witnesses, a focus on the appearance of female court participants, unequal extension of professional courtesies to female lawyers, and a failure by judges to intervene when lawyers or court employees display bias. The committee also found that child support awards tend to be too low, judges rate a family law assignment as their lowest preference, prisons do not meet the needs of institutionalized women, and "when domestic violence victims seek protection from the court, they are often further victimized by the process." Most of the 12 other states that have issued gender bias reports—Florida, Maryland, Massachusetts, Michigan, Minnesota, Nevada, New Hampshire, New Jersey, New York, Rhode Island, Utah and Washington—have reported similar findings.

Only in New Jersey, however, has any real study of the impact of the report been made. Now "there is a widespread understanding that gender bias is a problem judges need to take seriously," says Lynn Hecht Schafran, an attorney who directs a gender bias project sponsored jointly by the NOW Legal Defense and Education Fund and the National Association of Women Judges.

Norma Wikler, a sociologist at the University of California at Santa Cruz who was Schafran's colleague on the New Jersey study and who advised the California panel, says that the changes in court environment in New Jersey had not been accompanied by steps the report had recommended. As a result of Schafran's and Wikler's study, New Jersey Chief Justice Robert Wilentz has created a standing committee of judges and bar members that will oversee implementation of the initial report's recommendations.

Most other states have implementation committees that have had varying success at pushing the courts to initiate new studies or procedural changes. Only California has a formal mechanism to see that its report's suggestions are carried out. Once the Judicial Council approves recommendations, they become official court policy, and the council's standing committees are automatically charged with overseeing implementation.

School Finance Cases

School finance cases are active in at least the following states: Alabama, Alaska, Idaho, Illinois, Indiana, Louisiana, Massachusetts, Minnesota, Missouri, Nebraska, New Jersey, North Dakota, Ohio, Oklahoma, Oregon, Tennessee, and Texas. There are probably others.

To prevail in these cases, plaintiffs must fulfill three basic conditions: (1) bringing the litigation through the trial stage and any appeals, (2) convincing the courts that the state constitution requires the state to provide roughly equalized spending in individual school districts, and (3) getting the courts to take action sufficient to require the legislature to act. Not all these conditions will be fulfilled in every state where litigation is a topic.

The decision to undertake litigation on school finance carries some hazards for the litigants. The action is costly to the districts involved. It will often incur the wrath of some of the other school districts and their teachers, as one of the potential results is to reduce state aid that would otherwise be available to them. In the process, it may destroy a united front in dealing with the legislature on school aid allocation issues—carrying both the risk of lower school funding in total and the risk that the funding made available won't be favorable

to the districts in court. The existence of litigation, particularly at the appellate stage, can also provide a rationale for relatively low school aid allocations as the legislature waits for the court's guidelines before infusing substantial new money into the school aid formula. For all these reasons, in some states it appears that districts are in a hurry to establish that litigation is being undertaken, but in no hurry to press for court decisions.

Getting a state court to decide that state constitutions require substantially equal per pupil spending, or equal spending with equal local tax effort, isn't easy either. The U.S. Supreme Court has decided the U.S. Constitution has no such requirement and about half the cases have resulted in comparable state court decisions. In the typical case, plaintiffs are trying to convince a state court that constitutional language to the effect that the state shall ensure that there be a system of free public education carries an equalization mandate. In Alabama's case, the problem is even more difficult as the language regarding the state's obligation to provide public education was eliminated from the state constitution at a

Reprinted with permission from *State Policy Reports* 9:1 (January 1991): 14-16.

time when the state was battling desegregation. It has never been reinstated.

Even if a state court system decides a school finance system is inequitable, quick remedies don't necessarily follow. In the Texas case, legislators were convinced (or acted as though they were convinced) that the courts would enjoin the distribution of aid under the old formula, thereby closing many of the state's schools. Some Texas legislators appear to have believed that the court would write its own school aid formula and find a way to require that funds be disbursed pursuant to it. But in West Virginia, it has been clear that the courts weren't about to attempt either of these remedial actions. The possibility for inaction on remedies are substantial. It typically takes at least a year to litigate a school finance case to final conclusion. During that year, the formula would likely be changed in the normal course of legislative action, creating a potential for a new decision on the merits and a new set of appeals.

. . . As the courts have become more involved in school finance, the emphasis has shifted from relatively simple views of equalization to more complex arguments over such subjects as measures of need and of local fiscal capacity.

Local fiscal capacity is easily measured by the property tax base per pupil. But some districts, such as high income residential suburbs, may have more discretionary taxpayer income than districts with somewhat higher per pupil property tax bases—or at least so it can be argued. Another problem arises when two districts have identical property value per pupil, but one shares its tax base with a high tax jurisdiction such as a central city while the other doesn't.

There is endless room for argument over how exactly "need" for education spending should be measured, once the concept that all pupils have identical needs for spending is abandoned. One of the major changes in New Jersey [in 1991] involved definitions of students requiring compensatory education. The new program defines "at risk" students by qualification for free school feeding programs, basically an income test that eliminates most suburban children. The old test was related to school performance, so it put considerable quantities of money into the suburban districts.

A New Path for School Funding

by Jean Dykstra

The Odyssey of Abbott v. Burke

The New Jersey Supreme Court's decision June 5 [1990] striking down the state's school-financing system not only concluded almost 10 years of *Abbott v. Burke* litigation, but nearly 20 years of school-finance litigation in New Jersey.

Marilyn Morheuser, executive director of the Education Law Center in Newark, deemed the decision "a great victory for school children." But the victory came only after a long journey through the state's legal system.

In 1981, the Education Law Center filed a complaint in state Superior Court on behalf of 20 children attending public schools in Camden, East Orange, Irvington, and Jersey City. (Raymond Abbott, whose name led the suit alphabetically, was 12 when it was filed. A high school dropout, Abbott was recently released from the Suffolk County Jail in New York, only to land in the Camden County jail for violating probation.) The plaintiffs argued that these 20 students, and other children living in poor, urban areas of the state, were being victimized by the state's inequitable system of public school finance, known as the "Thorough and Efficient Act."

The suit argued that the financing system, because of its reliance on local property taxes, resulted in educational spending disparities between property-rich, suburban school districts and property-poor, urban ones. These inequities, argued Morheuser, violated both the "Thorough and Efficient" and Equal Protection clauses of the state Constitution, as well as the Law Against Discrimination.

Superior Court Judge Virginia Long dismissed the case in 1983, on the grounds that the plaintiffs had failed to exhaust their administrative remedies. The Appellate Court reversed this decision in 1984, and on appeal, the state Supreme Court remanded the case to the Office of Administrative Law, in 1985, " . . . to promote development of a complete and informed record . . ."

In 1988, Administrative Law Judge Steven L. Lefelt handed down his often-cited 607-page decision. As an administrative law judge, Lefelt could not declare the state's educational system unconstitutional, but could only make a recommendation to the state's education commissioner, Saul Cooperman. Lefelt's ruling

Jean Dykstra is a former editor of *New Jersey Reporter*. This article is reprinted by permission of the Center for Analysis of Public Issues, © 1990, from *New Jersey Reporter* 20:1 (June-July 1990): 10-11, 13, 26-27.

found, however, that Chapter 212, "as it is being applied, can be found by a court to violate the New Jersey Constitution."

Lefelt further found that expenditure disparities were an inherent risk in the guaranteed tax-base formula, the basis of the 1975 law, and recommended a "high foundation" formula, which would direct every school district to spend a set amount for education—based on a foundation level which the state determines is sufficient to provide a thorough and efficient education. The state would make up the difference between what the poorer districts could raise and the foundation level.

Commissioner Cooperman rejected Lefelt's recommendations, arguing that educational disparities were district-specific, and that the "T&E" clause does not require absolute sameness in financing or programming. Furthermore, he rejected the finding that there was a strong relationship between educational expenditures and the quality of education.

After the state Board of Education ratified Cooperman's decision, it was appealed by the plaintiffs. The Supreme Court certified the appeal, and heard the case in September 1989.

In the Supreme Court's decision, Chief Justice Robert Wilentz found, as Lefelt had recommended, that the current system of school financing is unconstitutional. The ruling had a relatively narrow focus, however, finding that the plaintiffs had proven the system unconstitutional only as applied to 28 poor, urban districts. The court ruled that it could not find the system unconstitutional as it applied to any other districts.

The court, in effect, linked the state's poorest districts to its wealthiest. It directed that the 1975 law, at the very least, must be amended to "assure funding of education in poorer urban districts at the level of property-rich suburban districts."

The court identified 28 districts in which spending would need to be brought up to the average spending in the wealthiest districts through a classification system of "District Factor Groups," which had been formulated by the Department of Education. Those 28 districts educate approximately 25 percent of the state's children. The court left the Legislature free to use a different classification system, as long as the system was not based on how much a poorer urban school district is willing to tax.

In what Morheuser called an "important, serious difference" between the court's decision and [New Jersey governor James J.] Florio's [Quality Education Act] the court required that the funding of those poor districts be increased correspondingly as spending increases in the wealthiest districts.

"Whatever the legislative remedy," said the court, "it must assure that these poorer urban districts have a budget per pupil that is approximately equal to the average of the richer suburban districts, whatever that average may be, and be sufficient to address their special needs."

The court declared that, "The minimum aid provisions presently found in the act are counter-equalizing, and as such, are unconstitutional." Minimum aid, in the 1975 funding formula, guarantees state aid to even the wealthiest districts.

The court rejected Cooperman's argument that mismanagement, not lack of money, was the root of educational inequities. Wilentz noted that money can make a difference, if effectively used, toward providing students with equal educational opportunity. " . . . the education provided," . . . "depends to a significant extent on the money spent for it."

The court went further, declaring that the needs in poorer districts, in fact, warranted more money being spent for schools there than in the wealthy districts, where students begin their education with certain advantages. "The totality of the districts' educational offering must contain elements over and above those found in the affluent suburban districts," stated the decision.

Regarding state aid to the teacher pension and annuity fund (TPAF), the court said it is, "in effect, counter-equalizing," although it concluded that it would abide by a previous judgment in *Robinson v. Cahill* and leave TPAF contributions as they stand in the 1975 law—as a state contribution. It added, however, that it would not foreclose the possibility that such aid is "constitutionally infirm." Teacher pension contributions are paid in greater amounts to wealthier districts because they employ more experienced and highly paid teachers.

The court based its ruling on the 1975 funding formula's violation of the "T&E" clause in the Constitution, which guarantees "the maintenance and support of a thorough and efficient system of free public schools for the instruction of all the children in the state between the ages of five and eighteen years." It declined to rule on the plaintiffs' state equal protection claim, and found that the plaintiffs had failed to prove that the system of educational financing violates the state Law Against Discrimination.

Kentucky Starts From Scratch

New Jersey is not alone in its legal fight to reform its school-funding system. School-funding formulas are being challenged in nine other states, ranging from Alaska to Oregon, and [in July 1990] school-finance reform advocates in five more states were considering legal challenges to their school-funding systems.

"We tend to change things in microsteps in school-finance reform," says Chris Pipho, director of the Information Clearinghouse at the Education Commission of the States, in Denver, Colorado. "Court cases sometimes force a quantum leap."

The Kentucky Supreme Court proved

Pipho's observation correct [in] June [1989] by passing perhaps the most sweeping school-aid reform decision yet. It not only ruled that the unequal resources being provided by the state's school-aid formula were unconstitutional, but went much further, by declaring all aspects of the state's school system inadequate.

"It was a good move in the political sense," says Malcolm Jewell, editor of *The Kentucky Journal*. "Because the people who said we shouldn't be throwing money at a bad system were given a way to improve the system."

A 22-member task force was appointed by the Kentucky Legislature and Governor Wallace Wilkinson to draft a reform package in light of the court decision. Since the court had cited both the state superintendent and the state education agency as part of the problem, outside consultants were recruited.

Although the court deadline was July 15, [1990], Wilkinson announced that he wanted both the school-reform bill, and the approval of a revenue source to fund the bill, to be enacted during the regular legislative session, thereby pushing up the deadline.

For a variety of reasons, however, including the governor's stand against any increase in Kentucky's 5-percent sales tax, relations between the governor and the legislature were strained, and months of confrontational debate followed.

Nevertheless, one day before the end of the legislative session in March, the legislature signed a mammoth, 906-page education reform bill, which Governor Wilkinson signed into law April 12 [1990].

The Kentucky law establishes a new funding system designed to close the spending gap between poor and rich districts.

It also creates a system of rewards and punishments for schools, based on performance. In an effort to improve school quality, for example, students at the worst schools will be able to transfer to better schools, at state expense. A group, comprised of "distinguished educators," was formed to implement the takeover of deficient schools.

One of the most contentious provisions of the new law has turned out to be the absolute ban on nepotism in hiring teachers and electing school board members. Traditionally, nepotism has been widespread, particularly in rural parts of the state, according to Pipho.

The law also mandated site-based management, which is intended to provide more local control, an objective many school reformers are trying to achieve. School councils, consisting of teachers, parents, and administrators, are to be created to set local school policy.

A foundation level, similar to Governor Florio's proposal, was implemented to guarantee an adequate level of funding per pupil. The law established a spending level of $2,900 per student. Previously, spending varied in Kentucky's 178 districts from $1,800 to $4,200 per student.

Districts may exceed the foundation minimum by 15 percent, and the state will match those funds on a sliding scale. If the districts choose to spend another 15 percent above the foundation, however, the state will not match those funds.

Not surprisingly, one of the most difficult issues to resolve was the funding of the bill. Eventually, a $1.3-billion tax increase, most of which will go to education, was enacted. In order to raise these funds, the state sales tax [was slated to] rise from 5 cents to 6 cents, and the corporate tax rate ... by 1 percent.

According to Robert Sexton, executive director of the Prichard Committee of Academic Excellence, a non-profit education advocacy organization in Lexington, Kentucky, this reform was some time in the making. "This decision came after five or six years of intense public pressure," he said, adding, however,

"This Legislature went further than any other in response to the court decision."

Texas Feuds Over School Funding

When Governor William P. Clements Jr. finally signed the Texas Legislature's school-financing proposal June 7, [1990], it suggested that a long and often acrimonious impasse between the governor and the legislature over how to fund Texas' public schools was finally coming to a close.

The impetus for the debate over school financing was the state Supreme Court's October 2 [1989] decision, declaring the state's public school-financing system unconstitutional due to "glaring disparities" between rich and poor districts.

The Texas Supreme Court's decision in *Edgewood v. Kirby* was unanimous, a fact that surprised observers who thought the court had become extremely conservative in recent years. Education experts say that spending disparities in Texas were relatively minor compared to those in other states. The court, however, taking a similar stance to that subsequently taken by the New Jersey Supreme Court, looked at the disparities between the 100 wealthiest districts and the 100 poorest, and found them to be substantial.

As in New Jersey, the argument was made in Texas, this time by [then-] U.S. Education Secretary Lauro F. Cavazos, who was addressing one of the four special sessions of the Texas Legislature that were held to address the issue of public school financing, that money is not the answer to the state's education problems. This argument drew angry criticism from a number of Hispanic leaders, who also see the problem as a minority-rights issue, since many of the poorer, disadvantaged districts, as in New Jersey, are heavily populated by blacks and Hispanics.

While the Texas court found that expenditure differences could not correlate to local wealth, it also ruled that expenditures need not be exactly equal, but only "substantially equal," according to Mark Yudof, Dean of the School of Law at the University of Texas, in Austin.

The court originally ordered a new formula to be in place by May 1 [1990]. During March, seven plans were discussed, four of which involved a tax increase. The governor's plan involved reallocating already existing money by restructuring the current formula, but many legislators felt the plan did not add enough new money to the system to raise poorer districts' spending adequately.

When the governor and legislators failed to agree on a plan, the court extended the deadline for a month—with a warning. State District Judge Scott McCown said that he was appointing a "special master" to develop an alternate plan, which would go into effect if the legislature failed to pass their own plan. The special master, however, would not be allowed to raise any new funds, or implement a new funding mechanism. He or she would therefore be sure to take a "Robin Hood" approach—taking from the rich districts to give to the poor.

According to Yudof, "The idea was that the special master's plan would be so draconian that it would force the legislature into acting."

A legislative battle followed, during which the governor vetoed two bills. The legislature tried to override his second veto, but failed to get enough votes. Meanwhile, a special master, William Kilgarlin, a former member of the Texas Supreme Court, was appointed, and began formulating his own plan.

According to the court's decision, both the legislature and the special master were to formulate school-finance plans by June 1. If the legislature failed to pass a plan by the deadline—or if the governor vetoed its plan—the court would consider the special master's plan. Otherwise, the court would consider both plans in a hearing on June 25.

The legislature was into its fourth special session when the governor, who had vowed to reject any school-funding bill calling for more than $300 million in its first year, finally agreed to the legislature's plan to provide $500 million in state aid in the first year to relieve spending disparities in school districts.

The legislature's new bill [did] not drastically change the current funding formula—a guaranteed tax base formula. But it [did] increase the sales tax and a number of "sins taxes," such as the tax on cigarettes and liquor, in order to pump more money into the poorer districts ... and it raise[d] the basic allotments that districts are required to spend on their schools. ...

Although the end was in sight, the battle was still not over. ... On June 25, the Texas Supreme Court [heard] both the legislature's plan and the special master's plan.

Capital Punishment: Illinois' First Execution After 28 Years

by F. Mark Siebert

After a hiatus of 28 years capital punishment returned to Illinois on September 12 [1990] when Charles Walker was executed by lethal injection. This was the first execution under a law passed 13 years [earlier]. Predictably, a great deal of legal skirmishing over its constitutionality filled the intervening period, and it was still in progress at the time of Walker's execution. It was a race between final pronouncement on the law and Walker's execution. That the execution took place was in part possible because Walker had indicated that he preferred death to life imprisonment and wished no more efforts at delay to be made on his behalf.

Legal maneuvering for the individual fills the period between initial imposition of the sentence and ultimate execution. State and federal statutes together provide eight possible levels of appeal of death sentences. These ordinarily review procedure rather than evidence. One is automatic: Article VI, section 4b of the Illinois Constitution requires that the Illinois Supreme Court review all impositions of the death sentence.

It is hard to assess the situation for all those under sentence at any given time. For example, at the end of 1988 there were 109 Illinois death sentence cases at seven of the eight possible levels of appeal. By [1990] there were 126 inmates on death row, at various stages of appeal. Even after Walker had exhausted all possible appeals and had informed the Prisoner Review Board that he wished no efforts to be made on his behalf, there was a request from some sources for executive stay of the execution because another Illinois case raising constitutional issues might reach the U.S. Supreme Court.

The route . . . looks like this.

August 24, 1962: The last execution in Illinois took place in the Cook County Jail (coincidentally, Gov. James R. Thompson [1977-1991] was involved in this case in his role as prosecutor in the Office of the Cook County State's Attorney).

1972: The U.S. Supreme Court, ruling on a Georgia case, threw out the death penalty for the entire nation because laws in most states could result in unequal imposition and failure to consider mitigating circumstances.

1973: The Illinois General Assembly passed Public Act 78-921, placing imposition

This article is reprinted with permission from *Illinois Issues* 16:10 (October 1990): 26-27, published by Sangamon State University, Springfield, Illinois, 62794-9243. © *Illinois Issues.*

of the death penalty in the hands of a three-judge panel.

November 1975: The Illinois Supreme Court declared the law unconstitutional. The provision for a three-judge panel touched upon the operation of the courts, since sentencing had conventionally been exercised by a single judge. In effect the legislature created a court. The high court struck down the law as breaching constitutionally guaranteed separation of powers.

July 1976: In another Georgia case *(Gregg v. Georgia)* the U.S. Supreme Court ruled that capital punishment would be permissible under certain circumstances. This triggered a flurry of activity in many states to pass acceptable legislation.

June 1977: The General Assembly passed Public Act 80-26, modeled on the law found acceptable in *Gregg*. The law was described as "defendent-oriented."

June 1977: The governor signed the new law.

January 1979: A Cook County circuit court ruled the law unconstitutional because of the possibility of uneven application across the state. Amid the spate of death penalty laws passed across the nation, Illinois' is unique in its provision that the court can consider the death penalty only if recommended by the prosecution; the state's attorney can make this decision after conviction. This, said the circuit judge, could result in uneven application. (In the three-year period 1977-80 the state's attorney in Sangamon County refrained from requesting the penalty in all 10 cases in which he might have done so. During the same period his counterpart in Champaign County recommended the penalty in all eight possible cases; in Cook County the recommendation was made in 51 out of 80 cases.)

April 1979: The circuit court in Sangamon County ruled the law constitutional. In his opinion circuit court Judge Ben Miller,

now a justice on the state Supreme Court, said that it is not unconstitutional to grant discretion to state's attorneys. He also said that imposition was not automatic, and that the death sentence did not constitute cruel and inhuman punishment.

November 1979: The first case questioning the law, *People ex rel Carey v. Cousins,* reached the Illinois Supreme Court, which ruled it constitutional 4-3. The dissenters (Chief Justice Joseph H. Goldenhersh and Justices William G. Clark and Howard C. Ryan) established the battle lines for a controversy that lasted for the next 10 years. They criticized the discretion given state's attorneys. The majority held that while there might be uneven application—this ultimate penalty might be imposed for varying degrees of culpability—that it would not be arbitrary because in each case it would depend upon the strength of the conviction.

February 1980: The next case to reach the Supreme Court injected a highly emotional issue when the court ruled that killing a fetus during killing of the mother is not murder. The Senate rushed to prepare a bill on fetal murder.

April 1980: The court ruled for the first time on specific imposition of the sentence in *People v. Carlson.* It overturned on the grounds of lack of consideration of mitigating circumstances.

November 1981: In *People v. Lewis* the court upheld the sentence for the first time. By this time Justice Seymour Simon had replaced Justice Thomas E. Kluczynski. Simon agreed with the minority in *Carey v. Cousins* on the matter of unequal application and expected them to join him in finally declaring the law unconstitutional. They declined on the grounds of *stare decisis*—the legal principle that a decision once made should remain in place in the absence of unusual circumstances. Simon began a series of dissents from each death penalty decision, always raising the objection of unequal application in addition to other reasons he might find. (Interestingly, this sentence was later changed to life imprisonment when it emerged that prosecutors had used information they knew to be inaccurate at post-trial hearings.)

September 1983: The legislature changed the method of execution from electrocution to lethal injection.

October 1984: A sharp exchange between Simon and Ryan. Simon pointedly criticized the three early dissenters for not joining him, and Ryan responded with the *stare decisis* argument, saying that Simon's repeated dissents cause unrewarding delays. ...

February 1988: In five decisions the court clarified a number of issues relating to imposition of the death penalty. As usual, Simon dissented.

January 1989: In an opinion upholding the penalty Ryan criticized the almost automatic argument of ineffective counsel. Significantly, he also criticized the protracted appeal process, which probably reflected the "law and order" temper of the times.

May 1989: In an appeal *(People v Silagy)* a U.S. district court judge ruled the Illinois law unconstitutional because of the discretion given state's attorneys, the lack of guidelines and the fact that the permission for prosecution to recommend the penalty after conviction hindered the defendant's constitutional right to effective counsel.

April 1990: After a series of decisions broadening the possibility of imposing a death sentence, the U.S. Supreme Court ruled that friends and supporters cannot intervene for a person who does not wish to continue appeals procedures. This applied to Walker who had so signified in a statement to the Prisoner Review Board and in a press conference.

May 1990: A federal appeals court overturned the decision of the U.S. district court in *Silagy*.

May 17, 1990: The Illinois Supreme Court set the September 12 date for Walker's execution.

Summer 1990: Several hundred Illinois attorneys petitioned Gov. Thompson to delay Walker's execution pending a possible U.S. Supreme Court decision on *Silagy*.

August 1990: The Illinois Department of Corrections began preparation for Walker's execution.

September 1990: A U.S. district court judge denied a request for a stay of Walker's execution as part of a class action suit challenging the execution procedure. This arose out of doubts raised by the manufacturer of the apparatus for administering the lethal injection about its efficacy and questions about the legality of the drugs to be used.

In August, in his final "State of the State's Judiciary" address, Chief Justice Thomas J. Moran decried protracted appeals of the death penalty and blamed them on inexperience on the part of trial lawyers.

September 10: Gov. Thompson refused to delay the execution or grant clemency.

September 12, 12:12 a.m.: Walker was declared dead.

IX. STATE ISSUES

One might think that the goal of state government is to provide the services that citizens need and then raise the money to do so. Actually, the process is just the reverse: the governor and state legislature raise the money they can and then decide the extent of services the state can provide. It comes as no surprise, therefore, that financial issues are at the top of state policy agendas. How should revenues be raised—taxes, user fees, bonds, lotteries? What kinds of taxes should be imposed—sales, income, inheritance, property? Who will bear the burden of these taxes—the rich, the poor, the consumer, the property holder? These are the most important questions state governors and legislatures address.

During the nationwide recession in the early 1980s, state revenues dropped precipitously. The fiscal crisis necessitated layoffs, hiring limits, travel restrictions, and delays in expenditures. The budget crunch of the early 1980s greatly lowered expectations of what state government could and would do.[1]

At the same time, the states were waiting to see how the national government would handle the federal deficit, and how that decision would affect state and local finances. Then, in the mid-1980s, a major fear of state leaders' came true: the president and Congress decided to solve part of the national deficit crisis by letting the states pay for a considerable part of it. Saving a program that formerly was funded in whole or part with federal funds means increasing state and local taxes. And to many lawmakers, increased taxes can mean defeat at the polls.

Toward the end of the 1980s another problem developed in many states: the deterioration of their fiscal health resulting from reduced tax revenues. In 1988, eighteen states had to cut back their enacted budgets, and by April 1989, ten had to do so for fiscal 1989.[2]

Now the states faced new budget problems: keeping their budgets balanced. In October 1988, the National Association of State Budget Officers (NASBO) reported "states are in a precarious position" and cannot afford to have any bad economic news. "They have very little reserves to deal with shocks." [3] Note the irony here: the bad news for the states was their low budget surpluses; for the federal government it was the large budget deficit! But that is just the problem, according to a later NASBO report: the "federal government continues to try and solve its own problems by passing costs on to the states." [4]

What can the states do? As already noted, one option is to raise taxes. States also can seek new sources of tax revenue. For example, more and more states are considering instituting a state lottery, which seems to be a painless way to raise money. But recent research on state lotteries indicates that they amount to a "heavy tax"—one that is sharply regressive— because it is levied in part on those who cannot afford it. The economics of the state lotteries in 1988 indicate that of each dollar spent on a lottery ticket ($16 billion), 48 cents went for prizes, 15 cents for administration, including promotion and sales, and only 37 cents ($5.7 billion) for government purposes.[5]

As we move into the 1990s, finances dominate the agendas of most state governors and legislatures. After a couple of years of economists arguing whether the country was moving into a recession, it became clear that we had. State leaders observed that an economic slowdown had occurred, which has translated into decreasing state tax revenues or in a decline of the revenue growth they had experienced in recent years. This often means tax increases must be considered if programs are to be maintained at their current levels, let alone starting new initiatives.

In April 1991, it was reported in *Fiscal Survey of the States* that the states were "in the worst financial shape of the decade," with twenty-nine states having already cut $8 billion from their current budgets. They did this by implementing layoffs (eleven states), furloughs (seven states), targeted reductions (twenty-four states), hiring freezes (twenty-two states), and travel freezes (nineteen states). Twenty-six other states were in the process of raising more than $10.8 billion in new taxes, which would be the largest one-year increase since the survey started in 1978.[6]

But increasing taxes can lead to citizen and voter dissatisfaction. Three of six governors in economically troubled New England who were up for reelection in 1990 decided not to seek another term; one of the three who did run, lost. This is partially due to the problems in their states' budgetary situation, which necessitated tax increases and caused voter resentment. Some blame President George Bush's famous 1988 campaign promise of "Read My Lips, No New Taxes" as setting a tone that affects all levels of government. However, Maine governor John R. McKernan (R, 1989-) believes that reasoning amounts to "whining ... President Bush didn't say the governors shouldn't raise taxes...."[7]

Now, there are few states that are not facing serious budgetary problems. The budget deficits in some cases are enormous; California's is over $12 billion, and even shutting down the state's entire higher education system would still leave a large deficit to handle. Governors and legislatures are trying to erase these deficits with all types of "revenue enhancements," program and governmental cutbacks, and even are reverting to what the federal government has been doing: shifting some responsibilities downward, toward the local governments.

After money, what are the issues of greatest concern to the states? Or, to put it another way, what do states spend the most money on? Funding levels are a good indication of commitment.

Large sums are spent each year on education, health programs, state highways, economic development, and environmental protection. In 1989, state government expenditures topped $469 billion with education ($173 billion or 36.9 percent) and welfare ($93 billion or 19.8 percent) taking nearly 57 percent of these funds.[8] These figures included a projected jump of 6.3 percent in state expenditures between fiscal 1988 and fiscal 1989 with Medicaid as the fastest growing major program, and support for primary and secondary education growing faster than overall growth at 8.2 percent.[9]

Medicaid spending, called "the PAC-Man of state government," increased by 18 percent in 1990 and by 25 percent in 1991. Unfunded federal mandates adopted by Congress over the last four years are costing the states an extra $2 billion in 1991 alone. These rates of increase clearly are outpacing the growth rate in state economies and are "absorbing more than 50 percent of the growth in revenues in many states."[10]

Of course, different regions of the country have different priorities. In the Southwest, water policy is a dominant issue. In the Midwest, farm problems, the declining industrial base, and lack of economic development are major concerns. And under the prodding of the U.S. Department of Energy, the states have been grouped into a series of regional interstate compacts (legal agreements) to seek processes and sites for the disposal of radioactive waste within each region.

Issues also vary from one state to another. Policy makers in Florida must address the many social and environmental problems created by the state's population boom and breakneck development. Some of these problems have difficult age and ethnic aspects to them.

Connecticut and New York have different troubles, such as the deterioration of public highways and bridges, which was made evident by the collapse of the New York state thruway bridge into Scoharie Creek in 1987. These states have been suffering from a declining tax base as industry and people move out. And in Nevada and New Jersey the infiltration of organized crime in state gambling casinos has officials on the watch. More recently, these casinos have been losing money.

Setting the Agenda

How do particular concerns become priorities on the states' agendas? Although state constitutions provide for the education, health, and safety of citizens, events can trigger new interest in these issues. For example, the Soviets' nuclear disaster at Chernobyl revitalized the antinuclear power movement in some state capitals. The collapse of financial institutions such as insurance companies or state chartered banks can lead to citizen despair and action by state regulators. Campaign promises and court decisions also influence policy making. A gubernatorial candidate who promises to lower utility rates will try to keep this promise once elected. And if a state court finds that some citizens, such as the mentally handicapped, are not receiving the state services to which they are entitled, chances are the governor and state legislators will pay closer attention to this issue.

A public health issue state leaders are frantically groping with now is Acquired Immune Deficiency Syndrome (AIDS), a disease without a cure as yet. Between 1981 and 1987, AIDS was considerably more likely to be found in the larger urban states, such as California (8,348 cases) and New York (10,870 cases), while smaller rural states virtually escaped the disease, such as in North and South Dakota where only five cases each were reported in this period. But AIDS is on the rise and an estimated 1.5 million people carried the virus in 1987.[11] By 1989 there were nearly 78,000 diagnosed cases of AIDs, up 66 percent from 1988. This increase in diagnosed cases was nearly matched by a 58 percent increase in state appropriations for fighting the disease in the same period, compared to only a 34 percent increase in U.S. Public Health Service expenditures.[12] This public health crisis is being addressed by the medical profession, but AIDS also intrudes into other public concerns that state leaders must consider. [13]

Provisions of the U.S. Constitution also can force issues onto a state's policy agenda. Since the 1950s, there has been a series of U.S. Supreme Court decisions on "separate but equal" education, reapportionment, and criminal justice based on lawsuits challenging state and local government policies and actions as violations of the plaintiffs' constitutional rights. These decisions have caused state and local government lawmakers considerable anguish as they address and adopt often controversial and expensive new policies, which usually translate into tax increases.

Many states are under a federal court order to ease prison crowding. The states were expected to spend more than $4 billion in 1989 to expand existing prisons and build new ones.[14] With all the calls to get tougher on those involved in drug transactions, state prisons will only become more crowded, exacerbating already difficult problems.

The only alternative to prompt action by the states to relieve prison overcrowding is to have the federal courts take over this major state government function and mandate that the states take even more controversial and expensive steps. Neither the federal nor the state governments want this to happen.

However, the U.S. Supreme Court also can be supportive of state policy initiatives. For example, in an important 1989 decision, the Court upheld state antitrust laws that in

1977 the U.S. Circuit Court of Appeals had declared preempted by federal law. The winning argument indicated federal antitrust laws were supplemental and not preemptive of state laws, an important constitutional distinction in our federal system of government.[15]

In 1989, the U.S. Supreme Court in the celebrated case *Webster v. Reproductive Health Services* decided to return to the states some of the questions over abortion rights. This partially reversed the Court's 1973 decision in *Roe v. Wade,* which had taken the power to restrict abortions in the first two trimesters of pregnancy from the states. The ferment in the states began quickly when prolife and prochoice groups organized to press their positions on state legislators and governors.

Florida governor Bob Martinez (R, 1987-1991) called a special fall 1989 session of his legislature to consider legislation restricting abortion. The legislators, who were not happy with the position this placed them in, "bottled up all four of Martinez's abortion bills in committee and adjourned the session early." [16] In Pennsylvania, the governor and the state legislature were of the same mind on abortion and readily passed prolife legislation. In 1990, the Idaho legislature passed very restrictive prolife legislation, only to have their prolife Democratic governor, Cecil Andrus, veto it as being too restrictive. Now we see legislatures in several states considering and passing laws regarding abortion, some trying to achieve the label of being the most restrictive in the nation.

In addition to the basic philosophical and religious arguments in the abortion debate, some of the key issues being deliberated in the state legislatures are: public funding of abortions for those who cannot afford them; use of public facilities for abortions; requiring parental consent for minors; abortion as a method of birth control or sex selection; specifying time limits for an abortion and determining the viability of a fetus; and birth control and abortion counseling.

Federal program requirements also can play a role in state policy making and administration. For example, in the early and mid-1980s, the states had to raise the legal drinking age to twenty-one and limit interstate highway speeds to 55 miles per hour or face the loss of federal highway funds. However, federal encroachment on setting speed limits came to a head in a highly publicized and controversial vote to override President Ronald Reagan's veto of a multibillion dollar transportation bill in March 1987. The override allowed those states that wished to raise the limit to 65 miles per hour on rural interstates.

Innovations and programs in other states can influence a state's agenda, as a new form of activity in one state may lead to similar action elsewhere. Some of the specific steps taken by the states that had to deal with the AIDS crisis in the early 1980s are now being copied by other states. Some states are copying other states' attempts to develop technology centers to attract industry. This "copycat" method of decision making has proved to be very popular: How did State X handle this?

Events not only in another state but in another part of the world occasionally determine the issues that state governments must address. Although the recent decrease in tension between the United States and the Soviet Union has spawned the "peace dividend"—a budget windfall from cuts in the defense budget—the states will bear the cost of the dividend. Cuts in the defense budget mean the closing of military bases in some states, reducing military personnel, and cutting back or canceling contracts for military hardware and weapons systems and funding for military research. Many states and localities have greatly benefited from the defense budget in years past. Now, as times and concerns change, so will their economies and fiscal health.

Implementation

Once policy goals and priorities are set by governors and legislators, important decisions must be made concerning who will implement them. This not only means which agency in state government will have the responsibility, but which level of government—state, local, or both.

Implementation decisions are often made with the considerable interest and involvement of the federal government. State and local governments administer some federal programs: food stamps, child nutrition, social services, community action, and senior citizen centers. In other areas federal and state governments *share* administrative and fiscal responsibility: public welfare, Medicaid, interstate and federal highways, hazardous waste, and water supply and sanitation.

But in many program areas the federal presence is minimal or nonexistent—especially since the passage of the 1985 Balanced Budget and Emergency Deficit Control Act, commonly known as the Gramm-Rudman-Hollings bill after its sponsors. This intensely controversial legislation mandates extensive across-the-board federal budget cuts if deficit targets are not met. Even before Gramm-Rudman-Hollings, federal aid to state and local governments had declined 23.5 percent in real money terms between 1980 and 1985.[17]

Even leaner times are ahead. The federal government is picking up a smaller and smaller share of the state tab for primary and secondary schools, state and community colleges, public hospitals, police and fire protection, state prisons and local jails, local streets and roads, public utilities, state and local parks, public libraries, and facilities for the disabled. During the 1988 presidential election campaign we heard candidates address the problems created by the declining federal presence. The Bush administration has shown little indication of reversing these trends; in fact, the trend may become worse as Congress and the president try to reduce the national budget deficit.

Current Issues

To put today's issues into perspective, the top seven discipline problems in California public schools in 1940 were "talking, chewing gum, making noise, running in the halls, getting out of turn in line, wearing improper clothing and not putting paper in the waste baskets." In the 1980s, the top seventeen problems were "drug abuse, pregnancy, rape, assault, arson, murder, vandalism, gang warfare, venereal disease, alcohol abuse, suicide, robbery, burglary, bombings, absenteeism, extortion and abortion."[18] In the 1990s, many of the problems of the 1980s remain, but AIDs, racism, and a few others probably should be added to the list.

For the future, four powerful trends are taking shape: the growth of *environmental concerns* in the wake of a deteriorating environment; the rapid *racial diversification* of our population with the attendant tensions of racism; the *changes in the age structure* as the population grows older and society shifts programmatic needs and costs between generations; and the increasing amount of *physical and sexual violence* occurring within the family and society at large.[19]

The articles in Part IX focus on six issues currently on the states' policy agendas. Penelope Lemov of Congressional Quarterly examines how the states are returning to an old revenue source—taxing sin. Angie Watson of *Illinois Issues* discusses the problems the states are having with disposing of hazardous waste, even when they join together to do it. Karen Hansen and Tracey Hooker of *State Legislatures* look at the difficulties that the states face in helping those with AIDs. Jeffrey Katz of Congressional Quarterly looks at one of the states' important functions, regulation; in this case reforming auto insurance: Lester Grinspoon, in an article from *The Journal of State Government,* suggests a bold, partial answer to some of our societal problems—legalizing drugs, and then taxing them heavily. Finally, Lynn Olson of Congressional Quarterly reviews the home schooling movement, an alternative approach to educating children.

Notes

1. National Governors' Association, *The State of the States, 1985,* 6.
2. National Association of State Budget Officers and National Governors' Association, *Fiscal Survey of the States, 1989* (Washington, D.C.: April 1989).
3. *Fiscal Survey of the States, 1988* (October 1988).
4. Marcia Howard, author of *Fiscal Survey of the States, 1989,* quoted in John Bacon, "Strapped U.S. Passes the Buck," *USA Today,* May 10, 1989, 5A.
5. Peter Passell, "Duke Economists Critical of State Lotteries," *New York Times News Service,* reported in the *Durham Morning Herald,* May 21, 1989, 11A.
6. National Governors' Association and the National Association of State Budget Officers, "States in Worst Fiscal Shape of Decade," *Governors Weekly Bulletin* 25:16 (April 19, 1991): 1-3.
7. New York Times News Service, "Budget Woes Put Pinch on Many States," in [Raleigh] *News and Observer,* March 4, 1990, 1A.
8. Bureau of the Census, Department of Commerce, *State Government Finances in 1989* (Washington, D.C.: U.S. Government Printing Office, 1990), 21.
9. "State Spending," *Governors' Weekly Bulletin* 23:11 (March 17, 1989): 4.
10. National Governors' Association, 1-3.
11. Kate Farrell, "Cutting the Cost of AIDS," *State Legislatures* 13:9 (September 1987): 24.
12. Bureau of the Census, Department of Commerce, *Statistical Abstract of the United States, 1990* (Washington, D.C.: U.S. Government Printing Office), 117.
13. Ibid. and "Effective Policies to Combat AIDS," *Governors' Weekly Bulletin* 21:38 (September 25, 1987), 1-2.
14. "Population Explosion Fuels Prison Spending," *USA Today,* March 27, 1989, 6A.
15. "Supreme Court Upholds State Antitrust Laws," *Governors' Weekly Bulletin* 23:16 (April 21, 1989), 4. The cases involved were *Illinois Brick v. Illinois* (1977) and *California v. ARC America Corp.* (1989).
16. John Koenig, "Bob Martinez: The Governor of the Polls," *Governing* 3:8 (May 1990): 44.
17. Congressional Research Service, "The Effect of Federal Tax and Budget Policies in the 1980s on the State-Local Sector," *Governors' Weekly Bulletin* 20:9 (March 7, 1986): 2.
18. Remarks of William Bondurant, executive director, the Mary Reynolds Babcock Foundation, to the National Development Conference in Dallas, Texas, June 12, 1987.
19. Ibid.

States Are Running Out of Sins To Tax

by Penelope Lemov

Cars took it on the chin in 1989. So did the gasoline to run them. And so did cigarettes, alcoholic beverages, and hotel and motel rooms.

During the 1990 legislative season, state legislators, as they had in 1989, tried to fill in all or part of their revenue disappointments the easy way: by raising their rates on so-called "sin taxes" and similar excise taxes that put the tax pain on people's pleasures.

But that's not the likely scenario in 1991. Given the level of state activity in 1989 and 1990 and the federal government's full-court press on excise taxes this fall, many state legislatures will find that this revenue vein is just about played out.

There are other reasons why most legislatures won't be able to depend on the comparatively painless application of excise taxes to keep budgets in balance. Slowing economies in 1991 will mean flagging revenues just as federal and state mandates, court orders and political pressures spell rising expenditures, especially for education, Medicaid and prisons. Excise taxes on motor fuel, tobacco products and alcoholic beverages, which accounted for 9 percent of state tax revenue in 1989, won't be able to handle the increases. That means more states are going to be looking once again at the more controversial income and sales taxes, with the most likely target for serious consideration new or expanded sales taxes on services.

The situation was simpler in 1990, and there was action aplenty on sin and other excise taxes. Sixteen states passed excise tax legislation that is expected to raise $2.1 billion in fiscal 1991; more than half the legislatures raised rates on two or more types of these taxes.

In many states, excise taxes attracted the attention of legislators because they had been ignored for a long time and were seen as ripe for the picking. Rhode Island was typical. "Many of those we changed this year [1990] were fees and excise provisions that hadn't been looked at for 10 years and weren't keeping up with inflation," notes Senator Richard Patterson, a Democrat who chairs the Senate Finance Committee.

Florida legislators, facing a $700 million bill to balance the state's $27 billion 1991 budget, "went to every sin tax and piddled around," says Florida Representative Anne Mackenzie, a Democrat who chairs the House

Penelope Lemov is a staff writer for *Governing*. This article appeared in *Governing* 4:3 (December 1990): 21-23.

Finance and Taxation Committee. The piddles alone should raise nearly half of the shortfall. Gasoline taxes went up more than a penny per gallon; alcoholic beverages were slapped with surcharges of from 4 cents to 10 cents on drinks served in bars and restaurants. The tax on cigarettes was raised a hefty 10 cents a pack, to 33.9 cents, proving once again that the seven out of ten adults who don't smoke don't mind when legislators sock it to the three out of ten who do.

In addition to adjusting the sin and gasoline taxes, many states looked around for other easy targets. Hotel and motel rooms were one: Four states raised or enacted room or meal tax rates on the theory that it was easier to load a little of the tax burden on the shoulders of out-of-towners.

Florida found an easy-to-hit target in a tax that falls most heavily on newcomers to the state. Those who register cars that add to the total volume of automobiles already on the road now pay dearly for the privilege: $295 per car. The tax does not apply to Florida families who replace a car they already own; only those who add an additional car to their fleet must pay it. But that exclusion doesn't apply to new arrivals and their cars. "When you move to Florida and add another set of wheels to our public roads, we consider that an impact on our clogged roads," says Mackenzie. The tax will not go into a kitty for road improvements but directly into the general fund.

But excise taxes have probably had it for now on the state level. For starters, the sin tax base is dwindling as people smoke and drink less. The taxes also tend to be relatively unproductive, points out Steven D. Gold, director of the Center for Study of the States at the Rockefeller Institute, because they're usually based on quantity rather than value—that is, an excise tax on beer may be 5 cents per bottle rather than a percentage of the price.

Therefore, excise tax revenues don't rise with inflation, only with a legislative increase in the tax.

No matter how much of a boost the tax is given, excise taxes have their revenue-raising limits, especially in troubled times. "If the economy continues to soften and we see budget numbers like we're seeing in states like Virginia and Florida," says Harley Duncan, executive director of the Federation of Tax Administrators, "then it's not likely that budget holes of that magnitude are going to be solved by painless sin tax increases."

Legislators in the Northeast and in parts of the Sun Belt are already feeling the impact of Duncan's point. In Rhode Island, gasoline, cigarette and alcohol levies were increased in 1989; in 1990, a motor vehicle tax was increased and a one-year, 1 percent rise in the sales tax was passed. But that won't do for 1991, says Patterson. "We're facing some serious times and a big deficit in Rhode Island. We will have to look to other sources of revenue."

In Texas, where the 1990 hikes in tax rates on alcohol and cigarettes are projected to raise $204 million for fiscal 1991, the revenue shortfall for fiscal 1992 is expected to be somewhere around $3.2 billion. "I'm already getting a headache," says Senator John Montford, a Democrat who recently took over as chairman of the Senate Finance Committee. Another increase in excise taxes is, he points out, out of the question. "If they become too high, the [yield] curve takes a downward turn and you trash yourself out of revenue." Not only might there be a decrease in consumption, but in much of Texas, he notes, there is always the problem of bootleg operations out of Mexico.

Then there is the complication of the federal government's budget-deficit agreement. "Who knows how much the traffic will bear with the federal government coming in with new gas, liquor, cigarette and luxury taxes," Rhode Island's Patterson says. "How much can we tack on if the feds are going to do it?"

From Arizona Senator Doug Todd's point of view, the federal government's gasoline tax increase means that it will be that much harder for Western states to raise revenue to maintain and finish state highways. "Our ability to raise additional gas taxes now will be a major fight," says the Republican chairman of the Arizona Senate Finance Committee. Some states, like California, saw the writing on the wall and acted quickly to raise their gasoline taxes, he notes. "Many of us tried that in Arizona, but we were set in a corner and stomped on."

If excise taxes won't play a starring or even supporting role in the revenue-raising picture in 1991, where will legislators in revenue-pinched states find additional funds?

States such as Texas and Florida that raised general sales taxes to and beyond the 6 percent mark in 1990 probably won't be able to take that route again. With the Texas sales tax at 6.25 percent and local options raising those taxes to as much as 8.25 percent in many areas of the state, Montford believes the sales tax in his state is maxed out. "It's at a point where if it goes any higher, nobody is going to buy anything."

States with a sales tax closer to 4 percent have more room to maneuver, but the alternative to raising sales tax rates is broadening the base. For many states, that could mean taxing services.

In today's service-oriented economy, it's not surprising that a sales tax limited to commodities isn't producing the kinds of revenues state and local governments need. The revenue productivity of the sales tax has eroded: In 1960, each penny of the sales tax in the median state produced $0.69 of revenue per $100 of personal income; by 1988, that figure had fallen to $0.56. Part of that erosion,

Gold explains, stems from expanded exemptions from the tax, but it is also caused in increasingly large measure by faster growth in the consumption of services rather than goods.

What makes economic and fiscal sense doesn't necessarily play well politically, however. Whenever the subject of a sales tax on services comes up, state legislators point to the very public bloody nose Florida got in 1987 when it implemented a tax on services and then rescinded it six months later in the face of a storm of protest and controversy.

Despite the publicity surrounding the Florida fiasco, which made other states wary of taking on powerful lawyers, accountants, advertising agencies and the like, several other states have quietly been reaping revenue from sales taxes on services. Three states—Hawaii, New Mexico and South Dakota—have long had a service tax on just about every kind of business that does business in their states. In New Mexico, for instance, the law has been in place since the 1930s, and there are few exemptions from the tax, which is imposed on a business's gross receipts.

Three other states—Iowa, Washington and West Virginia—also have long taxed many services but exempted professional services. Among the other 39 states with sales taxes, 19 tax a few services; at the far end of the spectrum, 20 tax virtually no services. A good number of legislators in these states are advocating the extension or inauguration of a services tax. Few are suggesting that all services, including advertising and legal work, be taxed, but Gold has compiled a short list of services most likely to be taxed. His list includes less controversial services such as home video rentals, country club memberships, car washing, barber shops, cable TV, carpentry, photocopying and lawn care.

Massachusetts' legislature moved on the issue in July 1990 and broadened the sales tax to encompass nearly 600 services, including work done by engineers, architects, accountants and lawyers. Two bar associations are suing over the application of the tax to legal services, and other opponents of the tax, which was to go into effect on December 1, successfully petitioned to put the issue on the ballot in November. Voters elected to keep the tax, but Governor-elect William F. Weld, a Republican, . . . pledged to rescind it [and he did].

Meanwhile, in Maryland, the Commission on State Taxes and Tax Structure, appointed by Democratic Governor William Donald Schaefer, recommended in its report that the state expand the sales tax to include services. And even the legislature in Florida, where the topic is more than a little touchy, is among those that may look into service taxes in 1991. Mackenzie, the House Finance and Taxation Committee chairwoman, says businesses in her Fort Lauderdale district are more unsettled by constant changes in excise taxes than they are about proposals for service taxes. "We're losing our ranking in terms of providing a stable tax climate to companies and major businesses. A lot of them are in favor [of the service tax] because otherwise, with excise taxes, we're just nickel and diming them to death."

If the legislature does revisit service taxes, it will do things a little differently than it did last time, Mackenzie predicts. "We'll take more time to explain to the public how the taxes will be implemented, and we'll give it more time to be implemented."

Legislators in some other states say they are reluctant to go the service tax route. In Arizona in 1989, a state commission set up to recommend reforms in Arizona's tax structure recommended reducing the sales tax rate but broadening the base with taxes on services. "It met with high disfavor in the legislature," Todd reports, adding that his state, along with several others in the Sun Belt, is struggling with flattening economic growth.

Based on the commission's recommendations, Arizona did revamp its income tax code, simplifying it and making it more progressive, and in the process raising an additional $110 million. It was one of 17 states that revised personal or corporate income tax codes, or both, with an eye to increasing revenues.

Restructuring of income tax systems along Arizona's line, in addition to broadening sales tax systems, is what Gold predicts as the wave of the future for states that will be revenue-starved in the 1990s. It's better politically, he suggests, for money to come in automatically without legislatures having to raise rates every other year. "If they're smart, states won't just raise their rates, but they'll reform their tax systems and make those systems more responsive to economic growth."

Low-level Radioactive Waste: States Search for Disposal Sites

by Angie Watson

The groundbreaking of the nation's first nuclear power plant in Shippingport, Pa., was the media event of 1954. President Dwight D. Eisenhower and the nation welcomed the peacetime use of the atom. The decommissioning of the plant in the late 1980s met with less fanfare but reminded the nation that harnessing atomic energy has its price. The radioactive trash produced when generating electricity at nuclear power plants, when mining uranium and when using radioisotopes for medical research and cancer treatment must be isolated for public safety.

The "hot" wastes from nuclear weapons production, uranium mining, the spent fuel from nuclear power plants and their cores when decommissioned are federal responsibilities. The nuclear industry and other waste producers dump low-level radioactive waste at three privately operated sites in the country. But a law enacted by Congress in 1980 will turn the problem of low-level waste disposal over to all of the states in 1993 when the three sites close their doors to outsiders.

Illinois is among 14 states now trying to find and design a site for low-level wastes, which include the rags, cleaning materials, tools, protective clothing, etc., used in nuclear power plants, and the animal carcasses and other radioactive remnants used in research. Considered less hazardous than high-level radioactive waste, low-level wastes become safe for exposure to humans after 300 to 500 years of storage. A small percentage, however, takes thousands of years to reach safe levels.

Concerns over public safety have slowed efforts here and in other states in determining new sites for the waste by a 1993 deadline set by Congress. Illinois will meet the deadline, says Tom Kerr, former division chief of low-level radioactive waste management for the Illinois Department of Nuclear Safety (IDNS). Others disagree. Onlookers do agree that most states do not want to finish first because of the fear that the rules may change, that the first few sites opened will be the only ones to open. "We're way ahead of probably 40 states," says Sen. Jerome Joyce (D-43, Reddick). "We could do it. I just don't want to be first."

The Low-Level Radioactive Waste Act passed by Congress in 1980 was the result of a

Angie Watson was a public affairs reporting intern with *Illinois Issues*. This article is reprinted with permission from *Illinois Issues* 16:4 (April 1990): 20-22, published by Sangamon State University, Springfield, Illinois 62794-9243. © *Illinois Issues*.

showdown the year before when the governors of South Carolina, Washington and Nevada announced they would no longer take the nation's waste indefinitely. In 1993, the low-level radioactive waste disposal sites in Barnwell, S.C., Beatty, Nev., and Richland, Wash., now taking the nation's wastes, will no longer accept them from areas outside their designated compacts. Under the act, states must establish compacts among themselves and agree on which member state will be the "host" for a waste site. 1993 is the deadline for new sites or plans for storage or disposal; 1996 is the last deadline for sites to be operating. Any state without a site must take possession of the waste upon the generator's request or risk paying damages to the generators for failure to do so.

Kathy Tharp, a member of the Concerned Citizens of Clark County and a staunch opponent of the proposed Illinois site near Martinsville, says: "Illinois is too far ahead of the other compacts in this process. You get the feeling that the other compacts are waiting for this to go on line."

Among nine compacts and four states opting to go it alone, 14 states are searching for sites. ... Illinois and Kentucky formed the Central Midwest Compact in 1984 with Illinois agreeing to take Kentucky's waste as long as it is not more than 10 percent of the two states' total.

Illinois has 13 operating nuclear power plants, the most of any state in the nation. From October 1988 to October 1989 they produced 106,410 cubic feet of low-level wastes, ranking Illinois among the top 10 states, according to the U.S. Council of Energy Awareness in Washington, D.C. They also produced most of the waste in Illinois. According to IDNS, in 1988 nuclear power plants generated 83 percent of Illinois low-level wastes; medical institutions, hospitals and industry accounted for 9 percent; and fuel cycle

generators (relating to mining and refining of nuclear fuel), 8 percent.

... IDNS ... identified two potential Illinois sites, one in Wayne County (Geff) and one in Clark County (Martinsville), [when] the selection process [was put] on hold. [In] fall [1989,] information in geological studies was altered, allegedly by the authorization of IDNS Director Terry Lash. Gov. James R. Thompson appointed former Illinois Supreme Court Justice Seymour Simon to hold public hearings to re-review the suitability of the two proposed sites, and the Illinois Senate Executive Committee [was] to investigate the allegations against Lash. [Lash has since resigned as director of IDNS, and legislation has been passed taking the siting authority away from IDNS and creating a three person board to make siting decisions. The board is made up of a former state supreme court justice, an engineer from the University of Illinois at Urbana, and the state representative of the Sierra Club.]

Both sites have opposition. Opponents claim they were selected, not for their suitability as disposal sites, but because they are in economically depressed areas where local agreement could come easy. For the Martinsville site, opponents contend there is a threat of contamination to underground water (aquifers). For the Wayne County site, located near the New Madrid fault line, opponents point to aquifers and potential seismic activity based on investigations by independent geologists for the now disbanded citizens' advisory group, the Citizens' Review Committee.

Other states are having difficulty, too. Michigan, the host state of the Midwest Compact, is at war with Ohio officials who oppose the proposed site which is a half mile from the Ohio border and the city of Toledo in Lucas County. The Lucas County prosecutor is seeking an injunction to stop the siting process. Ohio officials claim they did not know the

State Recycling Laws

State legislatures have enacted hundreds of recycling and waste reduction measures in recent years, setting up a statewide infrastructure to support and encourage communities to recycle. While local governments are on the "front lines" of recycling, there is much for states to do as well.

A number of state laws set recycling/waste reduction goals, ranging from 25 percent to 50 percent to be met over the next five to ten years. At least five states have mandated citizen participation in recycling—Connecticut, New Jersey, New York, Pennsylvania, and Rhode Island. Others, including Florida, North Carolina, Oregon and Washington, require local governments to provide recycling programs.

Some jurisdictions have banned certain kinds of plastic packaging and food service items, particularly foamed polystyrene. Other laws, for example those in Florida, Louisiana, and North Carolina, restrict or ban certain nondegradable plastic packaging, such as six-pack yokes, grocery bags, and packaging made with chlorofluorocarbons (CFCs). In addition, many states now require plastic containers to be coded by resin type to aid sorting and recycling.

A few new laws dictate that newspapers contain some recycled newsprint. California requires publishers to increase their recycled paper content usage to 25 percent by 1991 and to 50 percent by 2000. Connecticut established a recycled newsprint goal of 20 percent of total newsprint consumption by 1992 and 90 percent by 1996.

Other trends in state waste reduction/recycling legislation include:

- Banning certain materials from landfills, such as lead-acid batteries, oil, tires, and yard waste.

- Assessing advance disposal fees on the purchase of hard-to-dispose-of products. Washington charged a $1 fee on new tire sales to fund a pilot tire recycling project, and Maine required a 10 percent deposit on lead-acid batteries.

- Encouraging or requiring composting of yard waste.

- Making the state a market for recycled goods by requiring or encouraging state agencies to buy products made from recycled materials, to use compost material whenever possible, and to recycle their own waste paper.

- Reducing taxes for companies or organizations buying recycling equipment. California provided tax credits of up to 40 percent on some purchases, with a cap of $250,000 for each piece (the credit expires in 1994). New Jersey enacted a 50 percent tax credit, and Maine a 30 percent credit.

- Providing some funding for market research and development (Pennsylvania and New York) and low-interest loans to recycling companies (Pennsylvania).

- Requiring recycling instruction in schools.

- Financing processing centers for recyclables. Massachusetts built a materials recovery facility (MRF) that opened in 1990. Communities can use the facility for free—if they require citizen participation in recycling programs. Rhode Island owns an MRF at which municipalities can deposit separated recyclables free of charge. And Connecticut provides grants to establish regional processing centers.

Source: "State Recycling Laws," *Governing* 3:11 (August 1990): 14A.

location of the proposed site and fear the possible contamination of nearby water supplies. There is another lawsuit pending in Michigan state court. Michigan opponents claim the site's location on drained wetlands could lead to contamination of well water used by nearby communities.

In Texas, lawsuits have slowed progress in finding a site. The Texas Low-Level Radioactive Waste Disposal Authority (LLRWDA) is deadlocked with El Paso County over a potential site in neighboring Hudspeth County. ... The suit [filed by the El Paso County commissioners] claims that the site, located 12 miles from the El Paso county line, is unsuitable because it is on a flood plain. Lee Mathews, general counsel for the Texas LLRWDA, says an El Paso citizens' group has spent about $2 million in legal fees and technical studies since 1986 to block the siting process.

Perhaps the most dramatic opposition has come from New York residents. Protests by the Allegheny County Non-Violent Action Committee ... kept the New York Siting Commission from setting foot onto the three potential sites in that county [between November 1989 and April 1990]. ... Opponents claim the siting commission has been deceptive and has lost its credibility. They claim the Genesee River, which flows through Rochester, sits on top of an important aquifer that could be contaminated by the prospective sites that are within a two- or five-mile radius of the river. Experts working for the commission do not consider the underground body of water to be a "principal" aquifer because it is a sandy layer that has not been proven to hold much water, says Jay Dunkleberger, executive director of the New York State Low-Level Radioactive Waste Siting Commission. [The strife over this situation became so difficult that the governor halted the process in April 1990 and legislation was adopted in August to change the process and management of the state's site selection process.]

Of the 14 states trying to establish a site, California is expected to finish first because there was little opposition to its selected site at Needles in the Mojave Desert.

Underlying opposition to the disposal sites is the question whether any state or federal agency has the knowledge or technology to guarantee the public's safety.

Scientific theories on the effects of low-level ionizing radiation on humans are in conflict. Studies released by the National Academy of Sciences in December [1989] state that the exposure to low-level radiation is at least three to four times more likely to cause cancer than previously believed. The study included 76,000 survivors of the U.S. atomic bombings of Nagasaki and Hiroshima. Scientists found that the amount of radiation the bombs emitted was less than originally thought, and that more cancer developed in recent years than had been expected from the lower levels. Dr. Letty Lutzker, president of the Greater New York Chapter of the Society of Nuclear Medicine, says the report is misleading and is causing unnecessary fear. "Low-level waste isn't very dangerous," she said. Lutzker notes that the study found an unexpected increase of about 5 percent and that the radiation exposure posed by a low-level radioactive waste site would be lower than those recorded in the study.

The precautions taken at a site and the design of a site can contain radiation to maintain public safety, says Kerr of IDNS. The above-ground facility proposed for Illinois would have about a seven-foot covering over its concrete vault. The covering would be in layers, for protection and drainage, with earth and liners of clay and a high density polyethylene, according to John Barcalow, section chief for low-level waste external affairs at IDNS. The waste, which would arrive in solid form at the site, would be stored in containers designed to last a minimum of 300 years. Each container would be encased in cement which lasts 500 years before being put in the vault. Chem-Nuclear, a subsidiary of Waste Management, has the contract to operate the facility and monitor it for 10 years after it is closed. The state must then monitor the site for 300 years or more, Kerr says.

Not satisfied by the IDNS guarantees is JoAnna Hoelscher of Citizens for a Better Environment. She and many others question the stability of a man-made structure, especially a concrete facility that must contain the radiation. A November 1989 report by the National Institute of Standards and Technology for the Nuclear Regulatory Commission (NRC) says that concrete has a "service" life of 500 years. Hoelscher refutes that conclusion. "Can we guarantee that some part of the concrete isn't going to crack and there be some leakage?" she asks. "We don't know enough about concrete to know if it'll last 500 years."

Environmentalists point out that it was only 40 years ago that low-level radioactive waste was dumped by the federal government in the ocean or buried in shallow trenches. "Technological arrogance has claimed that everything will be handled," says Dave Kraft, a spokesman for the Nuclear Energy Information Service in Evanston, a nonprofit organization that researches nuclear power alternatives and hazards. "I know these scientists are people who can only talk in probabilities, but when they go to these communities, they talk in more definite terms than is justifiable." Kraft does not believe low-level waste is "accorded the respect it deserves as a health and safety issue."

Low-level wastes are defined by the process of elimination. Anything that is not high-level waste is low-level, according to the NRC. Low-level waste is divided into three classes: Class A (the lowest), Class B and Class C.

Class A makes up about 97 percent of all commercial low-level waste and does not require remote handling. It decays within less than 100 years to levels acceptable to the NRC for safe exposure to humans. Class B and C waste make up the other 3 percent. Some of the Class C waste must be shielded and handled remotely because radioactivity levels tend to be 10 to 100 times higher than in Class B. Nuclear industry experts say that much of Class C waste is metal, which emits little radiation.

Environmentalists argue that Class C does not belong in any low-level waste dumps. New York Gov. Mario Cuomo is testing the argument in a New York lawsuit against the federal government. Diane D'Arrigo, director of the radioactive waste project for the Nuclear Information and Resource Service in Washington, D.C., agrees: "Anything hazardous more than 100 years should be redefined as high-level waste."

While the states grapple with sites for low-level wastes, the federal government has the same problems finding a site for high-level wastes. Meanwhile, high-level wastes are stored on site where they are produced, mainly at the 112 nuclear power plants in the nation. Eight years and $500 million has been spent studying a site at Yucca Mountain, Nev., but Nevada officials question the safety of a site located near a volcano and a fault line.

Distrust of the federal government is at the heart of much of the opposition to low-level sites in the states. "Even if the state does a good job, is the federal government going to make regulation changes that'll upset the whole apple cart?" Kraft asks. Ellen Beal of Don't Waste Michigan is also uneasy. "The trend in the nuclear industry is to deregulate waste. . . . [I]t saves them money. They've got no place to put high-level waste. . . . If at some date they want the class of waste accepted to include hotter wastes, we're afraid the state wouldn't have a legal right to refuse it."

Extremists among opponents in New York believe the low-level waste should stay on the site where it is created, mainly at nuclear power plant sites. "Let's not open up a new facility that's never been contaminated," says Ted Taylor, a nuclear physicist and member of Concerned Citizens of Allegheny County. Illinois' Sen. Joyce does not think that is the best solution: "This stuff lasts forever. That public utility may be gone in 100 years."

More likely to happen is some agreement to establish fewer disposal sites for the low-level wastes. From 1980 to 1988 the national volume of low-level wastes produced by nuclear power plants dropped by 72 percent, according to the U.S. Council for Energy Awareness. The logical question to ask is: Why have more than three sites to replace the three that will close?

To date, the most outspoken opponent of the number of waste sites being planned by the states has been Michigan Gov. James Blanchard. A Democrat, he wrote President Bush in December requesting the president limit the number of sites. Blanchard told Bush that plans to construct 12 to 15 sites is "economically and environmentally irresponsible" and that the states are "unable to resolve these serious flaws alone." Michigan plans to sue the federal government, challenging the number of sites being built and the constitutionality

of making the states take title to low-level wastes, according to Chris DeWitt of the Michigan Attorney General's Office.

Once Michigan files its suit, three lawsuits will be challenging the federal government's authority to make states liable for the low-level wastes. New York Gov. Cuomo filed his suit February 21, [1990,] preceded on February 9 by a federal lawsuit filed by the Concerned Citizens of Nebraska.

Will the pressure of court battles move Congress to amend the 1980 act? Many doubt it, but not Sen. Joyce. He points to the sluggish progress of the host states as proof that they will not meet the 1993 deadline, and that they may seek help from Congress to find a place for their waste. "Probably if 35 or 40 states don't have a place to put their waste, common sense tells you that Congress is going to find a place to put it," Joyce says.

Meanwhile, [37] years after President Eisenhower hailed the groundbreaking of the first nuclear power plant, Illinois and other states are struggling to bury atomic age leftovers. The struggle may not end with the 1993 deadline. Environmental concerns and the fear that Congress will dump the waste on a few states, has site opponents and some proponents pushing for a slowdown in site selection. "The first states to the finish line will undoubtedly end up taking the waste for the whole nation," Beal says. "It behooves any state to slow down."

Treating HIV:
An Expensive RX for States

by Karen Hansen and Tracey Hooker

Money, morals and medicine are at the crux of the nation's debate over how far we will go in treating AIDS. And the challenge of the '90s will increasingly center on all of the estimated 1 million people infected with the HIV virus, not solely on patients with full-blown AIDS. Following the conclusion of federally sponsored clinical studies in 1989 of the drug AZT for early treatment of HIV-infected patients, the health focus has effectively changed from the death-sentence disease AIDS, to the long term treatable "HIV disease."

New research by the National Institutes of Health shows that about half the Americans infected with the AIDS virus may prolong their lives by taking AZT—triple the previous estimate—and the Centers for Disease Control are urging HIV-positive patients to take the drug early to forestall the onset of AIDS. The NIH findings are a "significant milestone in the battle to change AIDS from a fatal disease to a treatable one," said Health and Human Services Secretary Louis Sullivan.

But in a society of limited resources and unlimited medical possibilities, where will the money to prolong 500,000 more lives with this drug come from? Not necessarily from self-insured health plans, which can severely limit

or eliminate AIDS coverage. Not from medically indigent state programs, which are woefully underfunded in terms of the numbers of people seeking assistance to buy AZT. Not wholly from Medicaid, which may only cover the drug for those patients with full blown AIDS or AIDS-related complex. Not from Medicare, which limits its coverage to people who have been disabled for two years or who are over age 65. And not from public hospitals, which are overwhelmed by indigent AIDS patients.

Over the past five years, state governments have increasingly taken on the responsibility of finding money to care for patients with AIDS. "State and local governments have been paying at least half the costs of treatment and are paying more and more with each passing day," says Daniel Fox, president of the Milbank Memorial Fund, a health services research fund. Earlier treatment of HIV-infected people will undoubtedly raise serious financing problems for states.

Just how much will it cost? This is difficult to assess. "Forecasts for treatment

This article is reprinted with permission from *State Legislatures* 16:4 (April 1990): 13-15. © 1990 by the National Conference of State Legislatures.

costs vary widely," says Fred Deering, chairman of Security Life in Denver. He estimates that the treatment bill for people infected with the AIDS virus will reach ... $35 billion by 2000.

But an investment in early AZT treatment may save states money in the long run. Because effective drug treatment can prolong the lives of those with HIV infection, perhaps as much as 10 to 15 years, they can continue working and keep any insurance they have, thus reducing their reliance on Medicaid and other social service programs such as disability pay, subsidized housing, food stamps and AFDC. In addition, they contribute to the economy as productive, taxpaying members of society.

AZT is an expensive drug, costing some $6,400 a year per patient. But the cost could be cut in half if physicians follow a new FDA recommendation to reduce the dosage by half. Expanding its use to the 500,000 people the NIH believes could benefit from the drug, however, would cost the nation some $1.6 billion to $3.2 billion a year (depending on dosage), may simply postpone the inevitable, and may not decrease the total lifetime cost of medical care.

"The uncertainties of the financial implications of a state-level AZT program are not so great as to justify a refusal to continue assisting those in need," says Robin Levin Penslar, research associate at The Poynter Center, Indiana University. She estimates that prescribing AZT for these people can actually reduce the costs of treating AIDS and AIDS-related complex by $386 million in just one year.

But money isn't the only issue states must be concerned with, says Larry Bartlett, director of Health Systems Research, Inc. "The major question is not whether states will pay for AZT through public programs. States have an additional responsibility to ensure that HIV-positive individuals do not lose access to current private sector coverage because of discriminatory activities—such as insurers refusing to extend coverage to certain occupational groups like florists and hair dressers or by carving out disease specific caps on HIV-related services or specifically excluding coverage of AZT in their drug benefits," he says. Self-insured plans are often culprits, since federal law exempts such plans from state regulation.

The CDC has taken an aggressive stance on HIV. It recommends that people at risk of HIV infection seek testing immediately, it recommends that those who are HIV positive have their immune system regularly monitored, and it recommends that doctors initiate early drug treatment for medically eligible patients (those with a certain level of CD4 cell counts). "There are a lot of unknowns, but to me the biggest—because it's likely to have the most radical change—is the impact of preventive therapy in infected people to prevent the onset of AIDS," says Dr. Timothy Dondero of the Centers for Disease Control.

As the disease enters its second decade, AIDS funding is coming into increasing conflict with other public health and social needs, casting a shadow over the future allocation of more state and federal money for HIV treatment. In the states, a host of issues—prenatal care, education, prison construction—compete with AIDS for money, as they do on the federal level.

"AIDS has generated attention all out of proportion to other diseases," says Stanford University economist Joel Hay, a researcher at the Hoover Institution. "It's new. It's fatal. It's associated with high-risk behavior that's outside the mainstream morals. That captures our attention. But if they had a quilt for victims of heart disease [similar to the famed AIDS quilt], it would cover Washington, D.C. in two months."

Fighting the Discrimination Disease

Often dubbed "the second epidemic," fear, misinformation and prejudice against both people with AIDS and real or perceived HIV carriers have increased at a rate comparable to the spread of the HIV virus. . . .

HIV-related discrimination is difficult to document because persons with HIV are less likely to file a discrimination complaint and are often unsure of the remedies available to them. Also, people with AIDS may find the complaint resolution process too long and not responsive enough when dealing with a terminal illness. Nevertheless, numerous people have testified that they have been discriminated against after others learned that they had AIDS or had tested positive for HIV, or were related to someone with the disease. Some had lost their jobs, lost their housing, or lost their health insurance. Some had been denied dental or medical treatment, others had been victims of violence. . . .

Most states have laws forbidding discrimination against the handicapped. Over half these states have formally extended their protections to include people with AIDS, AIDS-related complex and HIV infection; not quite as many have also extended these protections to people perceived as being HIV infected. Most have done this through written statements from their human or civil rights commission, or with attorney general opinions; a few have statutorily extended their protections of the handicapped.

Employment, health care and housing are the areas most often covered under states' handicapped protection laws extended for HIV infection.

Most of the provisions protecting against discrimination by employers prohibit the use of HIV tests as a condition of employment or prohibit employers from discriminating against someone solely because he has taken an HIV test.

In health care, laws generally prohibit denial of admission to health care facilities based on AIDS or HIV status, prohibit denial of care based on failure to give informed consent and forbid the use of HIV tests as a condition to receive unrelated care.

Public ignorance about the disease and how it spreads has resulted in needless fear and prejudice. The best cure for discrimination is education, but scores of education programs during the nine years since the first recorded case of AIDS have failed to reach everyone.

Source: Julie Lays, "Fighting the Discrimination Disease," *State Legislatures* 16:4 (April 1990): 20-21. Reprinted with permission. © 1990 by the National Conference of State Legislatures.

Hay and other critics point to the following statistics:

Federal spending for AIDS has increased from $5 million in 1982 to some $1.6 billion today for the disease that has so far struck some 118,000 Americans (although another 900,000 are estimated to be infected and expected to get AIDS).

At the same time, the federal government spent some $1.6 billion on cancer, which killed 500,000 Americans in 1989, and about $1 billion on heart disease, cause of death for 770,000 Americans [that] year.

But the response to these statistics by President Reagan's Commission on AIDS and Congress' . . . National Commission on AIDS is that this disease is different because it's infectious, epidemic and it can be contained quickly.

And Health Systems Research's Bartlett argues that AIDS should serve as a catalyst to focus attention on health care access for all chronically ill people.

"We should look at access to treatment for the HIV-infected in the same way as the broader access problem. Treat it as you would treat any disease," Bartlett says.

Yet even strong AIDS advocates, like Dr. Phillip Lee, head of the Institutes for Health Policy Studies at the University of California at San Francisco, do not believe in lobbying solely for funds to treat AIDS. "There are 37 million uninsured Americans. You can't say you're going to deal with AIDS before you deal with someone who's pregnant and needs prenatal care."

Former Colorado Governor Richard D. Lamm, who held the Presidential Chair at the University of California-San Francisco School of Medicine, echoes those sentiments. "In a nation that doesn't cover basic health care for all of its citizens, doesn't vaccinate all of its children, doesn't provide prenatal care to all of its women, it is very unlikely that public policy can justify paying [so much money] for a drug that does not cure but only alleviates symptoms.

"This is not a moral judgment, but instead a judgment of health policy."

Yet some would argue that morals do enter into this complex public policy decision. Colorado Senator Dottie Wham observes that there is a conflict between public funding for HIV and other diseases because of a prevailing belief that AIDS patients "bring it on themselves." And although AZT does improve the quality of people's lives, the disease is terminal.

And that is the crux of the argument for many. Medicaid in 1989 spent an estimated $120 million on AZT and is expected to pay $275 million for the drug in 1993. . . . An advisory committee of the FDA unanimously recommended in January [1990] that the use of AZT be expanded to HIV-infected people without AIDS symptoms. FDA approval [followed].

AIDS is the greatest cause of death for men ages 25 to 44, and the fastest growing cause of death for women in the same category. By Dec. 31, 1989, there were 117,781 cases of AIDS in the United States, and 70,313 people had died from the disease. In addition, there were 1,995 reported cases of AIDS among children under age 13, and 1,080 deaths. AIDS advocates argue that if AZT is not made more available to HIV-infected people and funding assistance is not provided, those AIDS numbers will increase, with a cost to society estimated by researchers at between $541,000 to $623,000 per person in foregone earnings associated with premature death. (The foregone earnings of intravenous drug abusers is probably far below average U.S. earnings, but homosexual and bisexual males may have above average earnings.)

These estimates are nine to 10 times as large as the $60,000 in lifetime medical costs per AIDS patient. Foregone earnings of the 245,000 AIDS cases projected to occur between 1981 and the end of 1991 imply a loss to society of some $132 billion to $153 billion.

"Thus most of the economic impact of AIDS will occur via the loss of future output and only to a lesser extent via the diversion of scarce resources to medical care for AIDS patients," writes David E. Bloom, Columbia University economist, and Geoffrey Carliner, executive director of the National Bureau of Economic Research, in the February 1988 issue of *Science*.

"The principle of equity unquestionably demands a government-supported AZT purchase program," says Indiana University's Penslar.

Congress has appropriated $29.6 million through the Department of Health and Human Services to help states purchase AZT for low income AIDS patients.

Yet many people who are infected with HIV but have not been diagnosed with ARC or full-blown AIDS are not eligible for Medicaid coverage, according to Richard Chambers, director of intergovernmental affairs for the Health Care Financing Administration. Except for those who are eligible because of category, such as single parents with dependent children and those with other non-AIDS disabilities, Medicaid often covers health care only for the financially eligible who are diagnosed with AIDS or AIDS-related complex.

The uninsured and the underinsured HIV-infected population will have to rely on federal and state funds for their preventive care. And to some degree, states are responding. According to a report from the Intergovernmental Health Policy Project at George Washington University, state-only, non-Medicaid funds for HIV patient care increased 160 percent in fiscal year 1989. But if states don't have comprehensive strategies for indigent care, access to care by HIV-infected people will be a problem with serious consequences for public hospitals.

AIDS already threatens to overwhelm public hospitals in New York, San Francisco, Miami and Houston—where the virus hit and silently spread in the early 1980s. San Francisco health officials, for example, estimate that it will cost the city's public hospitals and clinics nearly a quarter of the $100 million that may be spent from all sources, including insurance companies and charity organizations, to provide medical care and home support.

AIDS patients are already forcing some public hospitals to take the difficult stand of telling patients who "don't have urgent or semi-urgent conditions to come back in a few months," according to Dennis Andrulis, president of the National Public Health and Hospital Institute. If AIDS patients are turned away, there is clearly no room for assisting HIV patients

New Jersey was the first state to act on the CDC's guidelines for identifying and providing early AZT treatment for the estimated 50,000 to 70,000 state residents infected with HIV. California, with one of the nation's highest incidence of AIDS, was also quick to respond to the recommendation to begin early AZT treatment for its estimated 200,000 HIV patients by appropriating $2.7 million for HIV drugs and $2.3 million for treatment services for the uninsured. And Texas, with the fourth largest number of AIDS patients, established an HIV Medication Program to help people, hospitals and clinics and local health clinics to purchase AIDS medicine. In all three states, the emphasis is on providing more cost-effective care outside the hospital.

In all, 10 states appropriated their own funds for AZT programs last year, including states with low rates of infection such as Hawaii and Utah. Some states—Maryland among them—are expanding coverage of AZT through Medicaid programs at their own expense.

The proportion of the health care costs for AIDS patients paid by state Medicaid programs has increased from 36 percent in 1983 to 49 percent in 1988, according to UC-San Francisco's Dr. Lee. In Michigan, for example, even though only about 10 percent of the state's citizens are eligible for Medicaid, fully 50 percent of the AIDS patients are. If states choose to expand their assistance to HIV-infected people, their share of Medicaid and indigent funding will continue to rise. The new federal assistance for AZT requires a 50 percent match by states. Many states depend on this money to help pay for treating their uninsured patients. "The whole problem is funding," says Louisiana Representative Mitchell Landrieu, chair of the state's AIDS Task Force. "Louisiana is not going to be able to pick up the tab for AZT" but will try to "have those matching funds in place" to take advantage of the federal program.

Low incidence states have "an opportunity to get ahead of the issue," says Dr. Charles Konigsberg, a member of the National Commission on AIDS and Kansas director of health. But while many states have expressed interest in planning for HIV treatment, few have actually developed comprehensive plans.

By the end of the decade, AIDS could be a manageable chronic disease perhaps with increased life expectancy, according to researchers at the National Institutes of Health. Inevitably, then, all states will be affected by the increasing demand for early intervention. And although AIDS is expected to claim fewer lives, for every reported case of AIDS there could be as many as nine people with HIV infection, putting policymakers in the position of having to provide preventive medical services to a large and growing number of people.

Auto Insurance Reform:
The Never-Ending Story

by Jeffrey L. Katz

When consumers across the country demand better auto insurance policies, they often hear about Michigan. Drivers there receive relatively generous medical benefits and prompt compensation after accidents. Yet their premiums are lower than the national average.

So why is it that, even in Michigan, consumers are feeling pinched? Why are Michigan Democrats, and even some Republicans, supporting mandatory cuts in auto insurance rates? Because average auto insurance premiums in the state rose nearly 42 percent between 1984 and 1988—three times the national increase in overall consumer prices.

Nationally, auto insurance premiums per passenger vehicle rose an average of 47 percent from 1984 to 1988, the latest year for which figures are available. Ten states and the District of Columbia experienced increases of more than 60 percent.

Those increases have come despite several rounds of reform across the country, all aimed at holding down premiums. The public seems madder than ever. "There's a major consumer revolt going on, particularly in places with big cities," says Robert Hunter, president of the National Insurance Consumer Organization.

Insurers say premiums outpaced the con-sumer price index because of steep increases in auto repair and replacement costs, health care costs and attorneys' fees. They also blame a sharp increase in auto thefts and a growing number of uninsured drivers who force higher costs on those who are insured. Consumer groups concede that these factors drive up insurance costs and that some companies might lose money on auto insurance in some years. But consumer activists say the real culprits are the industry's inefficiency and quest for more investment income; the lack of strong government regulation; state and federal antitrust exemptions that allow insurers to share cost and rate information; and a system that relies too heavily on litigation.

Several states have followed the lead of a California initiative and tried to impose mandatory rollbacks of auto insurance rates. New Jersey has replaced a large and expensive state-run insurance pool with one that covers only high-risk drivers. Some consumer advocates are lobbying to remove the insurance industry's federal antitrust exemption, in hopes that more competition will bring down

Jeffrey L. Katz is a staff writer for *Governing*. This article appeared in *Governing* 4:2 (November 1990): 23-25.

rates, but the industry is not expected to lose this exemption any time soon.

Insurers expect more turmoil. "I see continuing movement in a lot of different directions," says David Snyder, a counsel to State Farm insurance and former counsel to the American Insurance Association. But at the heart of the debate, Snyder and many others agree, is the very structure of auto insurance. The rapid rise in insurance rates is reviving a long-standing dispute over whether consumers fare better under the traditional "tort liability" system, which places virtually no limits on the right to sue for damages resulting from an auto accident, or under "no-fault" insurance, which generally places restrictions on that right in an effort to reduce litigation.

Some states that don't have no-fault insurance are considering adopting it. And some that do have a form of no-fault are considering raising the threshold above which policyholders are permitted to sue.

For the most part, the hotbeds of consumer activism on the issue have been in the Northeast and other areas with large urban concentrations, where insurance rates are especially high. It was the support of voters in eight densely populated counties around Los Angeles and San Francisco in 1988 that carried California's Proposition 103, which called for rolling back auto insurance rates by 20 percent.

"Proposition 103 was our worst nightmare, the worst nightmare for anybody in business," says Sean Mooney, senior vice president of the Insurance Information Institute. Although many of the reforms that were also part of Proposition 103, such as creating a consumer watchdog agency and allowing financial institutions to sell insurance, have been upheld, the rate rollback has been delayed by the state Supreme Court.

That has not dimmed the popularity of rollbacks. Since 1988, legislatures have ap-

proved reductions of 20 percent in New Jersey, 15 percent in Nevada, 10 percent in Pennsylvania and 5 percent in South Carolina. Insurers have gotten court orders to delay the rate reductions in New Jersey and Nevada. Pennsylvania's reductions were accompanied by new limits on medical reimbursements and rate rollbacks of up to 22 percent for those consumers who generally gave up the right to sue for pain and suffering; South Carolina increased penalties for drunk driving and adopted a mandatory seat belt law.

Rate rollbacks are controversial even among those who take a consumer's viewpoint. Jeffrey O'Connell, a University of Virginia law professor who helped popularize the no-fault concept in 1965, thinks it's ludicrous for lawmakers to try to cut consumer prices. "It would be nice if we could have cheaper furniture," he says, "or picture-framing or cars or clothes. But anybody who knows anything about economics knows you can't pass a law saying you must roll prices back without doing anything about the underlying costs." A more effective way to lower the price of insurance and promptly pay accident victims, O'Connell says, is through true no-fault insurance.

The term generally applies to auto insurance plans that allow policyholders to recover actual financial losses from their own insurance companies, regardless of fault. While this is supposed to speed reimbursement for injuries, the trade-off to keep costs down is that policyholders are usually limited in their rights to sue for "pain and suffering," emotional trauma and non-economic damages.

Some consumer activists, most notably Ralph Nader, object to no-fault because it limits legal action and restricts consumers' recourse when disputing reimbursements from their own insurance companies. But it is the nation's trial lawyers who have led the fight against no-fault.

The trial lawyers vehemently object to

restricting a victim's right to sue. And they argue that those responsible for accidents ought to pay for them. "I don't believe that any consumers are crying out for no-fault," says Michael Maher, president of the Association of Trial Lawyers of America. "I think the industry sees it as a vehicle to make more money." The most damning aspect of no-fault insurance, Maher says, is that it hasn't reduced premiums. Advocates of no-fault argue that it hasn't been effective in most states because trial lawyers browbeat legislators into keeping the barriers to legal action too low.

What is called no-fault now exists in 26 states, the District of Columbia and Puerto Rico. However, in its strictest form, as it is referred to by the industry and others, the term applies only to those systems that also limit the policyholders' right to sue for recovery beyond out-of-pocket costs. The laws of fourteen states and Puerto Rico meet this criterion.

But even most of these states have set such a low dollar threshold for permissible suits that they have had little impact on insurers' costs and, consequently, their rates. In Connecticut, for instance, if an accident victim's medical expenses exceed $400, he can take the other driver to court for compensatory damages for pain and suffering plus out-of-pocket costs. Says O'Connell, "As long as there's litigation over fault and payment for pain and suffering, the system is going to be wildly expensive and out of control, especially in urban areas."

The three states considered to have the most effective no-fault provisions are Florida, Michigan and New York. Rather than permit accident victims to sue for pain and suffering and out-of-pocket costs when their medical expenses reach a specified dollar limit, these three states have established a "verbal" threshold. Michigan's law, for instance, limits litigation to cases where someone "has suffered

death, serious impairment of body function or permanent serious disfigurement."

No-fault coverage is mandatory in Michigan, and insurers provide unlimited compensation for the costs of medical treatment and rehabilitation, plus up to $2,939 a month for three years for lost income and up to $20 a day for three years for services that had been rendered by the victim.

But no matter how generous the benefits, Michigan policyholders are telling legislators that their auto insurance premiums have "gone up faster than my ability to pay," says Representative Mary Brown, a Democrat who chairs the House Insurance Committee. The Democrat-controlled House responded in 1990 by passing bills removing insurers' exemption from the state's own antitrust laws, thus restricting their ability to share rate information with one another, and rolling back rates by 30 percent across the board.

Both bills languished in the Republican-controlled Senate. Most GOP senators would rather control costs by limiting what doctors can charge and devising stricter guidelines for benefits, as well as offering lower-cost premiums that limit medical benefits, says Jurgen Skoppek, counsel to the Senate Commerce Committee.

Frustrated by their inability to move no-fault measures through legislatures, a coalition called Project New Start, which gets some funding from insurers, is trying to give the public a choice between no-fault and tort liability insurance. O'Connell, father of the modern no-fault auto insurance plan, is encouraged that states like New Jersey and Pennsylvania recently began offering consumers a choice, although he doesn't think that those who opt for no-fault save enough on their premiums. Project New Start's proposal, as considered in Arizona, would further restrict no-fault consumers' right to sue with the idea that they would reap more savings. Those who choose no-fault would be guaranteed savings of at least 20 percent for the first year.

O'Connell says the choice proposal forces trial lawyers into the position of having to say that no-fault is so bad that "nobody should be allowed to have it even if they want it."

Motorists who choose tort liability retain the right to sue any driver for damages and are liable to be sued by others. When a no-fault driver and a tort driver are involved in an accident, the no-fault driver turns first to his own insurer for compensation, but is also able to sue the tort liability driver for uncompensated losses.

While the insurance industry supports the choice proposal, Mooney says, it's complicated to explain to consumers the differences between no-fault and tort liability insurance. "It's a difficult job explaining it to legislators," he adds.

That is precisely the point the trial lawyers have seized on. "Most people do not understand their need for liability auto insurance or coverages under their auto policy until it's too late," says Maher of the trial lawyers' association. Consumers will be attracted to the lower-cost policy without fully understanding that they will be giving up their right to sue, he says.

A Harmfulness Tax:
Legalize and Tax Drugs

by Lester Grinspoon

In the era of the Volstead Act, H. L. Mencken said of the alcohol problem that between the distillers and saloonkeepers on one side and the prohibitionists on the other, no intelligent person thought there was any solution at all. The same may be true of the illicit drug problem today, with its traffickers and users on one side and its moralists and police on the other. Only the problem is perhaps more serious because the acceptable range of solutions is so narrow. The report of the President's Commission on Organized Crime and the more recently elaborated Bush-Bennett plan suggest how things are going right now. There is very little effective opposition to prohibition.

The American war on drugs began with the Harrison Narcotics Act in 1914 and has escalated in the last 20 years. Federal, state and local governments now spend an estimated $8 to $9 billion a year on direct drug enforcement activities and millions more to house and feed the drug dealers and users who comprise one-third of federal prisoners and contribute substantially to the need to build more prisons. It is said that the pendulum of public attitudes swings back and forth between harshness and leniency in drug control. If there was some swing toward leniency in the early 70s, it now

appears to be going the other way, as indicated by the September 1989 White House paper on National Drug Control Strategy. This Bush-Bennett plan calls for even more spending on law enforcement.

Drugs enter the United States at a growing rate despite the war effort, although that effort does inflate prices and keep the drug dealers' franchises lucrative. Another consequence is drug-related crime and violence, a product of the black market in drugs now as it was a product of the black market in alcohol in the 1920s. The threat to civil liberties grows as the warriors, already by necessity using entrapment and informers, make plans to send in the army and examine everyone's urine periodically. They are already testing the urine of federal employees randomly.

Any serious approach to this problem (as opposed to the present one) demands a recognition of complexity and ambiguity. We have to compromise between social reality and the dream of a drug free society. We may have to

Lester Grinspoon is an associate professor of psychiatry at Harvard Medical School. This article is reprinted with permission from *The Journal of State Government* 63:2 (April-June 1990): 46-49. © 1990 by the Council of State Governments.

acknowledge that the use of drugs and alcohol has benefits as well as dangers. The main obstacle to thinking about serious alternatives to present policies is that no one in government wants to give up the symbolism of the criminal law or the commitment that has been made over the last 70 years, not only in the United States but all over the world to treating drugs as a criminal problem.

Ambient Public Attitude

But there is a great deal of public ambivalence, or, to put it less kindly, hypocrisy, where this issue is concerned. The moral consensus about the evil of drugs is often passionate but sometimes shallow. We pretend that eliminating the drug traffic is like eliminating slavery or piracy, or sometimes as though it were like eradicating smallpox or malaria. But no one would suggest that we legalize piracy or give up the effort to eradicate infectious diseases, yet conservative authorities like economist Milton Friedman and the *Economist* of London have suggested legalization of drugs.

Despite the hysterical rhetoric we often hear, drug control is not a settled issue in the same sense. Or rather, the need for that kind of rhetoric is a sign that it is not a settled issue. On the one hand, it is accepted in public discourse that everything possible has to be done to prevent people from using any of the controlled substances. On the other hand, there is an informal lore of drug use that is more tolerant. At one time it looked as though the forms of public discourse and this private language were coming closer together. Now they seem to be drifting apart again. A type of pretense that we have long abandoned, in the case of alcohol, is still considered the only respectable position where other drugs are concerned. Ambivalence (to put it kindly) or hypocrisy (to put it unkindly) have always been an undercurrent in public attitudes to-

ward drugs, even while the criminal control system becomes more and more entrenched. That undercurrent is what leaves room for the possibility of change.

A Plan for Legalization

I would like to suggest a proposal for a noncriminal approach to recreational drugs. Let currently controlled substances be legalized and taxed. The taxes would be used for drug education and for paying the medical and social costs of drug abuse. A commission would be established to determine these costs separately for each drug, and the rate of taxation would be adjusted to reflect the information gathered by the commission. Thus the government would acknowledge the impossibility of eliminating all drug use and use its taxing power and educational authority to encourage safer drug use. The drugs that are now legal, alcohol and tobacco, would not be distinguished from the others.

To illustrate the kind of calculation involved, it was recently estimated that direct health care costs plus indirect losses in productivity and earnings due to cigarettes amount to $65 billion a year, or about $2 a pack. (The exact figures depend on how costs are defined; for example, the economic loss from smoking may be balanced in a perverse way, by the lowered cost of caring for chronic disabling diseases of old age in a society where many die young of smoking-related illness.) Such a taxation policy might be regarded as a way of making people buy insurance for the risks to themselves and others because of their use of drugs. Life insurance companies already offer substantial discounts in their premiums for non-smokers, and this insurance preference is slowly being extended to fire and other insurance policies.

The program might be instituted in phases, so that we could adjust and learn more before committing ourselves fully. Phase one might involve alcohol, tobacco and cannabis: alcohol and tobacco because they are already legal; cannabis because it is probably the least dangerous drug used for pleasure. They all could be sold through specially licensed outlets at prices determined by the commission. Advertising would be banned. Present prices might be maintained at the start. Then, as the commission collected more information, pricing could change to reflect social costs. If this system works as hoped, data eventually would indicate that these drugs are causing less and less harm. At that point we could consider bringing other drugs into the system.

No More Drug Wars

The advantage is that we would no longer have the expense, corruption, chaos and terror of the war between drug traffickers and narcotics agents. In this war a kind of self-reinforcing cycle is developing. Drug enforcement operations begin to pay for themselves by funds confiscated from the drug traffickers whose operations they make enormously profitable. The taxing system suggested here would establish a different revenue cycle, in which society would pay for the costs of drug abuse by extracting them from the drug users in proportion to the amount they contribute to the problem. The commission that supervised this taxing system also would serve as an educator and guide to society—an educator not constrained by the present totally unrealistic assumption, built into the criminal law, that any use of certain drugs must be evil or dangerous, while other drugs have a range of benign and harmful uses. Honest drug education would become possible.

Is it plausible to think that this arrangement would work? Would it be possible to tax drugs enough to pay for their costs? Even if it were possible, would drug abuse increase so much that we would be paying too high a price in personal and social misery? Is the elasticity

of demand great enough so that taxing would substantially influence the amount of drugs consumed, especially by heavy users? Evidence on all this is very uncertain, even in the cases of alcohol and tobacco, where most research has been done. There is a large literature on the destruction curve of alcohol consumption among individuals in society, most of which concludes that any policy designed to cut total consumption will at least proportionately reduce alcohol use among problem drinkers and, therefore, the medical and social costs of alcohol abuse. The demand is elastic enough, even among alcohol users who create problems by their use, to be affected by a rise in price. In fact, there is some evidence that in countries where the price of alcohol is relatively higher there are fewer alcohol problems and the same is true for states within the United States.

Curbing Drug Demand

There also is some evidence of elasticity of demand for heroin addicts. Several studies suggest that addicts adjust the size of their habits to the price of heroin. One authority on heroin control has said that criminal law would be effective in cutting down heroin from five minutes to two hours. This is the "crime tariff." The criminal law makes it risky to manufacture and distribute the drug. This raises its cost to the consumer, who therefore needs more time to earn or steal enough money to obtain it and restricts accessibility, so that the consumer has to spend more time finding out where to get it. The question is whether through taxation we could impose a limitation similar to the crime tariff but more efficiently and with fewer monstrous side effects.

Inelasticity of demand is greatest in the case of tobacco, because nicotine is one of the most highly addicting substances. Nevertheless, it is clear that even here raising the price by taxes has considerable effect on consumption. Research suggests that for every 10 percent increase in cigarette prices, consumption will decrease about 4 percent. Some studies suggest that the price affects mainly the decision to start smoking regularly rather than the quantity smoked by an already addicted smoker. Thus the short run impact of extra taxation would be small, and it would reduce cigarette smoking only in the long run. Other studies find that as the average costs of tobacco is raised the income elasticity of demand increases, that is, poor people are more deterred from cigarette consumption than richer ones.

A problem raised by any system of authorized sales is the black market. The tax would have to be set low enough so that a black market would not be profitable. It is possible to do this and still reduce demand for the drug considerably, as the case of alcohol seems to show. On the other hand, it is not clear whether any tax low enough to prevent a substantial black market would be high enough to pay for the social and medical costs of the drug use. Certainly present taxes on alcohol are far from doing that. It might prove impossible to create a system that would make the abusers of a drug, or even its users, pay for the full costs of abuse. Maybe this problem is practically insoluble. Certainly the criminal law approach offers no solution for it.

We simply don't know the amount of drug use and the seriousness of drug problems that would exist under this kind of system— whether a legal taxation system would have the same effect as the current crime tariff. One way to study the issue might be to examine the effect of gambling habits of the institution of state lotteries in competition with illegal numbers games. In any case, to undertake such a bold move we would have to decide that the deprivation of freedom and the damage wrought by prohibition is greater than the damage attendant on an increment of drug use, much as we did when we decided to repeal the Volstead Act.

Models for Legislation

There are already some models available for legalization or quasi-legalization. In Amsterdam, there is a union or organization of drug users and addicts that advises officials. Heroin addicts get free methadone and marijuana is sold at openly tolerated cannabis cafes. Alaska allows its citizens to grow marijuana for household use and several other states have reduced the penalties for marijuana possession to fines similar to traffic tickets. In one of these states, Maine, a $300,000 a-year outlay on law enforcement was converted to a $20,000 gain for the state treasury with no increase in marijuana use.

Many might agree that the harmfulness tax approach would work if it were limited to alcohol, tobacco and cannabis. But what about cocaine? Well, consider the present alternatives. The Bush-Bennett plan, perhaps because its authors realize that the demand reduction, particularly in the inner city, will be difficult to achieve, aims at eliminating production of cocaine. But the so-called Andean strategy of interrupting South American supplies is bound to fail for simple reasons of botany. The assumption seems to be that coca grows only in Peru, Bolivia and Colombia. In reality, the coca bush will grow in any place where certain conditions are met: an altitude of 1500 to 6000 feet, continuous high humidity, a uniform average temperature of 65 degrees throughout the year and soil free of limestone. Coca thrives on land that is too poor for other crops. In the past it has been grown commercially in Jamaica, Madagascar, India, Ceylon and especially Java. Even if, implausible, the coca bush could be destroyed in the Andes, it would soon be blooming again elsewhere, just as the cultivation of opium poppies increased in Iran and Afghanistan when it was curtailed in the Far East. Let's hope we don't have to see American soldiers coming home in body bags before we realize that the Andean strategy will never eliminate the supply of drugs.

Parenthetically, it is worth noting the absurdity of our national self-righteousness with respect to Colombian cocaine entrepreneurs. The United States manufactures 600 billion cigarettes a year and sends 100 billion overseas. The 500 billion cigarettes consumed yearly at home cause 400,000 deaths; by extrapolation, our export trade causes 80,000 deaths abroad—far more than the number of deaths cocaine produces in this country. Furthermore, the Colombian government at least offers no official encouragement to the cocaine traffic, our government subsidizes tobacco cultivation and cigarette exports with the enthusiastic support of some of the fiercest congressional anti-drug warriors. Our government has no right to be morally indignant.

Cocaine Use Down

What about cocaine demand? The barrage of drug-war publicity has obscured the fact that the number of people using cocaine is declining. The reason is that the middle class is giving up the drug, just as it continues to give up the even more addictive nicotine. When people who are not otherwise desperate become aware of the dangers of drugs, they begin to avoid them. The cocaine problem is not improving, because it is largely a problem of the inner cities. Conditions there are worse now than they were when the Kerner Commission made its report 20 years ago. Increasingly, cocaine users are people who feel hopeless, trapped and alienated, who are able to find only miserable jobs at low pay or no job at all. When these people are exposed to crack cocaine, they have three choices: a) they can ignore it; b) they can seek respite by using the drug for a 20 minute holiday during which they feel good about themselves and hopeful about their situation; it is an illusion but they have nothing better; c) they can decide to sell crack in hope of getting rich and buying the luxury products with which our consumer society tantalizes them. This, at least, is not always an illusion; crack provides a genuine entrepreneurial opportunity for a few.

The social, psychological and economic pressure moving young people in the inner city toward options b and c are enormous. Crack is powerfully attractive to demoralized people in a desperate social situation. Admittedly, the harmfulness tax is not an answer to this problem. But the answer is even less likely to be found in criminal law enforcement, which Bush and Bennett practically equate with prevention. No policy aimed directly at drugs and drug users can deal with the social issues that are the true heart of what is loosely, inadequately and propagandistically labeled the "drug problem."

Home Schooling Undergoes a Resurgence

by Lynn Olson

Bettie Ethell never expected to teach her children at home. But when her husband traveled for his job, she would pull her offspring out of school for two weeks, get their homework assignments, and the whole family would travel with him. "When my children came back," she recalls, "they were always a week ahead of the class. I realized they weren't missing anything; they were benefiting. So we tried home schooling on a one-year basis."

Eight years later, she has educated three children herself. In the process, Ethell has joined a growing number of staunch advocates of home education.

Since 1982, 32 states have changed their laws or regulations to make it easier for parents like Ethell to teach their children at home legally, a change that has come about largely because of pressure from the home-schooling community. Although many educators continue to worry about the quality of home instruction, it is clear that they will have to learn to live with it.

States whose compulsory-attendance laws once failed to grant any legitimacy to home education have modified their statutes to make the practice legal. Others have relaxed requirements that home-schoolers be certified as teachers, follow state-mandated curriculum or

get prior approval before pulling their children out of class.

A number of states, including Georgia, Minnesota, Missouri, Pennsylvania and Wisconsin, have been forced to amend their laws after courts ruled that they were too vague regarding the circumstances under which home instruction was illegal.

"The resurgence of home education in the last 10 years has required legislators to address this issue," says J. Michael Smith, vice president of the Home School Legal Defense Association, "to recognize the constitutional rights of parents to teach their children at home." Requirements for home instruction vary from state to state, with responsibility for enforcing them left up to local school districts. But typically, they require parents to give notice of what curriculum or course of study they intend to use, where instruction will take place, and the name and age of the child. Periodic standardized tests or other evaluations of the child's progress, as well as home visits by public- or private-school teachers, are also common. Some states, however, including Illi-

Lynn Olson is a senior editor for *Education Week*. This article is reprinted from *Governing* 3:10 (July 1990): 56-57.

nois and Texas, treat home-educators as private schools, on which they impose few regulations.

Estimates of the number of students nationwide who receive home instruction range from 500,000 to as many as 1 million, but everyone agrees that the numbers are growing, particularly in states where regulations have been eased. In Florida, where the law was liberalized in 1985, the number of pupils reportedly being taught at home grew from 4,700 to 5,300 between 1988 and 1990. In Virginia, with a new law passed in 1984, 2,934 children received home instruction in 1990, compared with 503 in 1984-85, not counting students who gained exemptions from compulsory-attendance laws on religious grounds.

Despite such growth, home-schoolers still constitute a small slice of the total school population. If 500,000 elementary and secondary students are being educated at home, that is only 1 percent of all youngsters in grades K-12.

One of the largest contributors to swelling home-school enrollments has been the rise of the Christian fundamentalist movement. The vast majority of parents who choose to educate their children at home are thought to do so for religious reasons.

But a sizable number of families are opting out of the public schools on other grounds. Mary Kay Albrittain, chief of pupil services for the Maryland Department of Education, estimates that as many as 40 percent of home-schoolers in her state may be educating their youngsters at home for nonreligious reasons. These include college professors, former teachers and others who think they can do a better job than the public schools, and parents who are choosing to keep their youngsters home for an extra year or two before submitting them to the pressures of public education.

In other instances, parents are reacting to specific disagreements with state-mandated curriculum. In Virginia, Charles W. Finley, the education department's associate director for proprietary schools, says many parents chose to educate their children at home after the state passed a mandatory family-life education requirement that would provide sex education in the schools.

Increasingly, parents seem simply to have lost faith in the public school system. "Twenty-five percent of the kids who go to high school never graduate," says home-schooler Ethell. "Twenty-five percent of those who do graduate are illiterate. So parents are saying, 'Hey, as a one-on-one tutor, even I could do better than that.'"

Although the National Association of State Boards of Education does not have an official policy on home education, its 1988 report on the subject advocates a "cooperative approach" in working with home-school families.

Nonetheless, pitched battles over home education continue. The site of one of the most prolonged struggles is Iowa, where home-schoolers have been trying to liberalize the state's policies for the past five years. Iowa is one of only two states that still require home educators to be certified as teachers. The latest effort to change that was defeated in the state senate in spring 1990 by a 25-to-24 vote.

In states that have liberalized their home-education policies, the next round of debates is likely to center on what outcomes are required to ensure that home-educated children are making sufficient academic progress. States like South Carolina and Tennessee, for example, require youngsters to perform above a certain level on standardized tests in order to continue their education at home. Home-school advocates have argued that those standards are unnecessarily restrictive. But, in general, both educators and home-schoolers favor moving the debate away from inputs—such as parents' level of education—and toward a focus on what students are actually learning.

In addition, home-schoolers are continuing their efforts to do away with mandates in states like Connecticut, Maine, Massachusetts and South Dakota, which require parents to get prior approval from a local school board or superintendent before they can pull their children out of school. Parents who view teaching their children at home as a right—not a privilege—are opposed to such laws. They also complain that the rules are carried out differently from one district to the next.

The biggest foe of home instruction is the National Education Association, which adopted a resolution in 1989 stating that "home-schooling programs cannot provide the child with a comprehensive education experience." Home schooling, the union asserts, should meet all state requirements, instructors should be licensed, a state-approved curriculum should be used and the students should be limited to members of the immediate family.

According to Christopher J. Klicka, senior counsel with the Home School Legal Defense Association, the NEA's rules "would outlaw 98 percent of home schooling in the country."

But educators worry about the ability of parents—some without high school diplomas—to provide children with a well-rounded education. In North Dakota, for example, the department of education has regulations that require certified teachers to supervise home-educated children one hour per week, unless the parent is a licensed teacher. State Superintendent Wayne G. Sanstead refers to it as a "quality assurance" effort. But he says it is meeting with fierce resistance from the state's home-school association.

"I said back in 1985 that the home-school issue would never go away until such time as they have no regulations," he says. "I think their bottom line is they don't want any."

Like his counterparts in other states, however, Sanstead is running up against an increasingly organized and vocal home-school community. Every state now has at least one home-school association, as well as a network of local support groups. Nearly all are connected by phone trees that can be put into operation for lobbying at a moment's notice.

Representative Tom Mims, a Democratic member of the Florida legislature, in attempting to tighten requirements for home education, introduced legislation that would bar individuals on the state's child-abuse registry from teaching their children at home; require that teachers, rather than a relative, test home-educated children on a periodic basis; and conduct such evaluations every six months instead of annually.

Mims says he introduced the bill because there are "people who cannot or should not be teaching their children at home." "I have gotten many letters from home-schooling people who use incorrect spelling, incorrect grammar," he says, "and to know that these same people are at home teaching their children in the same fashion is what does need to be addressed."

Mims quickly found out what he was up against. "I had literally hundreds of people call me and oppose the bill who had absolutely no idea what it even said," he sighs.

Even advocates admit that the recent boom in home education may slow down in the near future, however, largely because most home-educators today do not work outside the home and the number of women who are opting for that lifestyle continues to shrink. "I just don't think that there are that many people out there who really have the time to do it," says Smith. "So I think it's going to continue to grow, but at a much slower pace."

Reference Guide

SOURCES FOR ALL STATES

Advisory Commission on Intergovernmental Relations
Changing Public Attitudes on Governments and Taxes (1990)
Intergovernmental Perspective (published quarterly since 1975)
Measuring State Fiscal Capacity: Alternative Methods and Their Uses (1986)
1986 State Fiscal Capacity and Effort (1989)
The Question of State Government Capability (1985)
Regulatory Federalism: Policy, Process, Impact, and Reform (1984)
State and Local Initiatives on Productivity, Technology, and Innovation (1990)
State Constitutional Law: Cases and Commentaries (1988)
State Constitutional Law: Cases and Materials (1990)
State Constitutions in the Federal System (1989)
Significant Features of Fiscal Federalism (1990)
The Transformation in American Politics: Implications for Federalism (1986)

Committee for Economic Development
Leadership for Dynamic State Economics (1986)

Congressional Quarterly
Governing (published monthly beginning October 1987)

Council of State Governments
The Book of the States (published biennially since 1933)
The Journal of State Government (published quarterly since 1990,
  bimonthly from 1986 to 1989)
State Government News (published monthly since 1956)
State Government Research Checklist (published bimonthly since 1968)
Suggested State Legislation (published annually since 1941)

Government Research Service (Topeka, Kansas)
State Legislative Sourcebook (published annually)

Legislative Studies Center, Sangamon State University (Illinois)
Comparative State Politics (published bimonthly since 1979)

National Center for State Courts
State Court Journal (published quarterly since 1977)

National Conference of State Legislatures
Capital to Capital (published biweekly from Washington)
The Fiscal Letter (published bimonthly)
Mason's Manual of Legislative Procedure (1989)
State Legislatures (published monthly since 1975)

National Governors' Association
The Budgetary Process in the States (1985)
Fiscal Survey of the States (published biannually)
Governors' Weekly Bulletin (published weekly)
State of the States Report (published annually)

National Civic League
Campaign Finances: A Model Law (1979)
A Model Election System (1973)
A Model State Constitution (1968)
National Civic Review (published bimonthly)

State Policy Reports
State Policy Reports (published bimonthly since 1983)
The State Policy Reports Data Book (published annually since 1984)
States in Profile (published annually since 1990)

SOURCES FOR INDIVIDUAL STATES

State Blue Books (usually published by the secretaries of state)

State Journals
California Journal (published monthly since 1970)
Empire State Report (published monthly since 1975)
Illinois Issues (published monthly since 1975)
The Kentucky Journal (published 10 times a year since 1989)
New Jersey Reporter (published since 1971)
North Carolina Insight (published quarterly since 1978)

GENERAL SOURCES

Barone, Michael, et al., eds. *Almanac of American Politics*. Washington, D.C.: National Journal.

Published biennially since 1972; by National Journal since 1983.

Beyle, Thad L., and Lynn Muchmore. *Being Governor: The View from the Office*. Durham, N.C.: Duke University Press, 1983.

Duncan, Phil, ed. *Politics in America*. Washington, D.C.: Congressional Quarterly. Published biennially since 1981.

Elazar, Daniel J. *American Federalism: A View from the States*. 3d ed. New York: Harper & Row, 1984.

Gray, Virginia, Herbert Jacob, and Robert B. Albritton, eds. *Politics in the American States: A Comparative Analysis*. 5th ed. Glenview, Ill.: Scott Foresman, 1990.

Key, V. O., Jr. *Southern Politics in State and Nation*. New York: Alfred A. Knopf, 1949.

Legislative Drafting Research Fund, Columbia University. *Constitutions of the United States: National and State*. Oceana, N.Y.: Oceana Press, 1985.

Morehouse, Sarah McCally. *State Politics, Parties, and Policy*. New York: Holt, Rinehart & Winston, 1981.

Peirce, Neal R., and Jerry Hagstrom. *The Book of America: Inside Fifty States Today*. New York: W. W. Norton, 1983.

Price, David E. *Bringing Back the Parties*. Washington, D.C.: CQ Press, 1984.

Rosenthal, Alan. *Governors and Legislatures: Contending Powers*. Washington, D.C.: CQ Press, 1990.

Rosenthal, Alan. *Legislative Life: People, Process, and Performance in the States*. New York: Harper & Row, 1981.

Sabato, Larry. *Goodbye to Good-time Charlie: The American Governorship Transformed*. 2d ed. Washington, D.C.: CQ Press, 1983.

Van Horn, Carl E., ed. *The State of the States*. Washington, D.C.: CQ Press, 1989.

Wright, Deil S. *Understanding Intergovernmental Relations*. 3d ed. Pacific Grove, Calif.: Brooks-Cole, 1988.

SELECTED TEXTBOOKS

Berman, David R. *State and Local Politics*. 6th ed. Dubuque, Iowa: Wm. C. Brown, 1991.

Bingham, Richard D., and David Hodge. *State and Local Government in a Changing Society*. 2d ed. New York: McGraw Hill, 1991.

Bowman, Ann O'M., and Richard Kearney. *State and Local Government*. Boston: Houghton-Mifflin, 1990.

Burns, James M., Jack Peltason, and Thomas E. Cronin. *Government by the People: State and Local Politics*. 6th ed. Englewood Cliffs, N.J.: Prentice-Hall, 1987.

Dresang, Dennis L., and James J. Gosling. *Politics, Policy, and Management in the American States*. New York: Longman, 1989.

Dye, Thomas R. *Politics in States and Communities*. 6th ed. Englewood Cliffs, N.J.: Prentice-Hall, 1988.

Engel, Michael. *State and Local Politics: Fundamentals and Perspectives*. New York: St. Martin's Press, 1985.

Gray, Virginia, and Peter Eisinger. *American States and Cities*. New York: HarperCollins, 1991.

Harrigan, John J. *Politics and Policy in States and Communities.* 4th ed. New York: HarperCollins, 1991.

Henry, Nicholas. *Governing at the Grassroots: State and Local Politics.* 3d ed. Englewood Cliffs, N.J.: Prentice-Hall, 1987.

Houseman, Gerald. *State and Local Government: The New Battleground.* Englewood Cliffs, N.J.: Prentice-Hall, 1986.

Jewell, Malcolm E., and Samuel C. Patterson. *The Legislative Process in the United States.* 4th ed. New York: Random House, 1986.

Leach, Richard H., and Timothy G. O'Rourke. *State and Local Government: The Third Century of Federalism.* Englewood Cliffs, N.J.: Prentice-Hall, 1988.

Lorch, Robert S. *State and Local Politics: The Great Entanglement.* 2d ed. Englewood Cliffs, N.J.: Prentice-Hall, 1986.

Press, Charles, and Kenneth Verburg. *State and Community Governments in a Dynamic Federal System.* 3d ed. New York: HarperCollins, 1991.

Ross, Michael J. *State and Local Politics and Policy: Change and Reform.* Englewood Cliffs, N.J.: Prentice-Hall, 1987.

Saffell, David C. *State and Local Government: Politics and Public Policies.* 4th ed. New York: Random House, 1990.

Schultze, William. *State and Local Politics: A Political Economy Approach.* St. Paul, Minn.: West Publishing Co., 1988.

Staufer, W. B., Cynthia Opheim, and Susan Bland Day. *State and Local Politics.* New York: HarperCollins, 1991.

Index